The Migration Conference 2023

Book of Abstracts

Organised and hosted by

I0022917

U·H

Universität Hamburg
DER FORSCHUNG | DER LEHRE | DER BILDUNG

THE MIGRATION
CONFERENCE
2023 HAMBURG

ALBRECHT MENDELSSOHN BARTHOLDY
GRADUATE SCHOOL OF LAW

Refugee Law Clinic
Hamburg

INTERNATIONAL
BUSINESS
SCHOOL

Z **ZEIT-Stiftung**
Ebelin und Gerd
Bucerius

CLAUSSEN SIMON | STIFTUNG

◆ TRANSNATIONAL PRESS®
LONDON

Supporters of The Migration Conference

Universität Hamburg
DER FORSCHUNG | DER LEHRE | DER BILDUNG

ZEIT-Stiftung
Ebelin und Gerd Bucerius

Refugee Law Clinic
Hamburg

CLAUSSEN SIMON | STIFTUNG

INTERNATIONAL BUSINESS SCHOOL

THE OHIO STATE UNIVERSITY

UCDAVIS
GIFFORD CENTER FOR POPULATION STUDIES

UNIVERSIDAD DE BURGOS

SOCIUS
Centro de Investigação em Sociologia Económica e das Organizações

RUHR UNIVERSITÄT BOCHUM
RUB

BIU
WEST UKRAINIAN NATIONAL UNIVERSITY

ISTANBUL
TOPKAPI UNIVERSITY

UNIVERSIDAD LATINA DE MEXICO

University of Nottingham
UK | CHINA | MALAYSIA

MOSCOW CITY UNIVERSITY

YAŞAR ÜNİVERSİTESİ

HEBEI UNIVERSITY

SYMBIOSIS
Golden Jubilee
Celebrating 50 Years of Excellence

UTPL
La Universidad Católica de Loja

Ming-Ai (London) Institute
明 愛 (倫敦) 學 院

UAED
Unidad Académica en Estudios del Desarrollo

CREDI
Centre for Development Evaluation and Social Science Research

MIGRATION INSTITUTE OF FINLAND

GÖÇDER

WB-MIGNET
Western Balkans Migration Network

INTERNATIONAL JOURNAL OF RELIGION

AMERI

TRANSNATIONAL EDUCATION REVIEW

YEIYÂ

MIGRATION & DIVERSITY

GÖÇ DERGİSİ

BORDER CROSSING

DISCRIMINATION

TRANSNATIONAL PRESS® LONDON

Conference Series: 26

The Migration Conference 2023 Book of Abstracts

Compiled by The Migration Conference Team

First Published in 2023 by Transnational Press London in the United Kingdom, 13 Stamford Place, Sale, M33 3BT, UK.

www.tplondon.com

Paperback

ISBN: 978-1-80135-231-4

Digital

ISBN: 978-1-80135-232-1

Cover Design: Nihal Yazgan

The Migration Conference 2023
Book of Abstracts

compiled by

The Migration Conference Team

TRANSNATIONAL PRESS LONDON

2023

CONTENTS

Supporters of The Migration Conferences included:

- Faculty of Law, Universität Hamburg, Germany [TMC2023 Host]
- International Business School, UK
- Refugee Law Clinic Hamburg, Germany
- Claussen Simon Stiftung, Germany
- ZEIT Stiftung, Ebelin und Gerd Bucerius, Germany.
- Albrecht Mendelssohn Bartholdy Graduate School of Law, Germany
- Association Marocaine d'Etudes & de Recherches sur les Migrations (AMERM), Morocco
- Association Marocaine d'Etudes & de Recherches sur les Migrations, Morocco
- Austrian Air – Official Carrier for TMC 2016, Austria
- AVAR journal
- Border Crossing
- Centre for Development Evaluation and Social Science Research (CREDI), Sarajevo, Bosnia and Herzegovina
- Charles University Prague Faculty of Humanities, Czech Republic
- Danube University Krems, Austria
- Dipartimento di Scienze Politiche, University of Bari, Italy
- EKKE – The National Center of Social Research, Greece
- Faculty of Contemporary Social Sciences, South East European University
- Global Migration Research Centre, Social Sciences University of Ankara, Turkey
- Göç Dergisi
- Harokopio University, Athens, Greece
- Hassan II Foundation for Moroccans Residing Abroad, Morocco
- Hellenic Sociological Society, Greece
- Institut de Recherche, Formation et Action sur les Migrations, Belgium
- Institut de Recherche, Formation et Action sur les Migrations, Belgium
- International Business School, Mobility Research Centre, UK
- International Journal of Religion
- International Organisation for Migration, Italy
- ISEG and IGOT, University of Lisbon, Portugal
- ISTAT (Italian National Statistics Office), Italy
- IUSSP International Migration Expert Panel
- J. Hornig Coffee, Austria
- Journal of Ecohumanism
- Journal of Posthumanism

- Migration Institute, Finland
- Migration Policies Research Centre, Istanbul Topkapi University, Turkey
- Ming-Ai (London) Institute, United Kingdom
- Mohammed V University of Rabat, Morocco
- Municipality of Bari, Italy
- National Office of Social and Cultural University Works, Morocco
- Ordine Assistenti Sociali Regione Puglia, Italy
- Puglia Regional Administration, Italy
- Red Cross, Italy
- Regent's University London, UK
- Research Centre in Economic and Organizational Sociology (SOCIUS), Universidade de Lisboa, Portugal
- RGS Population Studies Group, United Kingdom
- Ria Money Transfers
- Ruhr-Universität Bochum, Centre for Mediterranean Studies, Germany
- Sino-German Economic Development and Innovation Research Centre, Hefei University, P.R. China
- The Council of the Moroccan Community Abroad, Morocco
- The Global Mobility Project, The Ohio State University, USA
- The Ministry of Education, Morocco
- The National Human Rights Council (CNDH), Morocco
- Tourism Office of Lisbon, Portugal
- Unidad Académica en Estudios del Desarrollo, Mexico
- United Nations Population Fund (UNFPA)
- Universidad de Burgos, Spain
- Universidad Latina de México, Mexico
- Universidad Tecnica Particular de Loja, Ecuador
- University of Bari Aldo Moro, Italy
- University of California, Davis, Gifford Center for Population Studies, USA
- University of Nottingham, Faculty of Humanities and Social Sciences, China
- University of Vienna, Austria
- Urban Development and Social Research Association, Turkey
- Vienna Convention Bureau, Austria
- Western Balkans Migration Network (WB-MIGNET), Bosnia and Herzegovina
- Yaşar University Jean Monnet Migration Chair, Turkey

migrationconference.net   @migrationevent

fb.me/MigrationConference

Email: migrationscholar@gmail.com

Host Institutions of The Migration Conferences

- Universität Hamburg, Germany (TMC2023 Host)
- Mohammed V University of Rabat, Morocco (TMC2022 Host)
- Association Marocaine d'Etudes & de Recherches sur les Migrations (AMERM), Morocco (TMC2022 Host)
- International Business School, UK (TMC2021 Host)
- Ming-Ai (London) Institute, UK (TMC2021 Host)
- South East European University, N. Macedonia (TMC2020 Host)
- University of Bari Aldo Moro, Italy (TMC2019 Host)
- University of Bari, Italy (TMC2019 Host)
- Universidade de Lisboa, Portugal (TMC2018 Host)
- Harokopio University, Athens, Greece (TMC2017 Host)
- University of Vienna, Austria (TMC2016 Host)
- Charles University Prague, Czech Republic (TMC2015 Host)
- Regent's University London, UK (TMC2014 Host)
- Regent's College London, UK (TMiE2012 Host)

People

The Migration Conference Executive Team

Prof. Dr. Markus Kotzur, Universität Hamburg, Germany (Chair)

Prof. Dr. Ibrahim Sirkeci, University of Salford, UK (Chair)

Dr. Ülkü Sezgi Sözen, Universität Hamburg, Germany (Coordinator)

Prof. Dr. Jeffrey H. Cohen, Ohio State University, USA

Prof. Dr. Philip L Martin, University of California Davis, USA

Dr. Andrea Romano, University of Barcelona, Spain

Transnational Advisory Committee

Prof Deborah Anker, Harvard University, United States

Prof Gudrun Biffl, Krems, Austria

Prof Lucinda Fonseca, University of Lisbon, Portugal

Prof Elli Heikkila, Migration Institute of Finland, Finland

Prof Beatrice Knerr, Kassell University, Germany and Hefei University, China

Prof Markus Kotzur, Universität Hamburg, Germany

Prof Jonathan Liu, International Business School, UK

Prof Apostolos G Papadopoulos, Harokopio University of Athens, Greece

Prof João Peixoto, University of Lisbon, Portugal

Prof Michela C. Pellicani, University of Bari "Aldo Moro", Italy

Prof Giuseppe Sciortino, University of Trento, Italy

Scientific Review Committee

Africa

Agnes Igoye, Ministry of Interior Affairs, Uganda

Prof Mohamed Khachani, AMERM & Mohammed V University of Rabat, Morocco

Dr Rania Rafik Khalil, The British University in Egypt, Egypt

Dr Sadhana Manik, University of KwaZulu-Natal, South Africa

Prof Claude Sumata, National Pedagogical University, DR Congo

Dr Ayman Zohry, Egyptian Society for Migration Studies, Egypt

Americas

Prof Jeffrey H. Cohen, Ohio State University, USA

Dr José Salvador Cueto-Calderón, Universidad Autónoma de Sinaloa, Mexico

Dr Ana Vila Freyer, Universidad Latina de México, Mexico

Dr Pascual Gerardo García-Macías, Universidad Técnica Particular de Loja, Ecuador

Dr Carlos Alberto González Zepeda, Universidad Autónoma Metropolitana-Cuajimalpa, Mexico

Dr Torunn Haaland, Gonzaga University, USA

Prof Liliana Jubilut, Universidade Católica de Santos, Brazil

Prof Philip L Martin, University of California Davis, USA

Dr Carla Pederzini, Universidad Iberoamericana, Mexico

Dr Eric M. Trinka, Colby University, USA

Karla Angélica Valenzuela-Moreno, Universidad Iberoamericana, Mexico

Dr Hassan Vatanparast, Saskatchewan University, Canada

Prof Rodolfo García Zamora, Autonomous University of Zacatecas, Mexico

Dr Monette Zard, Columbia University, USA

Asia-Pacific

Prof Ram Bhagat, International Institute for Population Sciences, India

Dr Amira Halperin, University of Nottingham Ningbo, P.R. China

Dr Sadaf Mahmood, The Women University Multan, Pakistan

Dr Shweta Sinha Deshpande, Symbiosis School for Liberal Arts, India

Prof Nicholas Procter, University of South Australia, Australia

Dr Ruchi Singh, Tata Institute of Social Sciences, India

Dr AKM Ahsan Ullah, University Brunei Darussalam, Brunei

Dr Xi Zhao, Hefei University, P.R. China

Eastern Europe

Dr Merita Zulfiu-Alili, South East European University, N. Macedonia

Dr Suat Donmez, Istanbul Topkapi University, Turkey

Dr Olga R. Gulina, Benefit Research and Consulting, Germany

Dr Tuncay Bilecen, Kocaeli University, Turkey, UK

Prof Dilek Cindoglu, Kadir Has University, Turkey

Dr Yaprak Civelek, Anadolu University, Turkey

Dr Z. Banu Dalaman, Istanbul Topkapi University, Turkey

Prof Sevim Atilla Demir, Sakarya University, Turkey

Prof Vladimir Iontsev, Moscow State University, Russian Federation

Dr İnci Aksu Kargın, Uşak University, Turkey

Prof Sebnem Koser Akcapar, Ankara Social Sciences University, Turkey

Dr Armagan Teke Lloyd, Abdullah Gul University, Turkey

Dr Vildan Mahmutoğlu, Galatasaray University, Turkey

Dr Nermin Oruc, Centre for Development Evaluation and Social Science Research (CREDI), Sarajevo, Bosnia and Herzegovina

Prof Gökay Özerim, Yaşar University, Turkey

Prof Irina Savchenko, Linguistics University of Nizhny Novgorod, Russian Federation

Dr Onur Unutulmaz, Ankara Social Sciences University, Turkey

Dr Deniz Eroglu Utku, Trakya University, Turkey

Dr Pınar Yazgan, Sakarya University, Turkey

Dr Sinan Zeyneloglu, Kent University, Turkey

Western Europe

Dr Nirmala Devi Arunasalam, Global Banking School, United Kingdom

Dr Bahar Baser, Durham University, United Kingdom

Dr Gülseli Baysu, Queen's University Belfast, United Kingdom

Prof Aron Anselem Cohen, University of Granada, Spain

Dr Martina Cvajner, University of Trento, Italy

Dr Carla de Tona, University of Bologna, Italy

Dr Sureya Sonmez Efe, University of Lincoln, United Kingdom

Dr Deniz Cosan Eke, University of Vienna, Austria

Dr Alina Esteves, Universidade de Lisboa, Portugal

Dr Serena Hussain, Coventry University, United Kingdom

Prof Monica Ibáñez-Angulo, University of Burgos, Spain

Dr Gul Ince Beqo, University of Urbino, Italy

Prof Markus Koller, Ruhr University Bochum, Germany

Dr Emre Eren Korkmaz, University of Oxford, United Kingdom

Dr Oksana Koshulko, The Technical University of Munich, Germany

Prof Jonathan Liu, International Business School, United Kingdom

Dr Lan Lo, University of Nottingham, United Kingdom

Dr Altay Manço, IRFAM, Belgium

Dr A. Erdi Öztürk, London Metropolitan University, United Kingdom

Isabella Piracci, Avvocatura Generale dello Stato, Rome, Italy

Dr Sahizer Samuk-Carignani, University of Pisa, Italy

Prof Giuseppe Sciortino, University of Trento, Italy

Dr Selma Akay Sert, University College London, UK

Dr Caner Tekin, Ruhr-Universität Bochum, Germany

Irene Tuzi, Sapienza University of Rome, Italy

Dr Ülkü Sezgi Sözen, Universität Hamburg, Germany

Near East

Dr Yakhnich Liat, Beit Berl College, Israel

Dr Simeon Magliveras, King Fahd University of Petroleum and Minerals, Saudi Arabia

Dr Bradley Saunders, American University of Bahrain, Bahrain

Dr Paulette K. Schuster, Reichman University, Israel

Dr Omar Al Serhan, Higher Colleges of Technology, United Arab Emirates

Dr Md Mizanur Rahman, Qatar University, Qatar

The Migration Conference Technical Organisation Committee

Dr Aytac Yerden, Gedik University, Turkey (IT)

Ege Cakir, Middle East Technical University, Turkey (Admin)

Nihal Yazgan, Transnational Press London, UK (Admin)

Local Organisation Team at Universität Hamburg

Dr. Ülkü Sezgi Sözen (Coordinator)

Anastasia Pohler

Andrea Hearst

Berivan Dalgic

Chris Neuffer

Christian Kisczio

Clara Schulz

Constantin Velling

Dinah Cassebaum

Doreen Matthies

Elisabeth Enyonam Lösche

Erkin Özer

Eva Laas

Felicia Mäurer

Florian Lucks

Friederike Schwinn

Hannah Franz

Jan Koch

Jannik Luhm

Jara Al-Ali

Jennifer Steiniger

Justine Arnold

Konrad Limburg

Leah Mathiesen

Luisa Nembach

Lukas Heimann

Melanie Susantija

Melina Chana

Nina Henning

Pascal Schütt

Patrycia Skopinski

Pauline Weber

Serhii Lashyn

Shanice Omoghile

Stephanie Lange

Tabea Judith Borisch

Thea Tenckhoff

Verena Kahl

Zehra Betuel

Zeynep Güler Özer

Keynote Speakers

The Migration Conferences team are proud to have leading scholars and experts in the field as keynote speakers and panellists. This year, TMC will feature:

- Prof. Dr. Jürgen Bast, Justus-Liebig-Universität Gießen, Germany
- Prof. Dr. Luisa Feline Freier De Ferrari, Universidad del Pacifico, Peru
- Prof. Dr. Mario Savino, University of Tuscia, Italy
- Prof. Dr. Daniel Thym, Universität Konstanz, Germany
- Prof. Dr. Gabriele Buchholtz, Universität Hamburg, Germany
- Dr. Derya Ozkul Kusoglu, University of Oxford, UK

In previous years, The Migration Conferences entertained distinguished scholars delivering keynote speeches including:

Fiona B. Adamson, SOAS, University of London, UK [2019], Theresa Alfaro-Velcamp, Emeritus Professor, Sonoma State University, USA [2021], Joaquin Arango, Complutense University of Madrid, Spain [2018], Giuseppe Brescia, MP, Member of Italian Chamber of Deputies, Parliamento Italiano, Italy [2020], Caroline Brettell, Southern Methodist University, USA [2015], Pedro Calado, The High Commissioner for Migration, Lisbon, Portugal [2018], Barry Chiswick, George Washington University, USA [2014], Prof Jeffrey H. Cohen, Ohio State University, United States [2022], Martina Cvajner, University of Trento, Italy [2020], Jelena Dzankic, Co-Director of the GLOBALCIT Network, European University Institute, Italy [2020], Élise Féron, Tampere Peace Research Institute, Tampere University, Finland [2021], Nissa Finney, University of St Andrews, UK [2020], Elli Heikkilä, Research Director, Migration Institute of Finland, Finland [2020], James F. Hollifield, Director of the Tower Center for Public Policy and International Affairs at Southern Methodist University, Dallas, USA [2021], Agnes Igoye, Deputy National Coordinator Prevention of Trafficking in Persons, Ministry of Internal Affairs, Uganda [2020], Prof Markus Koller, Ruhr-Universität Bochum, Germany [2022], Michelle Leighton, International Labour Organization, Genève, Switzerland [2018], Philip L. Martin, University of California, Davis, USA [2019], Markus Kotzur, Universität Hamburg, Germany [2019], Douglas S. Massey, Princeton University, USA [2015], Helén Nilsson, Director, Nordic Council of Ministers Office in Lithuania [2020], Prof Mustafa Ozbilgin, Brunel University London, UK [2022], Karsten Paerregaard, Gothenburg University, Sweden [2019], Karen Phalet, KU Leuven, Belgium [2016], Rodolfo Cruz Piñeiro, Director, Departamento de Estudios de Población, El Colegio de la Frontera Norte, Mexico [2021], Prof Irudaya Rajan, IIMAD, Kerala, India [2022], Pia M. Orrenius, Vice President and Senior Economist Federal Reserve Bank of Dallas, USA [2021], Martin Ruhs, European University

Institute, Florence, Italy [2019], Oded Stark, University of Bonn, Germany [2017], Ruba Salih, SOAS, University of London, UK [2018], Sasskia Sassen, Columbia University, USA [2017], Giuseppe Sciortino, University of Trento, Italy [2017], Carlos Vargas Silva, University of Oxford, UK [2019], Ibrahim Sirkeci, International Business School, UK [2016], Hna. Leticia Gutiérrez Valderrama, Scalabrinian Missionary, founder of SMR and Sergio Mendez Arceo National Human Rights Prize in Mexico; Diocesan Delegate for Migration - Diocese of Sigüenza-Guadalajara-Spain [2021], Dr V.J. Varghese, University of Hyderabad, India [2022].

| 1A | Arts, Literature and Migration [EG17] |

Chair: Alicia Rusoja, University of California, Davis, USA

275   The refugee as the reverse side of the world of wealth in Uğur Gallenkuş's collages

Ewelina Kaczmarczyk

On one side, a perfectly green lawn and ideal glistening skyscraper reaching the clouds. A father and son control a drone. In the background, we can see people resting on blankets in the park. On the right, another father and child, but the image is totally different. The man lifts bloodstained corpse wrapped in a white sheet. Instead of grass – ruble. The drone from the left-hand picture transitions to an airplane on the right. There are no buildings and the explosion creates the shape similar to the tree from the first picture. This is what one of the first collages published on Instagram by Turkish visual artist Uğur Gallenkuş looks like. As the hashtag says, war and peace happens at the same time.

Refugees are the reverse of the wealth of Western culture – that is how Gallenkuş shows the crisis of borders and inequalities in the world. His collages depict two similar worlds, spaces, characters which strongly point in how different places of the world we live. However, is not such a „shock to thought" a procedure that duplicates stereotypes? Perhaps the refugee was treated here instrumentally as a ""remorse of the West"", an alien in whom a world without problems is reflected. As Susan Sontag wrote in ""Regarding the Pain of Others"": ""So far as we feel sympathy, we feel we are not accomplices to what caused the suffering. Our sympathy proclaims our innocence as well as our impotence"". So maybe the works of Gallenkuş show the connections between these worlds, which we should not forget? Or maybe the collages are an attempt to get closer to the Other, for whom we should provide decent conditions? How does the sight of someone else's suffering affect the viewer? In my presentation referencing to works of Susan Sontag, Achille Mbembe and Giorgio Agamben I will consider how art can create a narration about the experience of refugeeism, poverty and exclusion and how the strategy of the extract reflects the fragmented refugee identity.

561   Writing in Exile: Easterine Kire's Creative Responses to the Nagaland Conflict

Imti Watitula Longkumer

Nagaland, in the Northeastern region of India, has the longest and complex ongoing ethnic conflict rooted in the Naga Indigenous people's demand for autonomy. The conflict originated in the 1960s and 70s and peaked in the early 1990s. Prior to the advent of print culture, the Nagas had a rich tradition of oral literature, with history and culture passed down orally from one generation to another. With the advent of print culture, the Nagas began documenting their oral history and contemporary Naga writers started writing about the regional conflict and violence, reflecting the lived reality and experiences of the Naga people. The absence of a written history, allowed these works to gain currency and quickly garnered wide readership across the globe. This was not welcomed by the Indigenous freedom fighters and resulted in suppressing the writers. Easterine Kire, the first Naga to publish a work of fiction in English in 2003, faced threats and was forced into exile in 2005 due to her creative responses to the political violence and conflict. Kire writes in English and is the author of several books including poetry and short stories. Kire's creative works specifically addresses the Naga indigenous community to which she belongs, and uses the social, cultural and political narrative as backdrop to the stories. Kire began her writing career in her native home in Nagaland; however, due to the threats she was facing from the indigenous political parties operating in the state because of her responses in creative works to the political violence and conflict, she was forced to flee her home. Kire migrated to Tromsø's where she wrote most of her novels and spent ten years in exile before returning to her home country in 2015. Kire wrote six books in one year of her residency in Tromsø centering on Naga politics and these works have gained immense popularity. This essay looks at Kire's works that developed during exile and how the process of migrating from her home country had impacted her writing experience. Kire's significant literary output during her exile raises questions about how geographical distance shaped her creative process. Kire acknowledges this as she states the necessity for her as a writer to step back and write with an objective view when writing especially on sensitive subjects of the Nagas. In addition to exploring this aspect, this essay also examines how Kire's migration and exile allowed her to develop new strategies for writing and disseminating knowledge of a community with very little space of written literature.

123   Real Change Requires More from Us and Not Just More of Us: Latinx Immigrants in the U.S. Resisting Legal Violence by Reading, Writing, and Mobilizing Communal Organizing Literacies

Alicia Rusoja

The educational experiences of immigrant students in the U.S. are shaped by persistent anti-immigrant policies, practices and discourses (e.g. Campano, Ghiso, Welch, 2016; Gallo, 2017; Turner & Mangual Figueroa, 2019; Patel, 2012). They are equally shaped by the powerful community organizing against it of immigrant communities (Campano, Ghiso & Welch, 2016; Mangual Figueroa, 2015; Author, YEAR). Relatedly, education scholars have established that critical literacy plays a central role in the organizing of racialized and oppressed communities in the U.S. (Bishop, 2015; Horton & Freire, 1990; Author, YEAR; Yee, 2016), and in multiracial coalition building toward a shared vision of educational justice (Campano et al, 2013; Campano, Ghiso, Welch, 2016; Ghiso, Campano, Vazquez Ponce, Thakurta, 2022).

Building on and contributing to this scholarship, this practitioner inquiry (Cochran-Smith & Lytle, 2009; PI) paper examines what the author coins as the communal organizing literacies of Latinx immigrants organizing in Philadelphia, Pennsylvania. It draws from a subset of qualitative data – including fieldnotes, open-ended interviews, artifacts and photographs – from a larger year-long PI study that I, a Latina immigrant, carried out with an intergenerational group of eleven un/documented Latinx immigrants on our shared immigrant rights organizing practice. Through analysis grounded on a sociopolitical understanding of literacy and education, on Women-of-Color epistemology regarding the intersection and intermeshing of identity and systems of oppression, and therefore on the epistemic privilege of Latinx immigrants regarding how to fight against oppression, this study asks: "How do Latinx immigrants organize for their/our rights? and "What role does literacy play in their/our organizing?." Findings show that Latinx immigrants in this context organize through the pedagogical mobilization of communal organizing literacies whereby we critically and collectively read and compose communal organizing literacy texts, as well as enact communal organizing literacy events, facilitating intersectional political activism and grassroots education that enacts communal agency and communal being. Implications address how the communal organizing literacies of Latinx immigrant communities can be valued, leveraged and sustained in K-16 classrooms. Additional implications include the power of practitioner inquiry as a research methodology to resist coloniality.

68   Mappilas, Migration and Music: The Emotional Voyages of Kerala

Shibinu S and Mohamed Haseeb N

Integration and absorption of migrants and their descendants into society's cultural realm has long been a wonderful topic in the social fabric of Kerala. Kerala, India's southernmost state, has had a long-standing tie with the Arab world. Muslims make up around 42 percent of all emigrants from Kerala. In comparison to other religions, Muslim emigration is on the rise (Shibinu, 2020). Muslims in Kerala's northern regions are known as Mappila Muslims, and they have been moving in large numbers to Gulf countries for decades (Rajan, 2020). Migration, in general, provides a unique vantage point from which to examine emotions. Mappila songs in Kerala depict this mobility of emotions. Mappila songs are folkloric Muslim music-type songs in Arabi Malayalam by the Mappilas of Kerala, with lyrics set to a melodic framework (Muslims of the Malabar part of Kerala, India are known as Mappilas). These songs have a distinct cultural character inextricably related to Keralites and Arabs. The ability of Mappila songs to depict the cultural embodiment, exchange, and synthesis of both Kerala and Gulf countries is one of their distinguishing features. Second, the separation of a male migrant from his wife causes anguish, suffering, and disutility. Letter Songs are a subset of Mappila songs that express profound insights into the misery, pain, and desire that couples experience as a result of their physical separation of a male migrant and his wife. The psychological agony involved with the separation of a migrant parent from his children is the third factor that Mappila songs depict. There are different examples for these three major categories of Mappila songs. Despite the abundance of qualitative research on the subject, the emotional element of the migrant experience appears to be understudied. The current proposition is an attempt to comprehend the broad relationship between music and mobility in the cultural realm of Kerala's migrants. It will also provide a comparative analysis of three fundamental elements of Mappila songs in the emotional lives of migrant households'

1B Diverse Policy Treatments of Migrants, Asylum-Seekers and Internally Displaced Persons (IDPs): Critical Reflections from Greece, Spain and Ukraine [UG14]

Chair: Megan Denise Smith, Pompeu Fabra University, Spain

1001 Beyond Integration: Measuring the Quality of Life of People with a Migration Background in Barcelona Using the Capabilities Approach

Eva Fortes

European cities have been receiving a steadily increasing number of immigrants over the last 40 years, and the European Union has targeted these newcomers and their offspring with a series of policies and plans aimed at improving social cohesion and wellbeing through their integration. To measure that integration, the EU has developed indicators that focus mainly on employment, education, and housing. While these indicators may be useful as a rough measure for recent immigrants' ability to function in the receiving society, they fall short of the stated goal of social cohesion and wellbeing. Therefore, I propose the concept of quality of life (QoL) as a novel lens through which to measure progress towards the goal of social cohesion and wellbeing in the context of immigrant incorporation. This paper tests a new measure of QoL I created, using the capabilities approach, against existing measures of integration in a case study of Barcelona, considered an ideal case of city-level integration. With a nonrandom sample of 20 adults whose parents immigrated from outside Spain, I perform a case study in the city of Barcelona to measure my participants' QoL according to my validated list of human capabilities and compare it with their integration according to standard EU indicators. The results of my analysis highlight mental health and the lack of choice for people with a migration background, which includes control over their time as well as their political and material environment. This measurement also draws attention to the importance of going beyond the individual to look at their loved ones and community. These findings offer insights for future policies as Europe's population with a migrant background continues to grow.

1003   Rethinking Refugee Camps: Opportunities for Labour Force Preparation in Lesvos, Greece

Liana Wool

The economic integration of refugee populations has become an increasingly discussed topic internationally, resulting in policy supporting refugee integration into the European Union (EU) (OECD/EU, 2018), or reintegration into countries of origin ("UNHCR Policy Framework and Implementation Strategy: UNHCR's Role in Support of the Return and Reintegration of Displaced Populations: August 2008," 2009). Economic integration policies for refugees, falling under the wider policy umbrella of Active Labour Market Policies (ALMPs), tend to address the thoughtful workforce preparation and localised employment of refugee populations after they have been resettled into the host country. Before refugees are resettled, they must first await the confirmation of their refugee status to move countries, frequently in refugee camps. During this time, these individuals are deprived of any workforce interaction, in skills training or practical employment. Herein exists a practical and research gap of continued up-skilling and/or employment for refugee populations prior to resettlement. Therefore, this gap suggests the importance in examining three topics: 1. workforce training programs in current practice in refugee camps, 2. the labour force skills and interests of individuals residing in refugee camps, and 3. the attitudes and perceived barriers of local employers in hiring refugee camp residents.

1004   Responding to Displacement in Ukraine: Changing Socio-Economic Needs and Protection

Chissey Mueller

The full-scale invasion that Russia launched in Ukraine (as of February 2022) has resulted in wide-spread devastation, thousands of civilian casualties, and the displacement of millions of people who fled to safer parts in the country and abroad. The war has also impacted Ukraine's existing socio-economic systems, which had relied on agriculture, digital innovation and a sizable Ukrainian migrant population who often worked seasonal jobs in European countries, to name a few. Ukraine also had a well-established response to counter human trafficking, exploitation and abuse, which are harmful incidents that can be interconnected to socio-economic dynamics. This presentation reflects on the evolving socio-economic changes of internally displaced persons in Ukraine through three empirical case scenarios. It provides a snapshot of key demographic and socio-economic shifts that those displaced are experiencing and the unique needs of different forced-migration profiles including men and women, single-headed households, and other diverse sub-populations. The cases highlight the needs, barriers, material and emotional resources and the intent among different individuals and their migration decisions. The cases also explore how harmful incidents such as human trafficking, exploitation and abuse can prevail in times of crisis or thrive if ignored, necessitating the provision of specialised protection services and income-generating opportunities that support self-capacity development and the agency of individuals. Learning from what is occurring in Ukraine is crucial in mapping future migration policies, access to services and socio-economic options for those who are affected by a rapidly changing and multilayered crisis context.

1002   The Securitisation of Migration at Europe's Southern Border: Policies of Violence against Migrants and Asylum-Seekers in the Canary Islands

Megan Denise Smith

This paper is the first phase in a qualitative empirical study which explores how the securitisation of migration in the Canary Islands coalesces into these different forms of violence and the means through which migrants and asylum-seekers resist. It investigates the deviations in security practices and power dynamics at the local level and the role of contextual factors, such as resources and existing social networks, in shaping different forms of resistance. As Europe's southern border, Spain plays a key role in setting the precedent within European Union (EU) migration policies. This is observed through the bordering and security practices it establishes as the status quo, often in border zones such as the Canary Islands, designed to stem migration flows to the Spanish mainland. These practices can range from detention and deportation of individuals to more subversive forms such as the introduction of complex administrative procedures to regularise their immigration status or access their rights. What is referred to as the securitisation of migration encompasses a wide-range of techniques of power, characterised by representations of individuals migrating as either 'risky' or 'at-risk.' Such framings can create spaces where violence, discrimination and xenophobia are instigated and condoned against migrants and asylum-seekers. As a highly politicised borderland for migration to the EU, the Canary Islands provides an under-studied and emblematic case, central to understanding broader trends of migration governance and possible future social dynamics between migrants, asylum-seekers and host communities.

1C   Economics, Work and Migration 1 [BG 5/6]

Chair Stefan Schlegel, Bern University, Switzerland

392   Transactions on the market for Services as an institutional bypass: Implications for the regulation of migration

Stefan Schlegel

In this research, I start from the assumption that what makes migration such an impactful phenomenon is first and foremost that it grants access to institutions (like state institutions that may provide security and a degree of freedom; and private institutions such as private employers that may provide the opportunity of socially upward mobility). From this vantage point, a central role of migration law is the allocation of "entry tickets" to sets of institutions. Access to territory, in this view, is mostly an auxiliary for access to institutions. In many cases, having access to a territory is a precondition for access to sets of institutions.

One of the central aims of migration law is to regulate the amount of labor available in a given labor market and thereby control the price of labor. However, this technique to uphold the politically struck compromise between capital and labor relies on access to the territory being a precondition for access to a labor market. This regulatory technique is undermined at the moment in which institutions (like a market) can be accessed without having access to a territory. The more the place in which labor is performed and the place in which labor is sold can be geographically distant from each other, the more this central regulatory aim of migration law is in tatters. An important driver of this development is a shift from labor markets to markets for services. Where services can travel across borders but workers cannot, the shift from consuming a good as a service rather than consuming it as labor, allows one to circumvent the regulatory rigor of migration law. To understand the potential impact of technological disruption (esp. of digitalization) on this shift, I rely on the theory of the firm and the concept of transaction costs. I make use of the argument that in a world without transaction costs (highly unrealistic but nonetheless instructive), there would be no firms, no hierarchical relationships between employers and employees, and hence no labor market, only service providers. Put like this, labor markets are nothing but a transaction cost problem. They cannot but decline in relative importance (compared to markets of services) as technological innovations kick in and reduce transaction costs. In tendency, technological innovation, therefore, erodes the capacity of migration law to shape the relationship between labor and capital.

I argue that the restrictive access to labor markets that migration law in many countries establishes, paradoxically, may turn into a danger for the regulatory capacity of states if, thanks to technological disruption, access to a labor market can effectively be replaced by a cross-border service. The more restrictive the access to a labor market, the higher the incentives to switch to the service market instead. In the face of technological disruption that structurally alters transaction costs, states need to ease the access to their labor markets for potential migrants in order to keep at least part of their former governing power over the relationship between capital and labor.

290   The labour market integration of female immigrants: A cohort analysis on Germany

Tanja Fendel

Using data from the German Socio-economic Panel and two integrated studies (IAB-SOEP-Migration sample and IAB-BAMF-SOEP Sample of refugees) from 1992-2020, it can be shown that integration pattern of immigrant women improved over migration cohorts in terms of smaller differences in working hours and wages compared to native-born women for those who migrated more recently to Germany. Cohort effects remain after controlling for main determinants of integration such as education or years since migration. As a possible explanation of cohort differences, we examine the relevance of women's country specific human capital aquisition after migration proxied by language skills. We find the share of women with good language skills to be higher for those who migrated to Germany in more recent years. Based on a generalized structural equation model, with resampling bootstrap procedures we find a significant direct and total effect of language skills on integration indicators, as well as an indirect effect of language skills working through the firm size as mediator, being only significant for the largest firm size category. Furthermore, the cohort effects are insignificant in the specification considering a mediator effect. Hence language skills directly influence integration and for those who work in large firms also indirctly through the firm size as mediator and this appears to be a suitable explanaition why integration pattern differ between migration cohorts. Due to good language skills or other investments in country specific human capital, women of more recent migration cohorts appear to a higher share to be able to select themselves into larger firms that supply superior working conditions in terms of wages and working hours. The labour market integration of immigrant women therefore crucially depends on the extent they are able to acquire country specific human capital after arrival and especially skills which have high returns for large firms.

318   Spatial Mismatch and Migrant Employment in Germany: A Spatial Robust Durbin Model Analysis

Mohamed Ennebch and Moubarek Amine Berdaa

Migration has been identified as a major factor influencing economic growth in many countries[1]. In Germany, the migration of people between regions has been recognized as having an impact on the GDP of these regions. This study aims to analyze the relationship between migration and regional GDP in Germany using a spatial Durbin model. The model takes into account the potential spillover effects of migration on neighboring regions.

Relationships between migration and regional economic growth, with some studies suggesting a positive relationship while others suggest a negative relationship. Spatial mismatch theory was first introduced by John Kain[2] in the late 1960s, in response to the rise of urban poverty and the persistence of high unemployment rates in certain urban areas. Workers who live in areas with high unemployment rates may face difficulties accessing job opportunities[3], particularly if those job opportunities are located in different areas, due to a mismatch between job opportunities and the location of workers. In the context of Germany, Constant et al. (2009)[4] found that migrants face significant disadvantages in terms of job quality, career prospects, and earnings, compared to native workers[5]. This suggests the persistence of the migrant-native gap in employment outcomes and the need to address the structural and social barriers that prevent migrants from fully participating in the labor market[6]. These findings highlight the importance of understanding the relationship between spatial mismatch, migration, and migrant employment outcomes in the German context.

Using a spatial Durbin model on data from 2015 to 2016 were used to estimate the spatial Durbin model and create a weights matrix using a distance-based approach. With a spatial spillover effect that positively influenced neighboring regions. The results also showed a negative relationship between unemployment rates and regional GDP, indicating that higher unemployment rates have a detrimental effect on regional economic growth. Understanding the potential spillover effects of migration on neighboring regions can inform regional economic development strategies and help policymakers promote economic growth in a more effective and sustainable way. Mitigating high levels of unemployment should also be a priority for policymakers, as the results suggest that unemployment has a detrimental effect on regional economic growth.

Keywords: Spatial Durbin model, migration, regional GDP, spillover effects, unemployment rates, economic growth, regional economic development.

References

Lee, E. S. (1966). A theory of migration. Demography, 3(1), 47-57.

Kain, J. F. (1968). Housing segregation, Negro employment, and metropolitan decentralization. The Quarterly Journal of Economics, 82(2), 175-197.

Massey, D. S., & Denton, N. A. (1988). The dimensions of residential segregation. Social forces, 67(2), 281-315.

Constant, A., Kahanec, M., & Zimmermann, K. F. (2009). Attitudes Towards Immigrants, Other IntegrationBarriers, and Their Veracity. International Journal of Manpower, 30(1/2), 5–14.https://doi.org/10.2139/ssrn.1424986

Musterd, S. (2005). Social and ethnic segregation in Europe: Levels, causes, and effects. Journal of urban affairs, 27(3), 331-348.

Malpezzi, S., & Maclennan, D. (2001). Economic returns to social capital in the urban housing market. Regional science and urban economics, 31(6), 669-696.

491   Against the Tide: Opportunities for Capital Circulation among Transnational Entrepreneurs

Tanja Schroot and Roberta Ricucci

The constant growth of new economic realities founded by foreign citizens is undeniable with respect to the continuous decline of Italian entrepreneurs in the Italian context (Idos-Confronti 2021). However, Italy observes increased outflows of qualified labour, educated and specialised in the country, to a variety of contexts (ISTAT 2021). Recent scholarship calls for a change of perspective from static brain drain concepts towards research on potentials for brain circulation and transnational cooperation (Zimmermann 2014; Czaika, M.& Parsons 2018, Sarpong & Maclean 2021). The 'Italian problem' is not the emigration of a professional 'elite', but the scarce capacity of attracting high-qualified immigrants (Beltrame 2007).

Building on these premises, this work aims to contribute to the discussion on return/onward mobility and entrepreneurship, which is constantly growing but predominantly focusing on developing countries (Sinatti 2019) to analyse linked decisional processes within the paradigmatic life course framework and carve out potential benefits for the sending and receiving end.

Turin is in the centre of investigations, being a prime example of superdiversity when it comes to population composition and industry (Chamber of Commerce 2021). Even though declining, the city still represents one of Italy's main industrial centres with a long migration history (Rapporto Rota 2021). According to latest ISTAT data provided in January 2022, the share of migrants in the Metropolitan Area makes up approximately 10% of its current total population. As one of the leading business centres in Italy, Turin has a relevant network of international companies and organisations (UNESCO Center, ILO, ETF) as well as a notable number of high-quality academic institutions.

Following the research concern on potential facilitators for building trans- and cross-national entrepreneurship opportunities, secondary data on local entrepreneurship development (Infocamere 2021) over the last 10 years has been analysed and complemented with a qualitative investigation. The latter builds on a qualitative data analysis, rooted in host and home contexts, with 25 respondents (10 Italian Entrepreneurs from Turin living abroad, 15 Romanian and German Entrepreneurs living in Turin) and a theoretical framework that links international literature on brain circulation in the context of high-qualified migratory dynamics and life course development (Vlase and Voicu 2018). Data has been retrieved from semi-structured interviews that focused on the respondents' intentions to return to their origin contexts and thus to potentially expand or transform their business building on co-created skillsets along the path of self-employment.

Findings suggest two predominant tracks of professional integration in the labour host context characterised either by transcultural competence transfer and utilisation, or by professional re-invention and skills acquisition, whereas the latter occurred predominantly for study participants coming from less privileged national backgrounds. Furthermore, the analysis of results suggests a strong correlation between conditions caused by the global COVID crisis and the (re)definition of expected living standards in the host context, which are presumed to have a significant impact on future brain circulation.

1D   Education and Skilled Migration 1 [BG3/4]

Chair: Gökay Özerim, Yaşar University, Turkey

486   From Migrant Workers to Professional Teachers: The Reintegration of Overseas Filipino Workers (OFWs) through "Sa Pinas, Ikaw ay Ma'am, Sir" (SPIMS) Program

Jocelyn Celero and Rowena Hibanada

Overseas Filipino workers (OFWs) constitute one of the largest diasporas in the world, serving the global economy through various occupational niches. Extant literature often describes the emigration of the highly-skilled as a brain drain phenomenon, resulting in severe loss of human resources in sending countries such as the Philippines. However, a number highly-skilled Filipino venturing in labor migration face downward skill mobility, unable to capitalize on their education and competencies in destination countries. To mitigate this problem, the Philippine government has introduced recently programs that encourage return and reintegration of highly-skilled Filipinos.

This study focuses on the reintegration of education-trained Filipinos to the Philippine education system through "Sa Pinas, Ikaw ay Ma'am, Sir" (SPIMS), a multi-stakeholder program that aims to retrain OFWs with teaching competencies necessary for them to become professional teachers. One of the key aspects of this program is the Online Refresher Course (ORC), which allows OFWs to receive teacher training while abroad and preparing for eventual return to the Philippines.

Building on focus group discussions and key informant interviews, this qualitative research examines the relationship between the outcomes of SPIMS-ORC and the motivations of OFWs to return to the Philippines as teachers. It illustrates that contrary to the dominant literature, the labor migration of education-trained Filipinos is a case of brain waste (rather than a brain drain) phenomenon exacerbated by the prevailing rural-urban inequality in teaching opportunities, wage differences between the Philippines and abroad, and family burdens. Thus, SPIMS functions as a reskilling program for returning Filipino teachers aimed to successfully reintegrate them into the education sector. At the same time, it serves as a corrective through reversing the effects of downward skilled mobility and restoring their teaching competencies lost from venturing into non-teaching jobs abroad.

179   Alone or with support though? The role of private intermediaries in the migration of doctors - the case of Poland

Kamil Matuszczyk

The migration of medical personnel has received unflagging interest from researchers, experts, politicians and the media. Although the motives and circumstances of their migration are relatively well known, little attention has so far been paid to the commercialisation and organised facilitation aspects. Only a few studies shed light on the dynamic development of the actors that make up the so-called migration industry, helping to organise work and life in host country. These include employment agencies, recruiters, as well as other organisations dealing with, for example, the organisation of language courses or support in the nostrification of diplomas. Empirical research tends to be limited to the context and strategies used by commercial actors rather than explaining the motives of medical staff to use intermediaries. The importance of private migration intermediaries as an important factor influencing the migration decisions of doctors training in CEE countries remains an overlooked. Poland occupies a special position on the map of medical staff migration - on the one hand, a country with the lowest number of doctors per 10,000 inhabitants, and on the other hand, a country from which several hundred high-class healthcare professionals leave every year.

The aim of the presentation will be to explain the role played by private labour market intermediaries in organising and facilitating migration of young doctors. Attention will focus on a case study of Poland and sixth-year medical students at 14 public universities. The results of a quantitative survey (online questionnaire), conducted in February 2022 and February and March 2023 (partially repeated surveys), will be used. The use of closed and open-ended questions made it possible to capture, among other things, the factors that most pull or push people to emigrate. These included the context of migration intermediaries and their activities towards students before passing the final medical exam. In total, unique empirical material was collected among 770 students (including 100 repeated questionnaires to capture the change in the migration situation of students year-on-year). In addition, the results of surveys conducted among representatives of private intermediaries who recruit medical staff in Poland were used (several in-depth interviews conducted in spring 2023). This will also be complemented by findings from a qualitative analysis of the offers of these actors, available online (e.g. Facebook groups).

Preliminary findings shed light on the fact that students in their sixth year of study are not targeted by migration intermediaries. Only a few percent of respondents indicated that they had received a personalised offer to organise work abroad. More importantly, a much higher percentage (one in three) of respondents declare an interest in taking advantage of the rich service package offer in the future, when planning to go abroad. The most frequently indicated range was language courses, an adaptation course or legal assistance. The findings of the research are an important contribution to the ongoing discussion on the pull and push factors of migrants over several decades, especially in the context of the importance of commercial actors facilitating and mediating the migration of highly skilled workers.

317   Spatial Analysis of Youth TVET education, Insertion, Migration and Regional Economic Growth in Morocco Using GWR

Mohamed Ennebch, Moubarek Amine Berdaa, Ahmed Bassibas, Youssef Haddou Amar, Meryem Ragbi

This article discusses the role of vocational training in promoting economic growth and development in Morocco. The National Vocational Training Strategy (SNFP) aims to enhance the productivity and integration of young vocational training graduates[1] while valuing local resources and specificities by establishing "cities of trades and skills" across Morocco's twelve regions. Theoretical and empirical studies suggest that diversified and targeted education influences economic efficiency and growth in different ways. Empirical studies have also demonstrated the direct and indirect effects of vocational training on local and global economic growth. Using a Cobb-Douglas production function of the Solow model augmented by human capital and spatial interaction effects to study the spatial repercussions of youth employment on regional economic growth in Morocco. To address low employability, regional labor market imbalances, and globalization in Morocco, decision-makers and researchers are exploring new opportunities for young workers.

With a focus on reducing youth migration[2] and enhancing regional economic growth. The study analyzes the spatial dynamics of youth migration and economic growth[3] using a geographically weighted regression (GWR)[4] model that considers variables such as TVET enrollment, youth unemployment, and migration patterns. The results suggest that TVET enrollment has a positive impact on regional economic growth by increasing the productivity of young people and reducing the need for migration[5]. The study identifies significant spatial variations in the impact of TVET on economic growth and youth migration patterns, emphasizing the importance of considering the spatial dynamics of TVET when developing policies to address youth unemployment and migration. The findings have important implications for policymakers, educators, and researchers interested in addressing the issue of youth unemployment and migration in developing countries.

Keywords: vocational training, economic growth, youth migration, regional development, TVET, geographically weighted regression.

References

"Geographical determinants of vocational education and training in developing countries: a spatial analysis" by A. Raza, K. Siddique, and F. Rehman

"The role of technical and vocational education and training (TVET) in reducing migration and enhancing economic growth in developing countries: A review of the literature" by S. S. Adewale and T. O. Popoola

"Exploring the relationship between migration, education, and economic development in Morocco: A spatial analysis" by S. El Aidaoui and A. Boudhar

"The effects of technical and vocational education and training on migration: A geographically weighted regression analysis of Indonesia" by M. H. Abdul Ghafur and A. Wulandari

"The impact of technical and vocational education and training on youth migration in Uganda: a geographically weighted regression analysis" by S. K. Awio, R. Musoke, and F. Othieno

1126 Diversity and Gender Equality Plans for Managing Diversity and Preventing
Discrimination in Higher Education Institutions

Gökay Özerim, Burcu Kiper, Güldan Kalem

To build inclusive and equitable environments, higher education institutions must prioritize promoting diversity and combating discrimination. The implementation of Gender Equality Plans (GEPs) and Diversity Plans has become a strategic tool of managing diversity and addressing gender disparities in academia. Through the creation and execution of thorough Diversity Plans and GEPs, higher education institutions play a crucial role in addressing these issues. The connections between these plans, diversity management, discrimination prevention, and mobility must be understood, though. The goal of this paper is to examine how Diversity Plans and GEPs in higher education institutions can effectively manage diversity and stop discrimination, with a focus on how migration intersects with both of these issues. This paper aims to highlight the special complexities and opportunities that arise within the context of higher education institutions by looking at the connections between diversity plans, gender equality plans, migration, and discrimination prevention. Within this context, the study will conduct a literature review to identify the theories and research that have been done on how to manage diversity, prevent discrimination, and promote gender equality in higher education institutions. The paper will create a conceptual framework for understanding how Diversity Plans and GEPs can efficiently manage diversity and prevent discrimination, particularly in the context of migration, by analyzing and synthesizing this literature. This paper will look at case studies of institutions of higher learning that have successfully implemented GEPs and Diversity Plans aimed at managing diversity and preventing discrimination in order to offer practical insights. In order to better address the particular needs and experiences of people living at the intersection of migration and gender, the paper will highlight key principles and tactics that can increase the inclusiveness and efficacy of these plans. The focus of recommendations will be on doable actions that institutions can take to improve their Diversity Plans and GEPs, such as fostering a supportive environment, promoting intercultural awareness, and putting in place laws that guarantee equality and anti-discrimination.

1E   Migration, Law and Policy 1 [EG15/16]

Chair: Ülkü Sezgi Sözen, Universität Hamburg, Germany

166 It's the Politics, Stupid: Official Chinese conceptualizations of migration and mobility

Carsten Schäfer

From its beginning in the 1930s, the development of migration studies was closely interlinked with Western nation-state building processes. As a result, migration studies have reproduced notions originally defined by European and North American immigration politics - such as "refugees" or "asylum seekers"; its resources are mostly invested in measuring the degree of integration of immigrants. Yet, China's nation building process differs much from those of most European states. The same holds true for the country's experience with international migration. While Europe hosts the largest number of international migrants, China is the world's leading emigration country. Not surprisingly, the way in which "migrants" are categorized and imagined and migration is conceptualized, studied and politicized in China is quite different from European mainstream approaches. Chinese knowledge production is characterized by a strong China-centrism and methodological nationalism that produces essentializing discourses on race, culture and belonging. These paradigms also affect the establishment of migration politics and border regimes. Against this background, I aim to systematically reflect the cultural, political, ideological and historical contexts that shape the production of knowledge on migration in China as well as the thereby arising actions. This study is based on a qualitative content analysis of official Chinese documents, Chinese think tank publications and other Chinese research. We cannot understand international mobility without understanding non-Western notions of migration. By mapping different geographic "epistimologies" and their influences on migration, I want to understand the conditions of possibilities for future cross-cultural cooperation in both politics and research between Europe and China.

73   Securitizing migration in times of crisis

Laura Planas Gifra

Securitization processes have become more common in the past decades and have been used to further control areas in which the state believes has lost control. An example of these practices can be seen in the case of migration, as states have continuously passed laws and policies to establish harder control mechanisms at their borders, introduce administrative burdens, and even use private security companies to help them administer security services. These measures have often been taken in response to the terrorism, one of the main international security concerns of our era.

It is extremely important to be aware of securitization processes and understand how they happen. Because when we talk about securitization, we are talking about bringing a non-security issue to the security agenda of a country and, in this way, to justify the restriction of specific rights. That is why we need to be very careful when applying these measures to the general population, but also to especially vulnerable groups such as refugees as these can make their lives even more difficult than they already are. Regrettably, securitization practices in the field of migration are becoming more common in countries around the world.

At the EU level, for instance, we have seen that Private Military and Security Companies do not merely provide border security services. They now frame, shape and entrench militarized responses within the European Agenda. They contribute to the framing of irregular migration as a security threat which can only be addressed through emergency-driven military. They are also shaping European policies and thus accelerating securitization processes. In setting up EU priorities in defence and security they may also be contributing to framing irregular migration as a security threat, in other words, to reinforcing practices that lead to a securitization of migration.

Extraordinary measures should be proportionate and held only so long as the security threat persists. But once the threat is over, these measures should cease too. Is this the case of counter-terrorism laws? Is it justified to treat groups such as migrants through the lens of national and international security? If so, are these measures proportional and temporarily limited? Who is the actor responsible for pushing these measures? What is the role of private actors such as private security companies? Do legislators consider the implications on the rights of refugees when dealing with terrorism? What then is just and unjust when applying measures against the War on Terror? It is necessary to understand how securitization measures are taken, justified, and how they affect the rights of migrants, especially in times of crisis.

226   Labour Shortage, Open Door Policy and Sabah (Malaysia) State's Dilemma

Ramli Dollah

Malaysia is one of the Southeast Asian countries that host a large number of immigrants, with Sabah being the most affected state by this issue. As a result, immigrants in Sabah are often considered to be the 'mother of all problems' and the 'mother of all threats' in the state. However, the state's rapid economic development in all sectors, especially in plantation and construction, demands a large number of immigrants to maintain its economic progress. Apparently, the global neoliberal economy of a capitalist market in Sabah since the state achieved independence with Malaysia in the 1960s requires a significant workforce. Due to a shortage of local workforce, the government has pursued an open-door policy by allowing a large number of immigrants to work in all economic sectors in the state. This paper argues that any policy to reduce the number of immigrants in Sabah is difficult to achieve due to the state's high dependence on foreign workers.

Therefore, despite stepping up raids and deportations, Sabah needs more foreign workers to ensure the state's economic survival. The paper posits that as long as Sabah continues with the labour incentive economy, dependence on foreign workers will persist, creating a dilemma for Malaysia and Sabah in particular, as this over-reliance affects the government's policy for dealing with immigrants. As a result, any measures taken to address this issue will undoubtedly have major repercussions for the Malaysian economy, particularly in Sabah.

151   The Experience of First-Hand Contact with Street Level Bureaucracy among Long-Term Slavic Migrants in Poland

Jan Bazyli Klakla

This paper presents an excerpt from the results of research on the relationship between the experience of the legal and institutional environment by long-term Slavic migrants living in Poland and their acculturation process. It concentrates on the experience of first-hand contact with street level bureaucracy and its connection to acculturation processes.

Template analysis (TA; Langdridge 2007) was conducted on data from (A) five in-depth expert interviews with migration professionals, (B) 20 biographical and narrative interviews with migrants from European Slavic countries who came to Poland between 1989 and 2010, and (C) legal and policy documents.

The author's modification of the Relative Acculturation Extended Model (RAEM; Navas et al. 2007) for qualitative research was used as a template to guide data collection and analysis.

The findings provide information about (A) respondents' negative experiences in this context, (B) the attitudes of suspicion presented by the state and its authorities towards migrants, (C) the change that occurred during the migrants' stay in Poland and the positive experiences they also had, and (D) the relationship that occurs between the experiences of migrants in this context and their acculturation process.

The research argues the extent of successful integration can be attributed to patterns of interaction between immigrants and the bureaucracy rather than solely to foreigners' willingness to invest in the acculturation process.

References

Langdridge, D. (2007). Phenomenological psychology: Theory, research and method. Glasgow: Pearson Education.

Navas, M., Rojas, A. J., García, M., & Pumares, P. (2007). Acculturation strategies and attitudes according to the Relative Acculturation Extended Model (RAEM): The perspectives of natives versus immigrants. International Journal of Intercultural

Relations, 31(1), 67-86. https://www.sciencedirect.com/science/ article/abs/pii/S014 7176706000617

1F   Migration and Integration 1 [UG13]

Chair: Paulette Schuster, Reichman University, Israel

361   Empathic approach as a key for sustainable integration of migrants into the society and labor market

Amira Bieber, Mohammed Issifu, and Turker Saliji

The European society is extremely diverse in terms of cultures, origins, religions and sexual orientations, resulting in the quest for recognition by these various groups while, at the same time maintaining the European identity. This necessitates measures of empowerment and promoting integration of these groups in societies and the labor market. Reports available indicate that, there is widespread discrimination particularly against migrants and other minority groups within the European societies (EU Fundamental Rights Agency report, 2021), which tend to negatively affect people's opportunities, well-being and reinforcing ethnic inequalities which eventually leads to social exclusion which derails the integration process of migrants especially, in societies. It is to mitigate against this social ill and facilitate migrant's integration processes that the Pro Arbeit adopt approaches - Not about us, without us – to involve and walk in the shoes of migrants before designing intervention to support their integration processes.

These approaches, focus on different levels, including beneficiaries, employees and decision makers by implementing beneficiary-oriented projects aiming to improve society's perception on diversity, with emphasis on the fight against discrimination, the prevention of xenophobia and living together with differences. Through its international projects with other partners in different countries, we adapt and share practices, to improve itself and to share its experiences, through which it was realized that more knowledge about cross-cultural differences and empathy among public employees improves the quality of services provided to beneficiaries. Pro Arbeit also influences the decision-makers and local authorities in the 13 cities in county Offenbach. Using its extensive network, we are working intensively to ensure that institutions and organizations at the same level make concepts such as interculturalism, anti-discrimination and empathy for diversity part of their regular strategies, and that business schools, universities and vocational schools make these concepts part of their curricula.

As a local authority with the goal of enabling people to better integrate into the labor market and thus into society, we are constantly challenged to improve our strategies, use innovative approaches, and take relevance and demand into consideration. At the same time, we use our findings in a multidisciplinary way and within the framework of our networks.

In our experience over many years show that sustainable results are only achieved when the people concerned are addressed empathically. They feel taken seriously, understood, supported. At the same time, by changing perspectives, we create better frameworks, make decisions and take sustainable steps.

Our approach has further proven that empathy, interculturality, and similar concepts should not only be propagated in public, but should also be reflected in the day-to-day processes, approaches, and strategies of institutions and organizations, as well as in the rhetoric and practice of decision-makers.

The session at the Migration Conference will present the themes and results of current european projects dealing with migration, diversity and integration, but will also be a stimulus for discussion on the empathetic attitude of the public institution in working with migrants.

264   More than Learning the Lingo? A Review of the Literature on the Roles of Language Cafés in the Integration of People on the Move Settling in Europe

Majbritt Lyck-Bowen

The significance of learning the local language for successful integration of people on the move settling in a new community is well documented (OECD 2021). Research has established that mastering the language of their new community is not only important for people on the move's daily activities but also for their long-term integration especially into the labour market (Kanas and Kosyakova 2023 and Karlsdóttir et al 2020). Initial research focused on the roles of formal language classes in integration whereas more recent research tends to mainly explore how new technologies can be used to teach languages. Despite general agreement that informal learning spaces such as language cafes play an important role as an alternative or complementary to formal language classes in aiding integration, language cafes have been afforded much less attention in the literature (Johnston 2016 and Morrice; Tip; Collyer and Brown 2021). The main purpose of this article is to provide a critical integrative review of the literature that explores how language cafes contribute to the political, social, economic and cultural integration of people on the move that settle in new communities. This will include assessing the evidence base in this area of research to identify issues and areas where further research is needed. The article will argue that though studies have identified many different ways language cafes can potentially aid the integration of people on the move into their new communities, the evidence base is still weak and often relying on a few smaller research projects that have focused on one or a few case studies mainly from the Nordic countries.

References

Johnston, Jamie (2016) Conversation-based programming and newcomer integration: A case study of the Språkhörnan program at Malmö City Library. In Library & Information Science Research, 38:1, 10-17, https://doi.org/10.1016/ j.lisr.2016.02. 001.

Kanas, Agnieszka and Kosyakova, Yuliya (2023) Greater local supply of language courses improves refugees' labor market integration. In European Societies, 25:1, 1-36, DOI: 10.1080/14616696.2022.2096915

Karlsdóttir, A., Sigurjónsdóttir, H. R., Ström Hildestrand, Å. and Cuadrado, A. (2020). Learning to live in a new Country – everyday social integration. Stockholm: Nordisk Ministerråd. https://pub.norden.org/nord2020-036/#25770.

Morrice, Linda; Tip, Linda, K.; Collyer, Michael and Brown, Rupert (2021) 'You can't have a good integration when you don't have a good communication': English-language Learning Among Resettled Refugees in England. In Journal of Refugee Studies, 34:1, 681– 699, https://doi.org/10.1093/jrs/fez023

OECD (2021) Language Training for Adult Migrants, Making Integration Work. OECD Publishing, Paris, https://doi.org/10.1787/02199d7f-en.

419   Beyond the integration on social structures – Wellbeing and personal expectations on the integration of refugees in Portugal

Marta Lemos

The institutional strategy for the integration of refugees in Portugal is mainly focused on the registration in social structures needed for the activation of administrative, legal, and learning procedures, such as, in language learning, in the enrollment in employment services, in the National Health Service, in Social Security or in the search for housing. It is expected that after completing this "registration checklist" refugees actively seek their autonomy independently or with little institutional intervention from the host entity in charge of their integration during the first eighteen months in the country. Faced with chronic variations of bureaucratic and human resources constraints in portuguese public services together with financial and social challenges, refugees wait long periods of time, often beyond those stipulated by law, to have access to these services or commodities, many of them co-dependent. Ultimately the result of this framework is the failure of their autonomy, so often referred to as the main objective of the reception and integration of refugees.

During those months little or no refugee's personal expectations, physical and emotional needs are considered. All the efforts are made to answer state's expectation of integration removing the person from its own path and identity. As expectations are connected to the quality of life (Subaşi, 2021) this alienation along with the absence of resources and the structural violence (Galtung, 1969) imprinted by public services, this combination of aspects leads to frustration and anger condemning refugees to illbeing (McLeod, 2017) causing damages in different areas of their lives and compromising even more their autonomy. Tied by the circumstances referred above and using the lens of Ahmed (2004), refugees create ways to claim some control of their lives and fill gaps in the reception and integration system through self-promotion and re-creation of situations of physical and emotional wellbeing.

From ethnographic fieldwork and follow-up interviews this paper focuses on some examples collected from the experiences of single men arrived in Portugal through the Relocation Program between 2016-2017 till nowadays. Their experiences reveal how integration takes place beyond the structural and systemic regulatory requirements. Refugees' integration must not only rely on more technical and quantifiable matters, such as the ones mentioned in the beginning, but also on subjective and individual questions, that is, the creation, promotion, and maintenance of favourable conditions to the intimate, affective and emotional needs of refugees to achieve personal and identity goals, and to complement and support their integration.

169   Ethnic Eateries in the Carmel Market in Tel Aviv as a Microcosm of Immigration

Paulette Schuster

The open-air market (called a "shuk/souk" in Hebrew and Arabic, respectively) is a vital part of Israel's culinary and social ecology. In addition to providing local residents with access to fresh produce and other household goods, they serve as a showcase for the country's myriad ethnic cuisines, and offer a space to gather and sample these foodstuffs. With their cacophony of smells, tastes, and sounds, markets are a great way to tap into a community's personality.

Nearly every major city in Israel has some sort of market, ranging from established municipal markets housed in massive permanent indoor/outdoor structures, to impromptu ones that consist of little more than a few blankets spread out and covered with freshly picked greens.

For example, in Jerusalem, there are the Mahane Yehuda and Emek Refaim Markets; in Haifa, the Talpiot and Wadi Nisnas Markets; in Ramle you have the city market; in Netanya there is a Municipal Market; in   Beersheva there is a Bedouin Market and in Tel Aviv, there are several markets: Levinsky Spice Market, Hatikvah, port market, Farmers' Market and the biggest one: the Carmel Market which is the focus of this paper.

Israel is a melting pot of cultures and ethnicities. The Carmel Market houses a plethora of ethnic eateries that are represented in the form of fast-food stalls, sit-down popular restaurants, chef-owned upscale restaurants, pop-up booths, takeaway and delivery stands, and permanent stores. Among these, I found Mexican, Thai, Moroccan, Turkish, Yemenite, Peruvian, Brazilian, Hungarian, Romanian, Chinese, Korean, Persian, Iraqi, Polish and other ethnic kitchens.

Prashizky (2022) argues that physical place influences intergroup/ethnic relations that in turn reshape the symbolic meaning of urban spaces. This paper will explore the Carmel Market as an interconnected and eclectic urban space that fosters intergroup/ethnic relations among its patrons, vendors and customers.

1G   Göç Çalışmaları 1 [UG11]

Chair: Filiz Göktuna Yaylacı, Anadolu University, Turkey

416   6 Şubat Kahramanmaraş Depremleri Sonrasi Zorunlu İç Göç: Eskişehir Örneği

Filiz Göktuna Yaylacı ve Gül Sevi Üçüncü

FORCED INTERNAL MIGRATION FOLLOWING FEBRUARY 6 KAHRAMANMARAŞ EARTHQUAKES: THE CASE OF ESKISEHIR

On February 6, 2023, earthquakes with a magnitude of 7.7 and 7.6 occurred in the Pazarcık and Elbistan districts of Kahramanmaraş, Türkiye. According to official records, 11 provinces were directly affected, nearly 50,000 people lost their lives, a total of 1,971,589 people were forced to evacuate or to migrate to other cities by their own means. More than 20,000 earthquake survivors migrated to Eskişehir in 5 weeks, which is in the second-degree migration zone after neighboring provinces. The main problems of this research are the experiences of the immigrants in the migration process, what their survival strategies are, and what they experience in the decision-making process. In this context, in addition to migration experiences and decision-making processes, the research also covers their interactions with public and çivil institutions and how they are affected by the media. The study group of the research consists of 30 immigrated earthquake survivors determined through purposeful sampling. 30 migrant earthquake survivors directly affected by the earthquakes were reached by snowball method and data were collected through interviews based on semi-structured interview form. The obtained data were evaluated with descriptive analysis. In this respect, the first findings of the research are as follows: The consecutive earthquakes have caused material, moral and social losses. Severe aftershocks and late intervention cases in the region have caused widespread and intensive fears and anxieties among quake survivors. Losses such as homes and workplaces, the death of a large number of people, and the root effect of social ties in the region have been the main reasons accelerating the internal migration. Among the outstanding reasons for migration to Eskişehir are the ties of acquaintances, active solidarity networks, and the city's economically favorable living conditions. On the other hand, high rental prices in the cities close to the earthquake zone, the immigrant satisfaction of the neighboring cities, the proximity of Eskişehir to the big cities, the working discipline of the municipalities, the social structure in the city, the neighborhood relations, the active and organized progress of civil society activities have also been effective in the decision-making process for migration.

478   Seçim Sürecinde Sığınmacılar Uyum, Eğitim ve Gelecek: 2023 Seçim Sürecinde Partilerin ve Cumhurbaşkanı Adaylarının Göçmen ve Sığınmacılar Hakkındaki Görüşleri

Filiz Göktuna Yaylacı ve Ali Faruk Yaylacı

Türkiye has a long and rich history in the context of migration. In addition to being a country that sends immigrants to Europe since the 1960s, Turkiye has also been a target of immigration flows from different geographies. Türkiye's character as a country of migration, which reflects the distinctive features of being a country of migration more and more intensely, has undergone a remarkable transformation since 2011 with the massive Syrian-originated refugee movements. With the Syrian refugees, whose numbers have reached millions and are gaining a more permanent character, serious debates have begun to be observed in the public and political sphere in the context of asylum seekers. In Türkiye, which is home to over five million foreigners today, debates around themes such as migration, asylum seekers, education and integration, and return occupy the public sphere. As is generally observed in migration countries, such discussions come to the fore more during election periods, and political actors make different promises in this context. These discussions and the promises of political actors have an important role in the formulation and successful implementation of policies to be developed with regard to migration processes. In this respect, it is important to comparatively examine the promises of political parties and presidential candidates regarding migrants or asylum seekers, and their policy proposals on education and integration, especially during the election period. Accordingly, this research will examine the campaign declarations of the political parties participating in Turkey's 2023 Presidential and parliamentary general elections and the related statements of the presidential candidates in a comparative way, as well as discussing the foreseen future concerning immigrants or asylum seekers.

Keywords: Migration; Asylum Seeker; Syrian; Integration; Election; Policy

428 Brain Drain of Health Workers from Turkey to Germany and Its Results: Possibilities of Brain Gain

Fuat Güllüpınar ve Gamze Kaçar Tunç

In this study, the professional experiences of doctors and nurses before, during and after migration will be analyzed by focusing on the factors that cause doctors and nurses to migrate from Turkey to Germany in recent years. In this context, it will be tried to understand how doctors and nurses immigrated to Germany through which transnational networks, associations or institutions. Their intentions, feelings and thoughts before they migrated, their experiences during the migration process, and their feelings and thoughts that transformed in the face of the opportunities and difficulties they faced after migration will be analyzed. Within the scope of the qualitative research, in-depth interviews will be conducted online with 35 doctors and nurses who immigrated to Germany and are members of transnational social networks operating in professional, cultural and academic fields. Opportunities and limitations of doctors and nurses in terms of working conditions, social rights, profession and career opportunities will be compared through their experiences in Turkey and Germany. In addition, this study aims to understand the attitudes and strategies of doctors and nurses to transfer their technical skills and knowledge to Turkey by trying to understand the social, cultural and academic associations and transnational social networks they are members of and maintain their relations with Turkey. The study also aims to identify their potential and role in knowledge, experience and skill transfer. At this point, the incentive policies and programs of some institutions in Turkey regarding cooperation with Turkish colleagues abroad and temporary or permanent return opportunities will also be investigated. Finally, the experiences of doctors and nurses in adapting to Germany as high-skilled immigrants and their attitudes towards Turkey will be investigated, and the differences in attitudes before and after migration will be analyzed.

14:45-15:00 BREAK

2A   Wellbeing and Migration 1 [EG17]

Chair: Jeffrey H. Cohen, Ohio State University, USA

324   The mental health effects of asylum status for refugees in Germany from a longitudinal perspective: A Growth mixture model

Judith Masselmann, Maria-Therese Friehs, Maarten van Zalk

Background:

Postmigration stressors such as an insecure asylum status or long asylum processing times are serious risk factors for the mental health of refugees. With this person-centred reanalysis of German survey data, we aim to quantify and integrate these effects from a psychological perspective. The presentation will address the following research questions beyond others: How has the mental health of refugees in Germany, specifically regarding depression and anxiety, developed between 2016 and 2019? How is the asylum status of refugees related to their mental health across time? Does a change in asylum status predict changes in mental health? How do asylum status, gender, German language skills, employment, whether an official hearing has taken place, and whether a spouse or children live outside of Germany predict the mental health of refugees in Germany?

Methods:

We will use data of refugees in Germany who participated in the longitudinal IAB-BAMF-SOEP survey between 2016 and 2019 (N = 1,241). We will investigate the development of mental health depending on their legal asylum status and asylum processing time using Latent Growth Curve Models. The level of unobserved heterogeneity will be examined by computing Growth Mixture Models which examine whether the population can be subdivided in terms of differing symptom scores. Finally, we will explore whether established predictors of anxiety and depression in refugees also predict whether individuals are in higher symptom subgroups.

Findings:

We are currently running the described analysis and assure that we will be able to present final analytical results by July 2023.

424   Health-related issues in the forced migrations context: an intersectional and multi-level approach in the recognition of international protection, from the European to the Italian experience

Sara Battistello and Chiara Lucchini

In the context of forced migration, especially when referring to health-related issues (i.e. disability, mental illness, sexually transmitted diseases, and other viral diseases), it is possible to talk about intersectional multiple discrimination (Arconzo, 2022) - meaning specific interaction between two or more factors of discrimination - and not just a mere sum.

How often are institutions faced with situations of discrimination caused by more than one factor at the same time? Are social and legal workers able to recognize such a sort of discrimination? The authors believe that institutions, as well as social and legal workers, are not equipped enough.

This paper aims to investigate the lack of protection that results from a traditional sector-based approach to vulnerability with reference to forced migrants with disability or mental and physical illness, in the European and Italian context. To do this, the study also analyzes the legislative and welfare voids and how they affect the international protection system (Longo, 2022; Griffo et al., 2020). In fact, we suggest that international protection can be the most appropriate way to protect forced migrants who are also victims of multiple discrimination - complying both with the evolution of the refugee definition and specific case-law (ASGI, 2021; Arconzo, 2022).

Firstly, the work aims to overcome the traditional policy of granting people with disability or illness a complementary form of protection or a health-related residence permit (ASGI, 2021). To do so, an intersectional approach will be useful to examine and open up the definition of refugee (Arconzo, 2022), drawing also from international literature and European guidelines, that state the right to be recognized as a refugee when "sharing an innate characteristic or a common background that cannot be changed" (EASO, 2020).

Secondly, we argue that a further look into the context of forced migrations clearly shows that where different vulnerabilities coexist, different discriminations come together. This becomes even more evident when listening to the stories of migrants, where new risk factors of different forms of discrimination can emerge. The many levels of discrimination prevent people, and even more forced migrants, from being granted a specific position in the system and, therefore, jeopardize their access to right care and protection (Di Sciullo et al., 2021).

Therefore, it can be useful to analyze how scholars, social and legal workers have been recently looking at the data about nationality and health, suggesting that both the journey and the situation in the country of arrival can affect, to a large extent, the discrimination factors that already coexist (Scotti, 2023; Prestileo et al., 2022; Prestileo et al., 2021; Fakoya et al., 2016).

In conclusion, we underline how only an intersectional approach can deal with such a complexity, better reading the reality and understanding the context; also funneling into the path of the European Commission that recently drafted a Strategy for the Rights of Persons with Disabilities 2021-2030 - an intersectional approach for disabilities.

250   Determinants of Post Traumatic Stress Disorder (PTSD) in Syrian Refugees living in Turkey between 2011-2017: Analysis by Gender and City

Alime Tombak

Background:

Circumstances of forced migrations are associated with increased psychological distress, behavioural disorders, and increased prevalence of mental illnesses such as posttraumatic stress disorder (PTSD), depression and anxiety. Research indicates that Syrian refugees are highly vulnerable and likely to experience various mental diseases due to forced migration and war-related traumatic events. Also, female migrants, on average, experience higher prevalence rates of mental disorders, depression, anxiety, and PTSD than males. Furthermore, there are location-based differences in the psychological stress outcomes of refugees. On average, refugees living in large cities will have higher psychological stress than those in small cities/ periphery.

Objective:

This study is aimed to examine the differences in psychological distress / post-traumatic stress disorder (PTSD) due to circumstances of forced migration among Syrian refugees living in Turkey (N=785 respondents) by their location/living city and their gender. If it differs, what are its determinants?

Method:

To explore which group of factors had the most significant influence on PTSD, 785 respondents conducted multiple logistic regression analyses.

Results:

(Preliminary Results): Among the four cities (Istanbul, Turkish centre; Şanlıurfa province borders with Syria; Izmir large port city/transit hub; Batman as a periphery), the highest post-trauma stress symptoms are in Istanbul and Şanlıurfa (H1 +). There are differences in posttraumatic stress disorder outcomes among refugees living in cities reporting big city İstanbul and the province borders with

Syria city Sanlıurfa (serves as a natural entry place for Syrians) (H1 A +). Gender-based differences exist in the posttraumatic stress disorder outcomes of refugees who arrived in Turkey (H2 +). Syrian male refugees living in İstanbul experience more posttraumatic stress disorder than Syrian female males living in Istanbul (H2 A-). More than %20 of male respondents living in Istanbul experience posttraumatic stress. In Şanlıurfa, posttraumatic stress symptoms in female respondents are higher than in male respondents (24.36%, 28.21%, 32.05%).

Conclusion:

These preliminary findings point to the importance of assessing posttraumatic stress disorder due to the circumstances of refugees. Furthermore, these results show that male and female refugees feel the burden of the experiences they carry differently. Moreover, psychosocial health care can affect PTSD outcomes for refugees by gender.

[1] MSc Sociology and Social Research thesis student at University of Cologne (Universität zu Köln) in Germany

441   Improving Consents and the Delivery of Healthcare for Immigrants and Refugees

Benjamin Levy

Over the past 5 years, several clinics in Chicago have been working to improve patient centered medical care. Our goal has been to simplify the consent process through increased use of video interpretation services, in-person interpreters (frequently former refugees themselves who are physicians, nurses, and medical assistants), and translated consents.   Several techniques were identified and used to improve refugee and immigrant patient understanding of procedures, which could be easily applied to clinics in many diverse settings globally. Whenever possible, provide easy to understand diagrams for patients, which show the procedure steps. The diagrams should illustrate medical outcome goals without the use of words. In addition, provide patient education materials that includes descriptions written in a 5th grade level in the patient's native language. Ask patients if they can read. Work with family members (present at patient visit or allow patients to video call family members during the patient visit) to assist with procedure planning such as taking a colonoscopy prep, NPO status, and the management of diabetic medications and blood thinners.

2B   History and Migration 1 [UG14]

Chair: Caner Tekin, Ruhr University, Bochum, Germany

245   The "Long Duree" Practice in Exploring the Iban's Migration to the State of Sabah, Malaysia 1940-2011

Amrullah Maraining

History as a discipline in social science keeps evolving through multidimensional foci and transcendent in its discipline, attracting more investigative and empirical debates. Such diversity results from the ink of contemporary history, although sometimes this may only be limited to polemic debates. Despite this, the development of contemporary history remains of utmost importance in the inquiries of knowledge. This study seeks to explore the democratization of historical methodology, emphasizing the studies of ethnicity in the state of Sabah, situated in East Malaysia. By acknowledging investigative and empirical inquiries on history, this study posits that the investigate question on ethnicity in Sabah requires a more democratic and universal approach. This study aims at achieving three objectives. Firstly, this study highlights the Annales methodology as an alternative approach in understanding democratizing historical methodology. This study also aligned with the current history of the Iban community migration to Sabah. Secondly, this study analyzes the practice of "Longue Duree" to separate the history of migration of the Sabah's Iban community through the timeline. This timeline approach would ultimately influence the migration patterns and the history of Sabah's Iban community formation. Thirdly, this study aims to understand the social science's orientation, focusing on the strength of the Annales approach to unravel the aspects of cultural change. This approach highlights the process of adaptation, assimilation with local culture, social development, economic and political dynamics in explaining the formation of the Iban community in Sabah. This study will explore the Iban's community in two villages in Mukim Merotai Besar and Mukim Balung to further understand these inquiries of debates as previously mentioned. This study adopts the framework of Annale's approach through the concept of 'Longue Duree.' Through structural analysis as a platform of analysis, this study aims to explore the historical facts through the methodology of data collection conducted in the field. Overall, this study successfully proves that the Annales approach helps understand the history of Iban's migration to Sabah. In addition, this study provides a diverse point of view in challenging the existing orientation of social knowledge in the Iban community. This study concludes that the framework of Annales approach enables enhanced perspective and widens the dynamics of historical knowledge as time flies.

145   The Story of a Revolution: Czech and Slovak Migration from Historical Central Europe Lands to the U.S.

Sezgin Uysal and Martin Guzi

The "Forty-Eighters" case which started in the German Empire and expanded all parts of Europe refers to the revolutionary wave of 1848 in Europe. Political reforms turned into a series of civil conflicts that led to political instability, starvation and were triggered by large emigration from Europe to Australia, the United Kingdom, and the United States (U.S). The U.S at that time encountered high economic growth that attracted labourers from all the world. Therefore, Czech and Slovak migrants were forced to migrate to find new jobs, while others had to emigrate for political reform, institutional change, and conflict reasons.

Considering all these situations had heterogeneous migration intentions for immigrant groups. The U.S was an attractive destination for Czech and Slovak labour emigrants. As a matter of fact, between 1850 and 1910, approximately 325.000 Czechs and Slovaks immigrated for several reasons to the U.S. This paper will study the emigration of the Czechs and Slovaks to the U.S in the period 1850-1910. It will explore migration's economic and political motives using the microdata of emigrating individuals. On the other hand, the study aims to explore different migrants, such as Czech and Slovak migrant groups situation of residential, duration of persistence conditions, and labour market performance after the migration to the host country. The study takes data from American census records available in Ancestry and IPUMS (the Integrated Public Use Microdata Series) databases.

The individual records of Czech and Slovak immigrants to the U.S are obtained at the time of arrival. They include detailed information about gender, age, birthplace, mother tongue, occupation, industry, and education. The microdata obtained from IPUMS and Ancestry with the census records of each person will be compared in ten-year periods. It will emphasise on personal characteristics, social networks or geographical network structures that affect the permanent duration of immigrants in the host country.

369   Counterparts or Self-operating? Pro-AKP Migrant Organisations in Germany

Sezer İdil Göğüş

During the AKP era, a general re-orientation of Turkish foreign policy could be observed, which also impacted the outreach towards Turks residing abroad as part of "diaspora engagement" (Aydın 2014, Öktem 2014, Baser 2015, Baser/Ozturk 2019). This engagement of Turkey has manifested itself in various aspects from granting her citizens abroad external voting rights to a policy that encouraged institutionalisation (Mencutek/Baser 2018) . At the same time, the AKP started to stress identity bonds to a community outside of the place of actual residence. In the vein of this new diaspora engagement, certain political activities (Adamson 2012, 2019) could be observed amongst Turkish people in Germany. Inter alia, pro-AKP/Erdoğan groups and organisations such as Union of International Democrats (UID) and short-lived German small party with Turkish background Alliance German Democrats (AD-Demokraten) entered the political stage. These organisations appear to represent – at the least functional – local counterparts for Turkey's transnational cultural policy. They address Turkey-related themes, embrace the historical and national identity bods, and are able to reach many Turkish people in Germany through events and/or social media. They are not just passive receivers of the AKP's diaspora politics, but they are also active political agents (Arkilic 2020, Goksu/Leerkes 2022), who position themselves and root their activities locally in Germany. The data is collected through three years ethnographic research (participant observations, interviews, and virtual ethnography) among the pro-AKP organisations UID and AD-Demokraten, and offers a micro analysis on the activities, the motivations, and the agency of these diaspora organizations. This paper, therefore, aims to analyse the resonance of the AKP's diaspora politics from local level perspectives in Germany by studying the roles they play for their clienteles: How do those people of Turkish descent and their organisations who respond to the new diaspora politics frame and justify their related activities with an eye to their life in Germany?

2C   Mexico as a Source and a Destination Country [BG3/4]

Chair: Carla Pederzini Villarreal, University of Iberoamericana, Mexico

1116   Adaptation of a community health outreach model during the COVID-19 pandemic: The case of the Mexican Consulates in the United States of America

Pablo Gaitan Rossi, Mireya Vilar-Compte, Arturo Vargas-Bustamante

Amongst Mexicans in the US, an important strategy to get information and health care navigation support during the COVID-19 pandemic was seeking help from the Mexican Consulates. Particularly, the Ventanillas de Salud (VDS) have been found to be a culturally sensitive outreach program within the Consulates available to Mexicans in the US regardless of their immigration status. This study examines how the VDS in two Mexican Consulates in the US adapted their outreach services to better serve Mexicans in the US during the COVID-19 pandemic. We use the EquIR framework, a pragmatic guideline for conducting equity-focused implementation research in health interventions. We identify the key implementation processes that the VDS enacted to adapt and continue outreach services and document the specific needs and experiences of the population that used the VDS to cope with the COVID-19 pandemic. The qualitative study will assess implementation outcomes that aid in the strengthening and replication of the VDS model for future public health crises.

1117   Does Lighter means Healthier? Skin color and health status among Mexican immigrants

Erika Arenas, Luis Ruvalcaba, Graciela Teruel

A vast amount of research reveals a negative association between dark skin tone and individual's life chances (Keith & Herring, 1991; Klonoff & Landrine, 2000). Structural racism, at the macro level, and racial discrimination, at the individual level, are the main drivers suggested by the literature explaining this association. In terms of health outcomes, darker skin shades have been associated with worst outcomes among U.S. born Americans, and among lawful immigrants and permanent residents in the United States (Williams et al. 2003; Borell et al. 2006; Han 2020; Painter and Tabler 2022). Yet, there are no studies investigating this association among undocumented individuals, which account to 25% of the immigrant population in the United States (about 11 million). In this paper, we contribute to the literature by examining the association between skin tone and physical and mental health among a recent cohort of Mexican migrants that moved to the United States after 2002. We use data from the Mexican Family Life Survey (the MxFLS), which is a novel panel dataset that has followed respondents even if they moved to the United States. In 2002, when the MxFLS baseline was conducted all respondents (N=35,000) were residing in Mexico. In 2005, and in 2010, when the second and third waves were conducted, respectively, about 10% of the sample moved to the United States. Using the MxFLS for this investigation offers unique advantages to study the association between health and skin tone. First, about 80% of the MxFLS sample consisted of undocumented immigrants, a population that has not been previously examined. Second, the MxFLS collected information about the skin color of the respondents using a skin color palette. Interviewers would choose the skin color of the respondent based on this skin color palette. Third, the MxFLS included a wide array of health information (i.e., mental health, and subjective measures of health) that was collected every wave. This is a clear advantage over other surveys given that having pre-migration information about the health status of immigrants allows controlling for potential biases caused by health selection of migrants. Fourth, the MxFLS collected information about the context of reception of migrants. Finally, it included socio-demographic information that may influence the association between health and skin tone. This paper will contribute to the literature investigating how the existence of racial and color hierarchies shapes life chances among immigrants, in particular those undocumented.

1118 What do Mexicans think about newcomers? A qualitative analysis of immigrant local perceptions

Karla Valenzuela Moreno and Marilyn Román Bejarano

This article sheds light on the perception that Mexicans have about newcomers in three state capitals: Saltillo, Coahuila; Monterrey, Nuevo León and Guadalajara, Jalisco. By conducting focus groups with members of the community and semi-structured interviews with stakeholders, we were able to determine which factors influence local perceptions about migrant persons. Our findings agree with other studies that point to the importance of local characteristics in the integration process. We show that perceptions differ among subnational jurisdictions. Even though there are shared perceptions -such as immigrants being poor and therefore dangerous, and a strong preference for skilled newcomers-, local features -such as values and lifestyles- have a strong influence in the acceptance of immigrants.

1119 Labor force participation of Central American migrant men and women in Mexico

Liliana Meza González and Carla Pederzini Villarreal

The paper uses information from the 2000, 2010 and 2020 censuses as well as the 2015 Intercensal Survey to compare access to the labor market for men and women from Guatemala, El Salvador and Honduras residing in Mexico. Labor participation, main economic sectors, human capital and income levels of the men and women of each of the three nationalities considered are compared, seeking to identify from a gender perspective the differentiated labor participation of each nationality. We estimate a model of labor participation to identify the interaction of gender and nationality in the migrant population from Central America.

2D   Migraciones and Transnacionalismo 1 [BG 5/6]

Chair: Pascual Garcia, Universidad Técnica Particular de Loja, Ecuador

450 Biopolítica y migración: Un análisis de las condiciones del desplazamiento centroamericano por el Noroeste de México

Julio César Félix Chávez and Nayeli Burgueño Angulo

La presente propuesta es parte de una investigación, cuyo objetivo principal es el conocer sobre la situación del fenómeno de la migración de tránsito de origen centroamericano y aportar a los estudios regionales sobre la movilidad y cruce de personas por México. Desde el análisis socio-antropológico, se pretende conocer sobre la situación que viven los migrantes de tránsito en su paso por la región del Noroeste de México y de qué manera el discurso que se ha construido, desde el Estado-Nación, traducido en la aplicación de políticas antiinmigrantes de exclusión y criminalización, condiciona y legitima la situación de marginación y violación de derechos humanos de los migrantes. En el marco de las políticas de contención migratoria implementadas por los gobiernos de Estados Unidos y México, se presenta un discurso de criminalización de la migración no autorizada, que se acrecienta con el aumento de la migración de origen centroamericano en su búsqueda por llegar a los Estados Unidos (Del Monte y Mariscal, 2020). El presente trabajo analiza el impacto de las movilidades en este contexto, el papel de las fronteras y políticas migratorias, no solo en las condiciones y retos con los que se enfrentan los migrantes ante estas, sino entenderlas como resultado de un discurso que obedece a una visión etnocéntrica de exclusión y racismo, que se profundiza y legitima. Se utilizan los conceptos de biopoder y biopolítica, como herramientas conceptuales y metodológicas, lo que Foucault (2019) definió como la injerencia del poder sobre la vida, sobre los cuerpos y su existencia, el cual se manifiesta no solo a través de leyes e instituciones, sino que permea en toda la sociedad, través de múltiples relaciones de fuerza.

492   Ecuador de país emisor de migrantes a tránsito y destino de millón de venezolanos

Pascual Garcia

El presente artículo se enfoca en analizar y explicar las causas y dinamicas del continuum migratorio de Ecuador. Asi como también a través de metodología etnográfica y etnográfica virtual e investigación documental, exploramos las rutas, las redes sociales utilizadas para llegar a su destino. Esta investigación también es una reflexión crítica a la gobernanza de Ecuador y sus ciclos político-económicos y las respuestas por parte de la ciudadanía ecuatoriana bajo el marco conceptual desarrollado por Albert Hirschman de voz, salida y lealtad.

Según datos de Naciones Unidas, desde 2014 más de 7 millones venezolanos abandonaron el país de los cuales 6.3 millones se encuentran en América Latina y el Caribe (R4V 2022) este éxodo debido a la agitación política, la inestabilidad socioeconómica y la crisis humanitaria en curso crisis; Según la OIM (2019), el Corredor Andino es la ruta vía terrestre más utilizada y dinámica de Sudamérica. Donde anualmente cruzan 225 mil venezolanos por Ecuador y radican 520 mil aproximadamente según datos de (R4V 2023).

Por lo tanto, realizamos un estudio exploratorio para conocer las dinámicas migratorias, prácticas xenófobas que sufren los migrantes

mediante observación participativa y estudio de caso con migrantes venezolanos en Macará, Pindal, Alamor, Zapotillo y Huaquillas (pueblos fronterizos en el Sur Ecuador) sobre sus experiencias de movilidad en cuanto a racismo, salud y redes sociales.

Los datos empíricos se recogieron mediante 66 entrevistas semiestructuradas recogidas entre marzo 2022 y enero 2023 a venezolanos en los lugares mencionados gracias a un proyecto financiado por la Universidad tecnica Particular de Loja en Ecuador.

Los hallazgos muestran que sus trayectorias incluyen migración circular entre Colombia, Ecuador y Perú y también un ir y venir entre su destino y Venezuela, así como múltiples períodos de permanecer en diferentes lugares. Además, los participantes informarondificultades para garantizar sus medios de vida - subsistencia- en las sociedades de acogida y un aumento de la xenofobia en Ecuador.

431   Migración de transito de centroamericanos por Zacatecas México hacia Estados Unidos

Pascual Gerardo García Zamora and Juan Lamberto Herrera Martínez

En estos momentos de postpandemia las circunstancias económicas y sociales han hecho sinergia como elementos generadores de mayor precariedad en la satisfacción de las necesidades básicas y también un incremento de la inseguridad física de las poblaciones en la región, por lo cual las personas y familias completas se ven en la necesidad de buscar mejores condiciones de vida y desarrollo para todos ellos, enfrentando de manera diferencial los obstáculos que el proceso migratorio va   presentando según las condiciones socioeconómicas, redes sociales de apoyo, acceso a internet y la capacidad en la toma de decisiones en esta experiencia de vida. Según la cepal la pandemia del Covid-19 y la crisis social incrementaron la pobreza extrema   en la región de América Latina y el Caribe de 13.1 por ciento en 2020   a 13.8 por ciento en el 2021, porcentajes conformados por 81 millones a 88 millones de personas de personas que descendieron en la escala de pobreza (Cepal 2021) a El objetivo del presente estudio es identificar, a partir de los testimonios de los propios migrantes, las regiones de más riesgos para su integridad, asi como los lugares, instituciones y poblaciones que acogen de manera solidaria su paso por México, así abordamos como el problema complejo de la migración presenta diversos desenlaces, desde los que logran llegar al destino, hasta los que después de muchos problemas deciden quedarse en México o buscan como retornar a sus países de origen. La metodología implementada para recopilar y analizar la información es la etnográfica, aplicando entrevistas semiestructuradas en la ciudad de Zacatecas que se encuentra en la parte centro norte del país aproximadamente a 600 km de la frontera con estados Unidos. La Estructura de la entrevista se centra en conocer la experiencia vivida desde que ingresa por Tapachula Chiapas que es la frontera sur del país, hasta esta ciudad. El presente estudio nos permitirá conocer la diversidad de experiencias desde el ingreso a México las rutas que toman, sus motivaciones, estrategias de sobrevivencia, medios de transporte, interacción con la población mexicana, fuerzas armadas y acceso de servicios asistenciales. Además, identificar sus redes sociales, funcionalidad y presencia en lugar de origen y destino, percepción de riesgo e identificación de las fuentes de este. El producto del presente trabajo permitirá conocer las condiciones en que los migrantes centroamericanos realizan este viaje a través de México

Palabras clave: Migración, Rutas y Redes sociales

Cepal 2021; panorama social de américa latina 2021

313   Vivir de las remesas sociales: Historias de vida de 6 familias ecuatorianas migrantes

Martha Sofia Garcia Guerrero, Ruben García, Analy Guaman Carrion

La migración transnacional también enfatiza la construcción de la comunidad transnacional, la cual se encuentra asociada a los integrantes de un circuito migratorio y a la importancia que estos le den al lugar de origen, siendo el lugar al que siempre vuelven o el lugar en el que se encuentra establecida su familia (Goldring,1997). Otros autores identifican a la comunidad transnacional, como el conjunto de migrantes que provienen de un mismo lugar de origen y que a su vez desarrollan prácticas transnacionales que vinculan a las personas con sus localidades (Rivera Sánchez, 2007). La comunidad transnacional se enfoca en todos los circuitos que sostienen lazos sociales estrechos, de forma que la construcción de comunidad contribuye a que se establezca una relación de pertenencia de los migrantes hacia la comunidad. Goldring (1997) también menciona, que el parentesco es un factor importante, ya que los lazos que se mantiene en el circuito migratorio con la familia son más relevantes del que se mantiene con el lugar de origen.

El propósito de este trabajo es analizar las prácticas transnacionales de los migrantes ecuatorianos, tomando en consideración al transnacionalismo desde las bases, se llevará a cabo bajo el planteamiento metodológico cualitativo. Como menciona Casilimas (1996), los acercamientos de tipo cualitativo nos muestran realidades subjetivas e intersubjetivas. Lo que se pretende es comprender las distintas realidades, desde una mirada a partir de los actores sociales, mediante historias de vida y entrevistas a profundidad a seis familias ecuatorianas radicando en España, Italia y Estados Unidos y como mantienen lazos sostenidos con su lugar de origen mediante las remesas sociales

Los migrantes a entrevistar fueron seleccionados mediante bola de nieve, dentro de ella se identificaron a participantes claves, mediante etnografía virtual puesto que esta técnica abre un nuevo campo en la investigación, ampliando el análisis en los múltiples escenarios, permitiendo el uso de herramientas digitales para su exploración. Los hallazgos muestran que durante la pandemia se intensificaron estos lazos por medio de llamadas, envío de ropa, medicinas e ideas para emprender. Sin embargo se necesita proseguir en el tiempo con las entrevistas a las mismas familias para poder conocer en un mayor periodo de tiempo la evolución o cambios de las prácticas sociales y el transnacionalismo que viven estas seis familias en tres lugares de destino diferente.

2E   Migration, Law and Policy 2 [EG15/16]

Chair: Thomas Richter, German Institute for Global and Area Studies (GIGA), Germany

1127   Emotions and extremism: The connection of discrimination, anger and the acceptance of political violence

Rebecca Endtricht

1128   Effects of the perception of human rights violations and protests in Iran on Islamophobic attitudes towards Muslims in Germany: Results of two representative surveys and a survey experiment

Peter Wetzels and Thomas Richter

1129   Declines in Perceptions of Fairness and Legitimacy as Precursors of Political Radicalisation in Times of Crisis

Diego Farren and Katrin Brettfeld

2F   Migration and Environment [UG11]

Chair: Jara Al-Ali, Universität Hamburg, Germany

435   The European Union facing Environmental Migration: An Interpretive Policy Analysis of the report on "The Impact of Climate Change on Vulnerable Populations in Developing Countries."

Armelle Wafo

Since 1985, a growing body of research has shown that the congruence between migration and climate change has led to the emergence of a new form of migration:

"environmental migration" (Blocher, 2017; Cournil and Vlassopoulos, 2015). Today, nationals of "developing countries" are mainly affected by climate change. Indeed, according to the World Bank, by 2050, there will be 143 million internally displaced people due to climate change, mainly in sub-Saharan Africa, South Asia and Latin America.Climate change affects not only the place of residence of these people, their health, their livelihoods but also the overall balance of the affected regions (Moor, 2011). However, there is currently no legal framework that can guarantee protection to people who migrate for environmental reasons (Ni, 2015).

Issues related to environmental migration, occasionally debated since the late 1990s within the European Union, took about ten years to be formally included in the agenda of the European Commission. Indeed, on 16 April 2013, a working document made for the first time a link between migration and climate change. The latter is published as an annex to the communication on the European Union's climate change adaptation strategy. It was not until 2020 that a motion for a resolution, contained in an own-initiative report of the European Parliament entitled "The impact of climate change on vulnerable populations in developing countries" (González, 2020), proposed concrete measures to legally regulate and protect environmental migrants. These measures range from diversifying climate change adaptation policies to granting international protection or humanitarian visas to these people. To be approved, the proposal had to obtain a simple majority vote. Following the plenary debate that took place in May 2021 in Brussels, the proposal is rejected.

How can we understand the non-adoption of this proposal? What links can be established between the different political positions identified in the motion for a resolution and the final vote? Did the requests for amendments to this report play a role in the non-adoption of the resolution? It is these questions that this research aims to answer. To achieve this, the report will be analyzed using interpretive policy analysis (IPA) (Yanow, 2007). This approach invites us to question the meaning of public policies by focusing on the language used in political debates (Ibid.). In doing so, the IPA highlights the different actors involved in the decision-making process, their political positions and the contextual elements surrounding the drafting of the motion for a resolution (prior negotiations, debate, amendments, testimonies and political ideologies). This analysis ultimately makes it possible to understand the deep issues that hinder the evolution of European debates around environmental migration.

289   Environmental Inequities and Urban Migration: An Analysis of Climate Injustice for Syrian Communities in Istanbul

Elif Bengi Güneş and Osman Balaban

Anthropogenic climate change results in both systemic inequalities and global harmful repercussions. While it was long seen as an environmental catastrophe, it has now emerged as a source of social inequality. The most vulnerable populations in the city, including women, children, even unborn babies, the elderly, the disabled, and those with poor income, face considerably more severe issues. Nonetheless, in many countries in the world, migrants stand out as one of the groups that go through this process the most intensely.

Due to its geographical and strategic location, Turkey has been a frequent destination for regular and irregular migration, including mass asylum movements since the Ottoman period. Despite this, both central and local strategies have not been sufficiently effective in alleviating migrants' hardships and supporting their way of life. As the Syrian Civil War began in 2011, Turkey's open-door policy drew a caravan of 252 refugees, resulting in an influx of nearly 3.5 million people. Racial discrimination, an absence of Turkish language skills, fear of deportation, labor exploitation, and economic woes have all led to problems in the regular lifestyle of Syrians, and have limited their capacity to survive disasters.

This paper is based on an ongoing research that aims to expose the vulnerability of Syrian immigrants dwelling in Istanbul, a city at the epicenter of international migration and under severe climate stress, toward environmental consequences. In this context, a macro-scale map was produced by examining the relationship between the data obtained on the impacts of environmental change in Istanbul and the neighborhoods where Syrian migrants constitute a spatial concentration. Then, an equal-weighted score approach was used to implicate the vulnerability characteristics. In the second phase, field surveys was conducted in the 12 most risky quarters. In-depth semi-structured interviews were carried out in Turkish and Arabic with a total of 60 people, 5 from each neighborhood. The interviews with participating Syrians were transcribed and synthesized into a thematic framework using an iterative approach.

As a result, it is revealed that Syrian migrants in Istanbul suffer from lack of social status, risk ignorance, being neglected, lack of basic rights, distrust, and livelihood difficulties. These disempowering factors cause them to live mostly in critical areas of Istanbul in terms of climatic hazards and have inferior and feeble coping aptitudes. In particular, for Syrian communities, family structure, institutional insecurity, language barriers and home comfort are likely to exacerbate the pressure of climate impacts. Despite having access to services that support climate adaptation, such as health and education, Syrians in Istanbul are largely unaware of climate change, and they are diverting resources to more prioritized concerns and life activities.

In Turkey, which has a robust migratory tendency, it is critical to investigate and evaluate the issue of climate justice at the urban and community levels to comprehend current and prospective social issues. Furthermore, addressing the unequal distribution of the consequences of climate change on populations and adopting pragmatic, adaptable, and successful utilitarian policies would make a substantial contribution to the literature.

61   Climate Induced Migration and Sexual Reproductive Health & Rights (SRHR): A descriptive study based on climate induced displacement in Pakistan

Syed Imran Haider, Muhammad Ali Awan, Shahzad Ahmed Shiz

Pakistan is amongst the countries most vulnerable to climate change and the most recent are the floods and torrential rains during 2022. According to the Global Climate Risk Index, from 1999 to 2018, Pakistanis experienced 152 events of extreme weather which caused 9,989 lives. An important, but usually ignored in policies and plans, climate impact is climate-induced migration. The last decade has seen a growth in climate migrants, and the patterns of forced climate displacement and migration can be observed in every province of Pakistan. Impacts of climate-related displacement are challenging and complex. Studies show that climate change has direct implications for SRHR. An increase of one degree Celsius in the week before delivery increases the likelihood of still birth up to six percent [1,2]. Climate disasters result in loss of livelihood and decreased yields which impacts maternal health due to decreased nutrient intake because of limited availability [3,4,5]. The present study has been an attempt to assess the issues of SRHR after a climate induced displacement. The study focused on the 02 district of Sindh province including Larkana and Shikarpur which are amongst the worst affected by floods in 2021. The data was collected from displaced women (24) and relief workers (04) through in-depth interviews which was later analyzed thematically. Results present a strong impact of climate migration on the SRHR situation especially of women and young girls. It was found that such movement of families further strengthens the culture of gender inequality. The situation challenging the traditional gender roles by pushing women and girls to search for food and other relief items creates many complications and increases protection challenges. The situation disrupts the already limited access of women to sexual and reproductive health care. Lack of access to routine hygiene and menstrual management items increases the risk of reproductive tract infections. Most of the participants reported that already limited economic opportunities of women get further decreased impacting adversely on their ability to purchase the required items. Women using contraceptives are pushed to discontinue due to non-availability and more focus on the livelihood than other things. This situation creates very difficult scenario for the pregnant women, and this can impact on their pregnancy outcome as well as the health of mother and child. A highly reported issue was the inadequate service delivery from public sector intervention in the camps and displaced sides. Even the limited interventions were gender blind and lacking to demonstrate notion of gender mainstreaming resulting leaving behind women needs particularly related to SRHR. The study recommends a high need for provision of climate and environment education to masses, mobilization and capacity building around disaster risk reduction and active engagement of government and civil society for protection and SRHR initiatives.

517   Climate Im(mobility) under the lens of climate justice

Marília Papaléo Gagliardi

Although climate change is a natural phenomenon, it has already been proven that it was greatly aggravated by human activities, which increased greenhouse gas emissions and thus accelerated and intensified its consequences. As a result, there is the worsening of disasters (here considered in their natural and social dimensions) which are more intense and frequent than ever, and that affects the way of life of certain communities and even their possibility of survival. In this context, it is noteworthy that, although the phenomenon is global, it affects certain regions and societies disproportionately, depending both on their geographic position and on the intrinsic vulnerabilities related to that particular population. E.g. those who live in the Global South suffer more from the impacts of climate change. Despite the greater contribution of the Global North to this scenario, and its climate and environmental debt, the richest regions not only tend to try to limit and prevent the movement of the most vulnerable people affected by those events to migrate from the Global South (which is already not the main route to migrate in this situations), but they also tend to lack a strategy to protect those more vulnerable within their own countries. In this scenario, the relationship that indigenous peoples and local communities have with their land is taken into account when considering not only the damage suffered but also the right of remain that is being violated. This study seeks to analyze how different populations, in different regions are being affected by climate change, how this can lead to their national or international displacement and what measures have been taken to mitigate these effects and allow the permanence of populations already in a greater state of vulnerability, either because of their situation as climate migrants or because of their immobility (derived from the lack of resources or their deep connection with the territory). To do so, this paper seeks to make a comparative analysis on how this phenomenon is being protected at the national/ federal level in both South American and European countries, contrasting the global North and South, from the perspective of climate justice.

2G   Migration and Integration 2 [UG13]

Chair: Banu Dalaman, Istnabul Topkapi University, Turkey

308   A latent profile analysis of Germans' psychological responses to refugees: Patterns of threat perceptions, attitudes, intergroup emotions, and their antecedents

Saskia Schubert and Tobias Ringeisen

Members of receiving societies can respond to the arrival and resettling of refugees very differently. Research has shown that person-centered factors related to social identity can affect the level of perceived threat towards refugees, which in turn are linked to the intensity of negative and positive intergroup emotions and attitudes toward refugees (Stephan & Stephan, 2000; Stephan, 2014; Kauff et al., 2017). However, it is largely unknown to what degree members of receiving societies display differential yet distinct patterns of cognitive-affective-attitudinal responses towards refugees.

The current study used latent profile analysis to examine whether a sample of Germans (N= 910) may be classified into distinct response profiles. Participants completed a cross-sectional online survey, which covered threat perceptions (symbolic threat, realistic threat, negative stereotypes), intergroup emotions (anxiety, hope, anger, and happiness), attitudes towards refugees, and antecedents related to social identity (identity as German, prior intercultural contact, cognitive empathy).

We could identify four different groups of Germans, which showed distinct response patterns regarding cognitive-affective-attitudinal responses, yet partly regarding antecedents. "The threatened angry" (13,1 %) displayed high threat perceptions, strong negative intergroup emotions and negative attitudes towards refugees, while reporting low intercultural contact experiences. "The hopeful approachable" (28,6 %) showed antagonistic patterns with generally more positive perceptions and attitudes. "The moderately threatened" (41,4 %) displayed moderate threat perceptions, intergroup emotions and attitudes toward refugees. The forth profile, "the moderately threatened and anxious" (16,9 %) showed a slightly elevated but otherwise similar pattern to the largest group regarding threat perceptions and intergroup emotions, except for a stronger display of intergroup anxiety. None of the four groups differed significantly in their level of social identity as German.

In essence, the majority of respondents report generally positive attitudes towards refugees (86,9%) and a rather low sense of threat (70%). Knowledge about different perceptions and intergroup emotions can help to create effective interventional programs and information campaigns with group-specific approaches.

References

Kauff, M., Asbrock, F., Wagner, U., Pettigrew, T. F., Hewstone, M., Schäfer, S. J., & Christ, O. (2017). (Bad) Feelings about Meeting Them? Episodic and Chronic Intergroup Emotions Associated with Positive and Negative Intergroup Contact As Predictors of Intergroup Behavior. Frontiers in psychology, 8, 1449. https://doi.org/10.3389/fpsyg.2017.01449

Stephan, C.W., & Stephan, W.G. (2000). An Integrated Threat Theory of Prejudice In S. Oskamp (Ed.), "The Claremont Symposium on Applied Social Psychology" Reducing prejudice and discrimination (p. 23–45). London: Lawrence Erlbaum Associates Publishers. https://doi.org/ 10.4324/9781410605634-7

Stephan, W. G. (2014). Intergroup Anxiety: Theory, Research, and Practice. Personality and Social Psychology Review, 18(3), 239–255. https://doi.org/10.1177/10888683145 30518

429   Migration. Integration? Trends, impacts and solutions and the aftermath of the Covid-19 pandemic in Italy

Mariann Dömös

Italy is one of the key actors in international migration processes in the Mediterranean region. Due to its historical and geopolitical location, the country has always been involved in migration trends, just the direction of this migration varied from era to era. At the end of the century, it became a country of destination, and from the 2000s, immigration began to increase to such an extent that it caused problems and difficulties in managing the phenomenon. At the political level, this issue was handled in different ways, but mainly as a border police issue. However, integration is essential for a successful immigration policy to reduce existing tensions and problems and to prevent new ones from arising; it is also necessary to enable immigrants to integrate as successfully as possible. In the case of Italy, there is a wide broad of organisations in civil society, and some of them try to handle the mass migration at the local level. An essential goal of the presentation is to demonstrate that if the migration policy at the decision-making level is incomplete or inadequate, the civil sphere can (at least partially) alleviate the problems. Another essential research question related to the topic is the importance of the organisations and the activities they are engaged in to reduce integration problems. Thanks to the research, a typology of the organisations was also completed, describing them according to their main characteristics.

Since February 2020, Italy has also been hit hard by the Covid-19 pandemic, which had a multi-level impact on immigration. In the first period, immigration stopped, but then it continued again, causing new challenges in migration issues for Italy. During the pandemic, the Italian government primarily strengthened border security and closure policies, facing the problem from a 'not in my backyard' approach (quarantine on cruise ships) without considering integration. On the other hand, due to the pandemic, these treatment strategies were questioned at several points, and new approaches were brought. As a result of the pandemic, civil organisations had to face new challenges too; for example, accessibility to health care was more difficult, and the already existing inequalities have increased and gotten worse in certain sectors of the economy. Another focal point of the presentation is the effect of the Covid-19 pandemic on Italian immigration and NGOs. How the Italian situation regarding immigration has changed after the pandemic, and what kind of conclusion does this period provides?

In my presentation, my main focus will be on the challenges of Italian integration policy, just like the impacts of the Covid-19 pandemic on Italian immigrant communities through the lens of Italian NGOs. Based especially on empirical experiences, the lecture results from various years of research in Italy with different scholarships. I mainly use qualitative methods and primary sources to analyse Italian civic society. My fieldwork has been taken since 2016, and I participated in the work of civil organisations and did observations, interviews and case studies.

246   Plurale Agencies zur Geschichte der Flucht im 21. Jh.: Agency-Konstellationen und Symmetrisierungen von Fluchtbewegungen nach Deutschland

Andres Otalvaro

Im Rahmen der seit 2015 laufenden Fluchtbewegungen nach Europa entstehen wissenschaftliche Fragen, die sich auf die Geschichte und den Alltag der geflüchteten Menschen beziehen: Wie soll diese Geschichte erzählt und geschrieben werden? Wer erzählt diese Geschichte? Welche Rolle spielen Stimmen und Körper, Bedürfnisse, Emotionen und Affekte von geflüchteten Menschen bei der (Mit-)Gestaltung dieser Geschichte? Was bedeutet also eine Geschichte mit den Stimmen und Körpern der Geflüchteten? Welche sind die strukturellen Hindernisse und Möglichkeiten für die Entwicklung einer solchen Geschichte und die Verstärkung der politischen und geschichtlichen Teilhabe von Menschen mit Fluchterfahrung?

Diese Überlegungen weisen auf eine ältere Frage hin, die Gayatri Spivak 1987 formulierte: Can the subaltern speak? Dazu gehört die Eruierung des Forschungsfelds „agency", was hier als Handlungsfähigkeit oder Handlungsmacht definiert wird. Dementsprechend werde ich in meinem Vortrag interdisziplinäre Ansätze zur agency rund um den Neuen Materialismus beanspruchen. In diesem Rahmen wird nicht nur die agency von Menschen mit Fluchtgeschichte, sondern auch die agency von fluchtbezogenen Netzwerken, Prozessen, Mobilisierungen, Organisationen und Dingen beschrieben. Daher ergeben sich was ich Agency-

Konstellationen der Fluchtrealitäten und entsprechende Symmetrisierungen nenne.

Im Mittelpunkt meiner Präsentation stehen also die Menschen mit Fluchterfahrung und ihre Geschichten. Zu beachten ist infolgedessen die agency bzw. die Handlungsfähigkeit von geflüchteten Menschen als vulnerable und marginalisierte Gruppe in einem bestimmten historischen Zeitraum (Europa im 21. Jh., konkret Deutschland seit 2015). Darüber hinaus ist es notwendig, um eine anthropozentrische Herangehensweise (menschliche Exklusivität) zu überwinden, zusätzliche Verflechtungen mit anderen Formen der agency in Betracht zu ziehen. Die Berücksichtigung von pluralen agencies beabsichtigt die Überwindung der Fokussierung auf Geschichten oder agencies von großen Strukturen (z.B. der Staat), Institutionen, Ideologien, prominenten Persönlichkeiten und hegemonischen Narrativen. Unter einer sogenannten Symmetrisierung gewinnen die Geschichten „von unten" der durchschnittlichen Menschen mit Fluchterfahrung an Relevanz.

Mit Blick auf das sehr dynamische Phänomen der Flucht in Deutschland bzw. in Europa im 21 Jh. möchte ich fünf Agency-Konstellationen mit ihren pluralen involvierten Akteur:innen, Prozessen, Komponenten und Artikulationen erstmal flexibel abgrenzen: a) Agency-Konstellation der Unterstützung, Solidarität und Gastfreundschaft sowie des Humanitarismus; b) Agency-Konstellation der Gewalt, des Rassismus und der Verletzbarkeit; c) Agency-Konstellation der staatlichen und kommunalen Strukturen; d) Zusätzliche geographische und soziokulturelle Agency-Konstellationen e) Andere materiellen Netzwerke, technologischen Assemblagen und Umgebungsverhältnisse.

Die konstitutive agency von Menschen mit Fluchtbiographie hat ihre eigenen Alleinerstellungsmerkmale. Körper, Emotionen, Affekte, Begehren, Sprachen (Mehrsprachigkeit), Handlungs- und Wirkmächte von geflüchteten Menschen sowie ihre alltäglichen und dauerhaften Selbstorganisationen und Kooperationen durchqueren aktiv und fortlaufend die oben genannten Konstellationen als Kernausdrücke ihrer agency bzw. als die sogenannte Autonomie der Migration. Diese (relative) Autonomie der Migrierenden erlaubt es ihnen, einen eigenen Referenzrahmen zu etablieren bzw. eine eigene „walking and talking" Alltags- und Erfahrungsordnung mit eigenen Begriffen, Normen, Werten, Kodierungen und Erfahrungen angesichts sehr dichten und gewaltsamen Migrationskontrollen und Grenzregimes (vgl. De Genova 2017, 1-35; Papadopoulus und Tsianos 2013, 178-196; Andrijasevic, Bojadnijev, Hess, Karakayali, Panagiotidis, Tsianos 2005, 345-362; Rosenthal, Bahl und Worm 2016).

366   Examining Leftist background and Ethno-national Identity in Political Attitude of Kurdish Immigrants in Western Europe

Sabah Mofidi

As part of a larger project that examines the changes in the political identity of first-generation Kurdish political immigrants from Iranian/Eastern Kurdistan (Rojhelat) with leftist political background living in Germany, The Netherlands, Sweden and France, this article analyses changes in their ideological-political attitude/orientation, and the influence of their Kurdish identity and leftist ideas on it in European politics, especially partisanship and voting for election candidates. In this regard, it tries to answer this question: What ideological-political changes have Kurdish leftist immigrants experienced, and to what extent their Kurdish identity and leftist ideas/thought influenced their political attitude towards European political parties? It supposes that a change in their political-ideological space by moving away from Iran with its closed society and also from the political Kurdish parties, where they were under the rigid political-military control, towards Europe with its political individualism and higher cross-ideology political density, leads to change in ideological-political attitude. However, their ethno-national and ideological background influence their political orientation yet. The research has focused on the members and ex-members of Komele and Communist Party of Iran. It is based on data collected through 25 personal interviews. The results show that in addition to considering the interests of Kurdish community in Europe, the political participation of Kurdish people is actually the continuation of their lobbying politics to influence the European politics regarding the Kurdish rights in their country of origin.

1000   Syrian Refugees' Behavior in Jordan, Egypt, and Germany: Experimental

Evidence Stefan Voigt

END OF DAY ONE

Day Two 24 August 2023 - 09:00-10:30

3A   Insecurities and Migration 1 [EG17]

Chair: Zeynep Banu Dalaman, Istanbul Topkapi University, Turkey

143   "How do I run a business in South Africa without foreigners?" Movers' Right to Work

Theresa Alfaro-Velcamp

The nationalistic and xenophobic movement Operation Dudula has been leading demonstrations throughout South Africa claiming that foreigners are taking South African jobs and that there are 'no wars in Africa' to warrant African immigrants special treatment. This xenophobic movement blames the movers (an umbrella term for immigrants, cross-border migrants, asylum seekers and refugees) for societal collapse and challenge the legality of their border crossings. They call the movers "criminals" and pressure domestic government officials to criminalize the movers through "statelessness." This notion that "no foreigner must be employed ahead of a South African" is at the crux of the debates around movers' right to employment. Yet, there has not been an examination into how movers' employment affects the South African economy. What would happen if there were no foreigners employed in South Africa? What would this look like? Through interviews with non-governmental (non-profit) organisations (NPOs/NGOs), employers, industry associations, government officials, and labour attorneys, and an examination of international and domestic laws and norms, this paper suggests the reframing of the employment narrative with respect to movers. It is estimated that "for each foreigner with a scarce skill, it is probably correct to say three locals will accompany them in obtaining employment." (Bagraim 7/27/2022). According to the South African Constitution of 1996, (Section 22) states that "[e]very citizen has the right to choose their trade, occupation, or profession freely." However, the "practice of a trade, occupation or profession may be regulated by law." In 2003, the Watchenuka case confirmed the asylum seekers' right to work in South Africa. The ruling wove the right to work with human dignity (Section 10). Movers' right to work is intrinsic to international human rights accords; however, in the Global South, states are often constrained by high unemployment rates of nationals, as noted by Operation Dudula and other xenophobic movements.

172   Mexican migrants, mobility and insecurity: Does criminalization matter?

Jeffrey H. Cohen

Mexican migrants destined for the US are increasingly criminalized and degraded by xenophobic voices in the media as well as politicians who seek scapegoats to blame for any ill imaginable. While the lasting impacts of these xenophobic voices may be debatable, it is clear that the rhetoric has changed the way the nation reacts to migrants, refugees and asylees. This is perhaps nowhere more apparent than in the limits that the government places on foreign arrivals and the increasing criminalization of movers for crossing borders regardless of their predicament.

While the xenophobic voices grow in strength, the criminality that fills their messages often misses the very migrants they call out. In fact, whether the goal is to promote "self-deportation", a limit on border crossing or to instill a fear of arrest, the xenophobic characterization of migrants as criminals has not slowed the flows. A recent study notes that border crossing from Mexico remain at near record levels; and this is not a new phenomenon.

In this paper, I explore insecurity and the response of Mexican immigrants to their criminalization using interviews with movers as well as secondary data from resources like the Pew Research Center and Migration Policy Institute. I track attitudes toward increasing criminalization and note some of the critical ways that criminalization impacts daily lives. Does criminalization matter? Day to day concerns with work, opportunities and futures typically replace the fears of deportation and a criminal record for most movers, nevertheless, it is clear that criminalization does limit Mexican migrants in the US, even those migrants who have spent decades living quiet, peaceful lives.

495   Negotiating home and host country belonging among Turkish-origin students in Germany aftermath of the earthquake in their home country Turkey

Hande Erdem Möbius

On February 6, 2023, a massive earthquake of magnitude 7.8 and 7.5 struck south-central Turkey and northwestern Syria. Over 50,000 people died in Turkey, turning it into the deadliest natural disaster in the country's modern history. Previous research has shown that such disasters in the home country enhance immigrants' transnationalism, strengthen their homeland belonging (Lundy, 2011; Takeda, 2015), and negatively affect their well-being (Smid et al., 2018). In addition, the responses and actions of the native community may influence the lives of immigrant groups during the post-earthquake period (Esnard & Sapat, 2011). The present study utilizes qualitative in-depth interviews to explore how university students of Turkish origin in Germany negotiate their home and host country belonging in the aftermath of the earthquake in Turkey. The theoretical underpinnings of the research are transnational identity (Ehrkamp, 2005; Kaya,

2018; Vertovec, 2001), intercultural communication (Arasaratnam, 2015; Ichikawa, 2021), and boundary drawing in terms of reconstructing "us" versus "them" in the context of migration (Barth, 1969; Sanders, 2002). The findings are discussed, taking into account both host country aspects (intra-ethnic and inter-ethnic group contacts, perceived/received support at personal, group, and institutional levels, cross-cultural aspects of bereavement) and home country aspects (transnational ties and practices, feelings of post-traumatic stress) in the negotiation of sense of belonging. The study contributes to research on the impact of home country disasters on the transnational identity formation and well-being of immigrant students and highlights the role of higher education institutions in the provision of support.

References

Arasaratnam, L. A. (2015). Research in intercultural communication: Reviewing the past decade. Journal of International and Intercultural Communication, 8(4), 290–310. https://doi.org/10.1080/17513057.2015.1087096

Barth, F. (1969). Introduction. In F. Barth (Ed.), Ethnic groups and boundaries: The social organization of culture difference (pp. 9–38). Universitetsforlaget.

Ehrkamp, P. (2005). Placing identities: Transnational practices and local attachments of Turkish immigrants in Germany. Journal of Ethnic and Migration Studies, 31(2), 345–364. https://doi.org/10.1080/1369183042000339963

Esnard, A.-M., & Sapat, A. (2011). Disasters, diasporas and host communities: Insights in the aftermath of the Haiti earthquake. Journal of Disaster Research, 6(3), 331–342. https://doi.org/10.20965/jdr.2011.p0331

Ichikawa, A. (2021). Unsilencing the migratory grief of international students. Journal of International Students, 11(4), 988–994. https://doi.org/10.32674/jis.v11i4.3032

Kaya, A. (2018). Turkish origin migrants and their descendants: Hyphenated identities in transnational space. Springer.

Lundy, G. (2011). Transnationalism in the aftermath of the Haiti earthquake: Reinforcing ties and second-generation identity. Journal of Black Studies, 42(2), 203–224. https://doi.org/10.1177/0021934710394444

Sanders, J. M. (2002). Ethnic boundaries and identity in plural societies. Annual Review of Sociology, 28(1), 327–357. https://doi.org/10.1146/annurev.soc.28.110601.140741

Smid, G. E., Drogendijk, A. N., Knipscheer, J., Boelen, P. A., & Kleber, R. J. (2018). Loss of loved ones or home due to a disaster: Effects over time on distress in immigrant ethnic minorities. Transcultural Psychiatry, 55(5), 648–668. https://doi.org/10.1177/1363461518784355

Takeda, A. (2015). Intensive transnationalism amongst Japanese migrants after the Great East Japan Earthquake: Voices from diasporic blogs. Studies in Ethnicity and Nationalism, 15(3), 492–507. https://doi.org/10.1111/sena.12162

Vertovec, S. (2001). Transnationalism and identity. Journal of Ethnic and Migration Studies, 27(4), 573–582. https://doi.org/10.1080/13691830120090386

390   The Impact of 6 February Earthquake on Internal Migration in Türkiye: A Comprehensive Analysis

Zeynep Banu Dalaman

The 6th February 2021 earthquake in Turkey caused widespread destruction and displacement, leading to significant migration within the country. The earthquake affected eleven provinces and about 18 million people living in the earthquake zone, and according to preliminary estimates, about 3.5 million people migrated from the region to safer places. This study aims to provide a comprehensive analysis of the patterns and determinants of internal migration in the aftermath of the earthquake and the policy implications of these findings.

There are three types of internal migration trends after disasters. The first is to neighboring villages with less damage, the second is to nearby provinces without damage, and the third is to metropolises and cities with greater opportunities. Using data from various sources, including government records and surveys, this study examines the demographic and socioeconomic characteristics of earthquake-induced migrants, the destinations and origins of migration, and the factors that influence migration decisions.

The findings suggest that the earthquake significantly impacted internal migration, with a large proportion of migrants relocating to urban areas. The study also reveals that income, education level, and employment status are the most critical factors that determine migration decisions. Based on these results, the study proposes several policy recommendations aimed at mitigating the adverse effects of earthquakes on internal migration, including the provision of affordable housing options, the improvement of infrastructure in rural areas, and the promotion of economic opportunities in disaster-prone regions.

3B   Göç Çalışmaları 2 [UG11]

Chair: Deniz Yetkin Aker, Tekirdağ Namık Kemal University, Turkey

418   Toplumsal Cinsiyet ve Göçmen Kadınlar: Eskişehir Örneği

Filiz Göktuna Yaylacı ve Gül Sevi Üçüncü

Gender and Migrant Women: Case of Eskişehir

Gender has increasingly come to be the focus of institutions and organizations, policy formulation and academic studies on migration. Discussing the validity of discourses that migration reinforces women's status as fragile others and their secondary position is one of the main issues of the gender context of migration. In this regard, this study has been prepared based on the BAP project to be carried out within Anadolu University, which focuses on the experiences of immigrant women in the context of gender. Eskişehir constitutes the field dimension of this study, as it is one of the satellite cities and hosts individuals who have immigrated from many different countries. It is expected that the results to be obtained within the scope of the project will contribute to the field and be a guide in terms of migration policies and social work interventions to be developed specifically for women. The main purpose of the project is to reveal the experiences of women who came to Eskişehir through immigration from different countries before, during and after migration, and in this context, to examine the life strategies of immigrant women in response to their daily life practices, interactions and immigration situations. Based on this main purpose, the research will adopt the feminist approach and use the research techniques offered by the qualitative research method. To this end, this research was designed as a qualitative research in order to consider the narrative and the acceptance of different realities. As part of the research, in-depth interviews were conducted with women under international protection and temporary protection status residing in Eskişehir. The research participants were reached through snowball and purposive sampling, and the study group of the research consisted of approximately 30 female participants from different countries. Drawing on the results of this project, this study will present the research fingdings in connection with various dimensions of migrant women's daily life practices.

409   Konya'da Çok-Etnili Mekânlarda Etnografik Bir Çalışma: Sınırlar, Bedenleşme ve Hayaletler

Gamze Kaçar Tunç ve Fuat Güllüpınar

Bu araştırmada Konya'da aynı mahallelerde yaşayan yerelden vatandaşlar ve mültecilerin oluşturduğu bir topluluğun bir arada yaşama pratikleri etnografik bir biçimde gözlemlenmiş ve kimliklenme, konumlanma, güç mücadeleleri gibi unsurlar görünür kılınmaya çalışılmıştır. Bu bağlamda alan araştırması Mayıs 2019- Mart 2020 arasında yürütülmüştür.   Türk, Kürt, Roman, Abdal vatandaşların ve Suriyeli (Arap), Iraklı (Arap ve Türkmen), Afgan (Peştun, Hazari, Özbek) ve Sudanlı (Arap) mültecilerin oluşturduğu 68 kişiyle derinlemesine mülakatlar yapılarak ve alanda katılımlı/katılımsız gözlemler yoluyla veriler elde edilmiştir.

Elde edilen verilere göre aynı mekânı paylaşan bu topluluğun üyelerinin grupsal olarak belirli çıkarlar bağlamında ayrıştıkları ve hiyerarşik bir yapılanma içerisinde oldukları görülmüştür. Grup sınırlarının çizilmesi ise en temelde yerel halk-yabancı ikiliği, etnisite ve ekonomik güç bağlamında gerçekleşmektedir.   Yerel halk olarak adlandırılabilecek Türk, Kürt, Roman ve Abdallar kendi içlerindeki ayrışmaya rağmen yabancı olarak adlandırılabilecek mültecilere karşı birlikte konumlanmaktadırlar. Bu yerel halk-yabancı ikiliğini ise ev sahibi-misafir metaforları üzerinden gerçekleştirmektedirler. Etnisite ise özellikle Romanların, Abdalların ve mültecilerin yer yer zorunlu olarak içerisine itildikleri yer yer de güçlü kalabilmek için kendilerinin tutundukları bir kimliğe dönüşmektedir. Ekonomik temelli sınıfsal ayrımlar, yine hiyerarşinin en tepesi ile en altı arasındaki güç dağılımını belirlemede etkili bir rol oynamaktadır. Bu hiyerarşik yapılanmada ev sahipleri, onların içerisinde ise Türkler, hiyerarşinin en tepesinde yer almaktadır. Hiyerarşinin en alt tabakalarını ise sırasıyla, Romanlar, Abdallar ve mülteci gruplar oluşturmaktadır. Mültecilerin kendi içerisinde de bir güç mücadelesine rastlanmış, bu mücadelede Suriyelilerin öne çıktığı görülmüştür. Bu hiyerarşik yapılanmada grupların ötekileştirme pratiklerine maruz kalma durumları araştırmada bedenleşme ve hayaletleşme metaforları ile karşılanmıştır. Buna göre Bourdieucu anlamda bir alan mücadelesinde diğerlerinin gözüne batma durumu bedenleşme, görmezden gelinme durumu ise hayaletleşme kavramlarına denk gelmektedir. Ev sahiplerinin kendi içerisine bakıldığında Romanlar ve Abdallar en çok göze batanlar olarak bedenleşmektedir. Misafirlerin de en güçlünün yanında yer almaya çalışarak Roman ve Abdalları dışlayıcı bir tutum sergiledikleri görülmüştür. Ev sahiplerinin tümünün gözünde ise Suriyeli mülteciler en çok bedenleşenler olmuştur. Özellikle Romanlar ve Abdallar için Suriyeliler en bedenleşmiş gruptur. Fenotipik özelliklerine rağmen Sudanlılar (ve onlar gibi diğer Afrika kökenli mülteciler) ise diğerleri tarafından yok sayılmaları bakımından mekânın hayaletleri olmuşlardır. Kamusal alanda sayıları ve pratikleri bakımından daha az yer almaları bunun önemli bir etkenidir, ancak daha önemlisi diğer grupların kimliksel (veya ırksal) bakımdan kendilerini onlardan üstün görmesi bu hayaletleşme sürecinin en önemli kaynağıdır. Onlar, hem ev sahipleri hem de misafirler için, alan mücadelesinde çok da yeri olmayan bir gruptur. Onlar, dünyanın pek çok bölgesinde en çok bedenleşen gruplar olmalarına rağmen, burada farklı bir tür ayrımcılıkla karşılaşarak "acınması gereken" bir grup insana dönüşmektedirler. Sonuç olarak bu çokkültürlü mekânda bir arada yaşamak, grup sınırlarını yok etmek yerine, grupların sınırları yeniden üretmiştir ve üretmektedir.

*Bu bildiri Gamze Kaçar Tunç'un "Etno-Kültürel Karşılaşmalar ve Toplumsal Kabul: Konya'daki Mülteci Çocukların Gündelik Yaşam Deneyimleri" adlı doktora tezinden türetilmiştir.

568   Türkiye'deki Mültecilerin Ekonomik Entegrasyonları: Tekirdağ Ferhadanlı Mahallesi Afgan Göçmenler Örneği

Deniz Yetkin Aker, İdris Akkuzu, Murat Deniz

Afganistan tarihi, yıllar süren işgaller ve savaşlar tarihidir. Stratejik konumu ve zengin yeraltı kaynakları açısından önemli bir ülke olan Afganistan; İngiliz, Sovyet ve ABD işgalleri altında kalmış, yaşanan iç savaşlar ve Taliban güçlerinin hakimiyet mücadelesi uzun yıllar süren siyasi ve ekonomik istikrarsızlık dönemlerinin yaşanmasına neden olmuştur. 2021 yılında ABD'nin Afganistan'dan çekilmesiyle birlikte yönetimi ele geçiren Taliban'ın baskıcı politikaları ve ekonomik koşulların olumsuzluğu milyonlarca Afgan'ın ülkelerini terk ederek göç etmesine neden olmuştur. Gerek işgal dönemlerinde gerek Taliban yönetimi döneminde kitlesel halde yaşanan göçler sıklıkla İran ve Pakistan'a yönelik olurken, küreselleşme süreci içerisinde dünyanın farklı bölgelerine yönelik göçler de yaşanmaktadır. Özellikle gelişmiş ülkelere yönelik göçlerin adresi Avrupa ve Avrupa'ya geçiş noktasındaki transit ülke Türkiye'dir. Türkiye'ye yönelik yaşanan göç hareketliliği genellikle düzensiz şekildedir. Genellikle İran üzerinden Türkiye'ye giriş yapılmakta ve kayıt dışı olarak ülkeye giren Afgan göçmenler, daha iyi bir yaşam umuduyla Türkiye'nin gelişmiş şehirlerinde kayıt dışı istihdama katılmaktadırlar. Türkiye'de bulunan düzensiz Afgan göçmenler sosyal ve hukuki haklardan azade zor koşullarda hayatlarını sürdürmektedirler. Afgan göçmenler genellikle beden gücü gerektiren inşaat, fabrika, tarım gibi alanlarda kayıt dışı olarak çalışmakta ve çalıştırılmaktadırlar. Dil bariyeri, kültürel uzaklık, yetersiz sosyal çevre gibi faktörler uyum sürecini zorlaştırmakta ve istihdam alanında daha düşük ücretlerle olumsuz koşullar içerisinde çalışmalarına neden olmaktadır. Türkiye'ye yönelik gerçekleşen göçlerin erkek ağırlıklı olması, yaşanan göçün daha ziyade ekonomik sebepler dolayısıyla gerçekleştiğini göstermektedir. Yaşanan göçün önemli duraklarından biri, İstanbul'a olan yakınlığı ve istihdam olanaklarının gelişmişliği sebebiyle Tekirdağ ilidir. Bu sebeple çalışmanın odak noktası Tekirdağ'ın Ferhadanlı Mahallesi'ndeki Afgan tarım işçileri örneklemi üzerinden oluşturulacaktır. Eğitim seviyesi, medeni durumları, mesleki yeterlilikleri, Türkiye'ye geliş süreçleri, çalışma koşulları, parasal transfer deneyimleri, Türkiye'deki dernek ve kurum ilişkileri gibi değişkenler üzerinden değerlendirmeler yapılarak çalışmanın ana hatları belirlenecektir. Tekirdağ ili içerisinde, tarım sektöründe çalışan düzensiz Afgan göçmenlerle nitel görüşmeler aracılığıyla yapılacak bu çalışma ışığında; Afganistan'dan Türkiye'ye yönelik gerçekleşen göçün nedenleri ve süreci anlaşılmaya çalışılacak, Afgan göçmenlerin Türkiye ekonomisi içerisindeki entegrasyon süreçleri incelenecek ve düzensiz göç sürecinde yaşanan deneyimler Türkiye ve Tekirdağ bağlamında değerlendirilecektir.

207 Mültecilerde Bağımlılık Riski Haritasının Oluşturulması ve Çözüme Yönelik Model Önleme Programı İnşası

Muhammed Refik Tekeli

Türkiye'nin 2011 yılı ve sonrasında artan bir şekilde karşılaştığı bir olgu olan yerinden edilmişlik / zorunlu göç beraberinde birçok sorunu ve hassasiyeti getirmektedir. Bu sorunlardan birisi olarak bağımlılık, göç ve göçün tetiklediği psikolojik sorunlar sebebiyle artışa geçmektedir. Bu durum birçok ülkede olduğu gibi göçmenlerde bağımlılık konusuna yönelik betimleyici ve korelasyonel çalışmaların yapılmasını gerekli kılmaktadır. Olgunun / sorunun mahiyetini tespit etmek ilişkili faktörlerin ortadan kaldırılmasına yönelik önleyici çalışmalar yapabilmenin ilk aşamasını oluşturmaktadır. Farklı kültürel ve coğrafi bagaj taşıyan göçmenlere yönelik, yerli gruptan farklı, koruyucu ve önleyici çalışmalar geliştirilmesi gerekmektedir. Bu noktalardan yola çıkarak, bu çalışmanın amacı göçmenlerde/ mültecilerde bağımlılık riskinin nitel ve nicel yöntemlerle belirlenmesi ve buna yönelik önleyici bir çalışmanın ortaya çıkartılmasıdır. Bunu gerçekleştirmek üzere bu proje dört aşamada tasarlanmıştır. İlk aşamada nitel saha çalışmasının gerçekleştirilmesi hedeflenmektedir. Bu aşamada 12 bağımlı mülteci ile yarı yapılandırılmış görüşme ve 24 bağımlı yakını mülteci ile üç ayrı odak grup görüşmesi yapılacaktır. İkinci aşamada nitel çalışmanın sonuçlarına dayandırılacak bir ölçek geliştirilecektir. Bu ölçek mülteci/ göçmen popülasyonun bağımlılık riskinin ölçümlenmesini amaçlayacaktır. Böylelikle geniş kitlelerde bağımlılığa dair risk faktörleri gözlemlenebilecektir. Üçüncü aşamada geniş çaplı, Türkiye'nin her bölgesini kapsayacak, bir nicel saha çalışması yürütülecektir. Bu çalışmada proje kapsamında geliştirilen ölçek kullanılacak ve Türkiye çapında bir tarama çalışması gerçekleştirilmiş olacaktır. Sonucunda Türkiye Bağımlılık Risk Haritası'nın mülteci popülasyon özelinde oluşturulması hedeflenmektedir. Son olarak ise tüm aşamaların çıktılarının nihai bir çıktı haline getirilebilmesi ve bu probleme bir çözüm önerisi sunulabilmesi için bir önleme programı inşa edilecektir. Bu aşama sonunda oluşacak Model Önleme Programı alanda uzman kişilerin desteğiyle çoklu katılım perspektifiyle gerçekleştirilecektir. Nihayetinde ise bu proje göçle artışa geçecek sorunlardan birisi olan bağımlılığı detaylı bir çalışma ile inceleme fırsatı verecektir. Literatürde bu konuda yeterli çalışmanın olmaması ve konunun güvenlikten sağlığa kadar birçok alanı içermesi konunun özgün bir çalışma alanı oluşturduğuna işaret etmektedir.

3C   Migration and Gender 1 [UG14]

Chair: Lan Lo, University of Nottingham, UK

358   Values of Ukrainian Refugees in Austria: Gender Roles, Attitudes toward Democracy, and Confidence in International Institutions

Bernhard Riederer, Isabella Buber-Ennser, Ingrid Setz, Judith Kohlenberger, Bernhard Rengs

Facing millions of Ukrainians who have fled the ongoing Russian war of regression to European host countries, it is crucial to know more about the arriving populations. Ukrainian refugees are predominantly women, children, and senior people. In addition, available evidence indicates a highly self-selective migration. We know that many refugees have a high socio-economic status. But much less is known about their opinion and values. What are the attitudes of Ukrainian refugees, compared to their home country and their host societies? Do they differ from previous refugees? Do we find East-West differences among Ukrainian refugees, and (dis)similarities to Russia?

The present study uses data from a large survey of Ukrainian refugees in Vienna, Austria (1,094 respondents of age 18+), conducted between April and June 2022. The survey included six items to measure gender role attitudes as well as political beliefs and opinions. We compare our findings with both international surveys, like the European Values Study or the World Values Survey, and prior refugee surveys on displaced persons in Austria. In our analyses, we focus on respondents between age 18 and age 59. Multinomial logistic regression models and decomposition analyses are employed to explain differences between Ukrainian refugees in Austria and (a) the Ukrainian population, (b) the Austrian population, (c) prior refugee groups in Austria, and (d) the Russian population.

Descriptive findings show that Ukrainian refugees in Austria report gender role attitudes that are more similar to those in the host society than to the population in the Ukraine in 2020. Socioeconomic differences explain a relevant part of the observed differences in gender role attitudes. Among refugees, gender role attitudes mainly differ by education, income, and degree of religiosity. Political opinions also differ. In particular, the confidence in the European Union is much lower in Austria than in Ukraine, with Ukrainian refugees showing extremely high confidence. Agreement to democracy as the right way of governing is, however, lower in the Ukraine, and also among Ukrainian refugees, than in Austria. Among Ukrainian refugees, it varies by age, income, and country of birth.

Furthermore, our analyses indicate somewhat more egalitarian gender role attitudes among refugees from the Ukraine than among refugees from Afghanistan or Syria. In particular, differences in gender role attitudes between women and men are much smaller among Ukrainian refugees than among other refugee groups. Large differences in political attitudes are found between Russia and Ukraine. The Russian population is less convinced of democracy and shows lower levels of confidence in international institutions than the Ukrainian population and Ukrainian refugees. Among Ukrainian refugees, however, a less positive view of democracy is found among refugees from the East of Ukraine. Overall, our analyses provide relevant insights for host countries.

527 The Economic Integration of Racialized Immigrant Women: A Community-Based Photovoice Study in Ontario, Canada: Migration and Gender

Bharati Sethi

Context: Despite the influx of immigrant/refugee women in Canada's labour force, much of the literature on economic integration is focused on men. Further, there is, an apparent lack of research that can illuminate the relationship between their work and health, especially for those residing outside Canada's large urban centers such as Montreal, Toronto and VancouverObjective: "Do you see what I see?" a community-based participatory research project, that used Photovoice -- a qualitative arts-based participatory methodology-- to explore how work impacted immigrant/refugee women's health in a middle-sized urban/rural region in Ontario, Canada.

Design: Following the key principles of Photovoice, twenty immigrant/refugee visible minority women were given digital cameras to record their work and health experiences. Intersectionality theoretical perspective that is concerned with understanding how social categories such as race, class, gender, ability, etc. simultaneously intersect to shape people's experiences guiding the research process.

Results: Analysis of 525 participant-generated photographs, women's diaries, and in-depth interviews revealed that the complex interplay of ethnicity, immigrant status (such as refugee) and geography (i.e. rural residence), intersected to influence women's health and work experiences. The participants experienced discrimination due to their race. Three key themes emerged: Expectations do not meet reality, Work and Health, Work and Family, and Resilience. From a methodological perspective, the results demonstrate that in the absence of language, Photovoice enables participants to communicate the nuances of their mental states (such as emotions and desires) and physical states (such as deteriorating health conditions).

Conclusions and Implications: The results have several policy and practice implications for immigrant women's economic and social integration in Canadian society. These include the individual, organizational, and family factors that lead to health-related absenteeism, stress and health problems such as backaches, muscular problems and depression. It is also critical that employers and policymakers pay attention to the link between discrimination and health as well as deskilling and health. Ultimately, failure to leverage competitive advantage and tap into a growing skilled, well-educated and culturally diverse female workforce in Canada's small towns and rural areas will lead to a loss of employer productivity and labour market deficiency.

63   Women's essential roles as change agents in humanitarian and development responses and post-conflict reconstruction/reconciliation

Candost Aydin, Nur Sultan Cirakman, Matthias Weissenbach

Women's essential roles as change agents in humanitarian and development responses and post-conflict reconstruction/reconciliation, as well as combatting the effects of climate change, are gradually recognised by the international community. The success of equitable development, peace and resilience efforts is therefore strongly contingent on tackling gender inequality and discrimination. Yet, the fact that conflict and disasters disproportionately affect women and girls remains unchanged. Women face a heightened risk of sexual and gender-based violence in conflict and crises, including forced displacement. They are frequently pushed to negative coping mechanisms for sustenance and are preyed on by human traffickers. In conflict, post-conflict, and other fragile settings, their access to resources and gainful employment is restricted due to several structural and practical factors that contribute to direct and indirect discrimination and limit their access to rights, resources and networks. Therefore, international refugee response measures can contribute to the operationalisation of 'realising rights', 'using resources', and 'improving representation' of women, operationalising and further developing a solid intersectional approach in project implementation. Towards this end, it is necessary to take stock of how the refugee response measures promote women's empowerment and resilience in tackling intersectional discrimination and deprivation and generate solutions to common but regional and country-specific challenges looking at the Türkiye case. As of August 2022, Türkiye accommodates 3.6 million Syrians provided with Temporary Protection (SuTP) status, and almost half of the SuTPs are women.

Therefore, looking at the cases in the world, the study wants to explore how the refugee response measures in Türkiye can develop their focus towards a "gender transformative approach" that addresses unequal social norms and practices, discriminatory attitudes and structural power imbalances based on gender. In this framework, exploring 'gender equality' in displacement contexts is expected to yield insights into the significance of rights-based approaches.

3D   Remittances 1 [BG3/4]

Chair: Zeeshan Hashim, Brunel University, UK

321   The spatial spillover effects of migration on sustainable development in the European Union: A Durbin model approach

Mohamed Ennebch, Nouhaila Kamsa, Moubarek Amine Berdaa, Aomar Ibourk

Migration is a significant challenge in the European Union (EU), where it has led to both opportunities and challenges for sustainable development. The EU has experienced a high level of migration in recent years, which has led to spatial spillover effects across different regions. The question is whether migration has a positive or negative impact on sustainable development in the EU and how these effects vary across different regions.

The study aims to investigate the spatial spillover effects of migration on sustainable development in the European Union (EU) using a Durbin model approach. The research hypothesizes that migration has a spatially-dependent impact on sustainable development, with varying effects across different regions. The research utilizes data from multiple sources, including Eurostat and the European Environment Agency, to construct a sustainable development index and relevant explanatory variables for the analysis. The study finds that migration has both positive and negative spillover effects on sustainable development, with variation across regions.

Keywords: Migration, Economic growth, Sustainable development, Spatial Econometrics, Spatial Durbin Model, Spatial Spillover effects,

References

Becker, S.O. and Muñoz, M., 2020. The effect of migration on destination countries: A review of the empirical literature. Journal of Economic Literature, 58(4), pp.930-1004.

Cai, R. and Wang, D., 2019. The impact of internal migration on regional economic growth in China: a spatial econometric analysis. Letters in Spatial and Resource Sciences, 12(1), pp.63-78.

Carling, J. and Collins, F., 2018. Aspiration, desire and drivers of migration. Journal of Ethnic and Migration Studies, 44(6), pp.909-926.

Kahanec, M. and Zimmermann, K.F. eds., 2016. Labor migration, EU enlargement, and the great recession. Springer.

Li, H. and Li, Y., 2019. Does migration facilitate regional green growth? Empirical evidence from China. Environmental Science and Pollution Research, 26(14), pp.13957-13968.

Martinez-Zarzoso, I. and Johannsen, F., 2018. Greenfield FDI and skill upgrading: A spatial analysis of local linkages in the automotive industry. World Development, 107, pp.357-375.

Qu, B., 2021. The spillover effect of migrant population concentration on economic growth in the Yangtze River Delta urban agglomeration. Cities, 110, p.103048.

Ratha, D. and Shaw, W., 2007. South-South migration and remittances. The World Bank.

Taran, P.A., 2018. Migration and global environmental change: opportunities and challenges for research and governance. Springer.

272   Trade-Based Informal Remittances System: Trade-Based Informal Remittances System: A Case Study of Afghan Migrants in Turkey

Mohammad Eyüp Babur

Trade-Based İnformal Remittances System: A Case Study of Afghan Migrants in Turkey

As its theories state, migration has different factors, origins, forms, and courses. In the field of migration factors, a new approach called the conflict model can be found to be more realistic. Conflicts at various levels and their repercussions, such as economic, social, and political challenges, have triggered mass migrations throughout history and geography. It's estimated that more than 7 out of 10 people in need of international protection, including refugees under UNHCR's mandate, originate from just five nations (Syrian Arab Republic, Venezuela, Ukraine, Afghanistan, and South Sudan). More than 72% percent come from only five countries.

Turkey has become the most prominent host of immigrants and refugees of various immigration statuses. According to the data of the Turkish Immigration Department, after Syrians, Afghans make up the largest group of illegal immigrants in Turkey. Moreover, Afghans have the most requests for asylum to the United Nations after Iraqi nationals.

As it was said, almost all Afghan immigrants in Turkey are in the status of illegal immigrants. On the other hand, due to the weak infrastructure in Afghanistan's banking system, especially after the Taliban came to power, Afghan immigrants in Turkey prefer informal channels for remittances to Afghanistan.

Hawala is one of the most widely used methods of informal remittances. In the age of technology and the use of technological infrastructures such as the Internet, and smartphones, the effectiveness of informal remittance has increased both from the point of view of speed and cost, making it more popular among immigrants. Among Afghan immigrants in Turkey, hawala is almost the only method of transferring remittances to Afghanistan.

Informal remittances (hawala) are illegal in Turkey, like in many other countries. Still, this process is carried out in various guises, such as call shops, markets where Afghans need most items, ticket offices, Afghan restaurants, and Afghan hair salons are doing. As it is known in the hawala, money is not physically transferred between countries. Instead, it is just a code consisting of letters and numbers between hawala operators in two countries, the sender and the recipient of the hawala.

In the research that used the method of in-depth qualitative interviews, three categories of people (Afghan immigrants in Istanbul, hawala operators in Istanbul, and Afghan importers from Turkey to Afghanistan) were interviewed as the target group. It was found that the massive amount of informal remittance (hawala) money that accumulates at the hawala operators in Istanbul is mainly used to finance Turkey's export of 270 million dollars to Afghanistan by traders In this way, on the one hand, the settlement between the hawala operators between Turkey and Afghanistan is settled. But on the other hand, the problem of Afghan business people facing issues in sending money from formal channels from Afghanistan to Turkey to finance their imports is solved.

Figure 1 shows the structure and mechanism of informal remittances from Turkey to Afghanistan and, conversely, trade-based informal remittances between Afghanistan and Turkey.

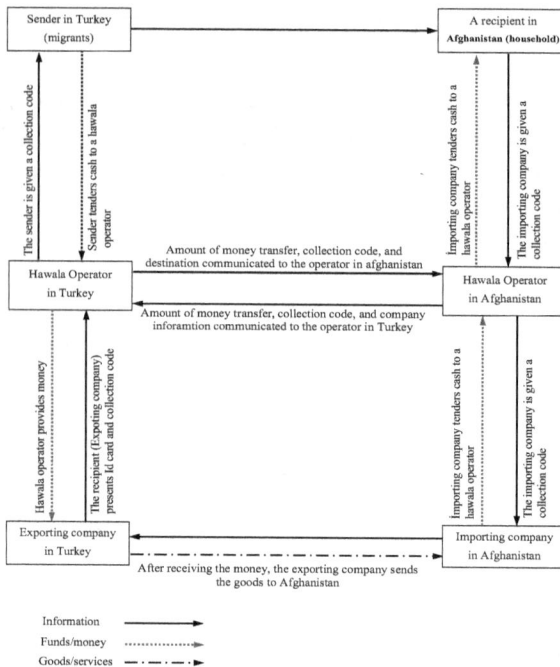

378   Emotional Earmarking: Insights on Overseas Remittances and Emotions from A Mixed Methods Study

Jeremaiah Opiniano

Overseas remittances improve the economic conditions of international migrants' families left behind. These monies also influence family relationships and the financial behaviors of migrant family members in both home and host countries.

The migration literature has yet to analyze the family financial dynamics of migrants and their households using the lens of household finance. Recent studies analyze the remittances-emotions relationship in a partial and static way, rather than holistically and dynamically. Studies are therefore insufficient to illustrate the complex and evolving relationships between overseas remittance-sending, using, and investing. Built on the Family Financial Socialization model and using a recent migrant household survey and object-centered interviews in two rural municipalities in the Philippines, this mixed methods research seeks to determine how emotions come into play when remittance-earning families decide to use remittances (including for productive purposes). The study finds that migrant households employ emotional earmarking to conjointly handle the economic and emotional benefits of remittances to prevailing family relationships.

488   The Pitfalls of Remittances Dependence –Non-linear Effect of Remittances on Institutions

Zeeshan Hashim

This paper explores how remittances influence political and economic freedom in developing economies. We investigate four channels of remittances – income effect, social remittances, voice after exit, and modernization effect – through which remittances promote liberalization and one channel – stability effect – which discourages liberalization. Endogeneity is a potential problem since lack of freedom is a factor associated with peoples' incentive to emigrate and economies' dependence on remittances, and the analysis can be plagued by measurement error in official figures of remittances and omitted variable bias. The results using the general to specific approach and the instrumental variable (FE-2SLS) model show that the impact of remittances on political and economic freedom is non-linear hump-shaped. Initially, an increase in remittances promotes democratization and economic freedom until a turning point is achieved, thereafter it discourages both freedoms. Some of the significant contributions of this research include demonstrating remittances' non-linear influence on political and economic freedom, showing how overreliance on remittances causes institutional decline; introducing an instrumental variable, exposure to natural disasters; and indicating how both political and economic outcomes are interconnected in developing economies.

3E   Migration, Law and Policy 3 [EG15/16]

Chair: Zeynep Üskül Engin, Galatasaray University, Turkey

78   At 'home' in Tel Aviv: Eritrean asylum seekers - forever status-less?

Arie Herscovici and Lilach Lev- Ari

Almost four percent (3.6%) of world population are migrants, most of them voluntary. They seek to improve their living conditions; others, forced migrants (about 100 million), migrate due to persecution, natural disasters, or severe poverty. Among the latter, it is possible to distinguish between asylum seekers applying for international protection in another country and refugees who are subject to proven fear of persecution on the basis of race, religion and nationality. Most immigrants prefer to come to "world cities" also known as "arrival cities," that offer more opportunities for economic, social and cultural integration. In these cities, policy ranges from granting temporary status to full integration in all areas of life. In the current study we focused on Eritrean asylum seekers in Israel, whose number is around 20,500 and over half of whom live in south Tel Aviv. The reasons for their migration are mainly the dictatorial regime in Eritrea and its prolonged war with Ethiopia. Since 2017, immigration from Eritrea to Israel has completely stopped. The main research question was: How do asylum seekers from Eritrea perceive their integration in Tel Aviv? Do they feel at 'home,' namely belonging to the city, or temporary and alienated? The research employed a qualitative method through semi-structured interviews with asylum seekers (N=10), officials in Tel Aviv municipality, and activists in civil organizations (N=12). Here we will present findings regarding asylum seekers only.

The main findings indicate that although asylum seekers from Eritrea are without status from the state's point of view, they are residents of Tel Aviv, and are entitled to receive education and welfare services. Civil organizations also come to their aid, providing legal and employment counseling, and act to advance their cause in public opinion, in governmental ministries and in the 'Knesset' (Israeli parliament). The interviews revealed that despite a certain feeling of integration into the life of the city and a sense of 'home,' there is also a sense of insult; they feel "transparent, not worth anything, thrown away." Implicitly, they feel in a kind of limbo - an undecided state of waiting for a decision, when they are subject to temporary employment conditions and low income; their children attend separate schools, and they are deprived of the most basic activities, such as enrolling in higher education or obtaining a driver's license. Therefore, and due to their living in Israel for over a decade, it is recommended to formulate a policy to redefine their status, similarly to what most European countries have done, particularly for those who are banned from emigrating and the younger generation, who were educated in Israel and perceive their future there.

292   Regularization as Strategy of Control: Reflections on Migration Governance in Mercosur, South America

Dorothea Biaback Anong

In times of globalization, migration control has been described as "the new last bastion of sovereignty" (Dauvergne, 2004: 588) of nation states. The exercise of nation states' sovereign right regarding migration is mostly located is states' decision, who can enter their territory and who can't, which is enforced through an increase in border control (Sassen, 1996; Bosworth 2008). Analyses of regional integration processes then, mostly taking the EU as an example, have stated that this sovereign right has partly been transferred to the regional level, resulting in more restrictive border control at external borders (e.g. Nita et al., 2017: xv). However, insights from my research on the governance of migration in the regional economic community Mercosur (Common Market of the Southern Cone) in South America, with the three member states Argentina, Brazil and Uruguay as case studies, raises questions as to the global applicability of these observations. The empirical research is inspired by interpretive policy analysis (Yanow, 2007) and comprises stakeholder interviews with 34 regional and national policy makers, civil servants, civil society and migrant organizations as well as an analysis of 153 policy documents.

The analysis shows that in the face of waning sovereignty states do not necessarily react with an increase of and more selective border and entry control. The regional context of Mercosur and the national cases of Argentina, Uruguay, and Brazil rather suggest that the realization of not being in complete control over borders can also be responded by "regularization" as strategy of control. This points to theories of the state that locate the condition of state power in the ability to 'grasp' or 'embrace' the population by means of registration and identification, as a pre-requisite to control and exert power (e.g. Torpey, 1998).

367   Investigation of Neighborhoods Closed to Migration in Terms of Sociology of Law: The Case of Istanbul

Dolunay Çörek Akyıldız, Zeynep Üskül Engin, Bengisu Mert

Turkey is a country established on lands that have been subject to migration throughout history due to its geographical feature. After the Ottoman Empire, there was an intense wave of immigration. In the Republican period, especially between 1989 and 1994, when the prime minister of the period was Turgut Özal, many of our compatriots from Bulgaria immigrated to our country. In recent years, after the war in Syria and the withdrawal of military forces from Afghanistan, immigration has begun to be received from the east of Anatolia. The last wave of immigration is different from the others. Because these people do not speak Turkish, they are referred to as citizens of another country, and they have difficulties in integration compared to other immigrants. Due to their increasing numbers, they are no longer allowed to be admitted to some neighborhoods, and the demographic balance has changed in some regions. In order to prevent this structural change, it is seen that the governorships took precautions by issuing some circulars. In this study, the legal basis of the mentioned situation will be investigated only on the basis of the city of Istanbul, as well as the literature review method regarding the neighborhoods where immigration is prohibited. Istanbul was chosen because it encompasses many identities in Turkey and is one of the most cosmopolitan and immigration-receiving cities. The aim of the study is to reveal the sociological connection of the phenomenon of migration with the law in Turkey by looking at the results of the researches, and to explain to what extent the legal regulations affect regional migration, together with the reasons.

3F   Migration and Integration 3 [UG13]

Chair: Karla Valenzuela, University of Iberoamericana, Mexico

259   Prospects for Inclusion of Immigrants and Refugees: The Case of Japan with Special Consideration of its "Cultural Coexistence"

Aoi Mochizuki

In 2022, the global population of forced migrants reached 100 million for the first time in history. Russia's invasion of Ukraine after February 24, 2022, has led to a new large-scale refugee problem. Daily reports have shown that European countries have warmly welcomed Ukrainian refugees. Japan, a closed country to refugees in general, has also instituted a policy of accepting a large number of forced migrants from Ukraine.

Currently, Japan is paying more attention to the refugee problem, and expectations are rising for a change in the restrictive acceptance policy of the past. In this presentation, I will focus on the concept of "cultural coexistence" in Japan and discuss Japan's refugee and migrant acceptance policy.

In the first part, I will examine the historical development of the concept of "cultural coexistence" in the country. "Cultural coexistence" is a key term the government uses in accepting foreigners in Japan. It is defined as "people of different nationalities and ethnicities … liv[ing] together as members of the local community while recognizing each other's cultural differences and trying to build equal relationships." In the 1990s, this term came to be used as a reflection of the discriminatory education of Korean ethnic groups living in Japan. In the 2000s, the Ministry of Internal Affairs and Communications has used the term as a slogan. In this presentation, I will compare the concept of "cultural coexistence" with multiculturalism in Europe and discuss its characteristics in Japanese contexts. In particular, I will examine how this concept was used in beneficial ways for Ukrainian refugees recently while the Japanese government has been reluctant to accept Syrian and Afghan refugees. It welcomed Ukrainian refugees with the new status of "evacuees."

In the second part, I will compare Muslim immigrants' and refugees' living conditions in Japan and European countries. In recent years, in Europe, the conflict between Muslim immigrants' and refugees' religious belongingness and the host society's values has been viewed as a problem. On the other hand, in Japan, Islamic values are not considered a problem, and Islamophobia is not as strong as in Europe. I examine how the concept of "cultural coexistence" is applied to Muslims in Japanese society.

Finally, I will draw from these analyses some implications. The definition of "cultural coexistence" has been criticized because it is very vague and may cover up a subtle assimilationist character. On the other hand, the concept underpins Japan's immigration and refugee policies and has led to the promotion of accepting foreigners by local governments.

6   Migration, integration and alienation: Migrants' reflections on acceptance and hospitality in Western Canada

Nathalie Piquemal and Faiçal Zellama

Canada defines itself as a country of immigration and a multicultural nation that supports and encourages the vitality and preservation of minority cultures and languages, as first codified in the Multiculturalism Act (1971), then in the Canadian Charter of Rights and Freedoms (1982). However, many immigrants, particularly racialized minorities continue to struggle with acceptance and belonging, as they navigate host-guest relationships shaped by cultural discontinuities, microaggressions, contested policies on foreign credentials, and unequal distribution of power and resources. In this presentation, we rely on critical multiculturalism to explain and analyze the persistence of inequalities in migration pathways, with special attention to othering practices and processes of minority immigrants by the Euro-Canadian society. Using a qualitative approach involving semi-structured interviews with 42 participants, we explore newcomers' perceptions of barriers and supports of integration related to cultural identity, host-guest interpersonal and structural factors, and stranger creation instituted by Euro-Canadian society. Our findings are organized in light of the four approaches to immigrants' cultural identity developed by Cohen and Kassan (2018), which we adapted to integration pathways as: Hybrid integration, dual/binary integration, contested integration and negotiated integration. We then analyze and interpret the simultaneous processes of integration of certain categories of immigrants into the Canadian social fabric and exclusion and relegation of other categories to its periphery. Finally, we discuss the complexity of hospitality in a multicultural context and offer critical insights on host factors that may produce, develop and nurture hospitable environments.

109   Economic news consumption and attitudes toward immigrant and ethnic minorities in times of crisis

Nonna Kushnirovich and Sabina Lissitsa

The study examined the relationships between consumption of bad or good economic news and attitudes toward immigrant and ethnic minorities during the economic crisis that developed during the COVID pandemic. The study considered attitudes toward two minority groups in Israel: high-income immigrant citizens from English-speaking countries, and Israeli Palestinian citizens, a low-income ethnic minority. This study is based on an online survey of 866 respondents, members of the majority population group.

The study found that during the global crisis, exposure to negative news was associated with better attitudes toward both high-income and low-income immigrant and ethnic minorities. Moreover, in times of global crisis, people focused mostly on local rather on global news. In contrast to competitive threat theory, the study revealed that feelings of economic threat during global economic crisis engender higher cohesion between different population groups and better attitudes toward minorities. Thus, in times of crisis bad news for the economy brings good news for social solidarity – people tend to rally around the flag; this phenomenon occurs even between groups in protracted conflict over the years.

284   Essential Hands, Invisible Worker: The Lives of Black Migrants in America

Yasin Kakande

Black migrants in the U.S. are subject to the same systemic racism as Black Americans, yet we're not accepted by Black Americans because our accents set us apart. For instance, not long ago, I was waiting for a passenger in front of South Station. As an Uber driver, you receive an exact address on your phone that tells you where to meet someone, and that's where I parked. As I was waiting, a policeman came up and rapped angrily on the window with his knuckles. I rolled the window down, wondering what I'd done wrong.

As a Black African, I have been told "Go back to your country!" or "Go back to Africa!" many times since coming to the U.S. Here, I describe several of those encounters, and highlight the particular—and often peculiar—nature of relations between Black Africans and Black Americans. For example, on my first day at work in a home for mentally disabled individuals, a Black American worker stormed into the dining coming from the office, yelling, "Why are all of you people running away from Africa and taking all of our jobs here? Go back to Africa!"

As I've delved deeper into discussions with Carl and other Black Americans I've met since coming to the U.S., I hear from many who think we are not brothers. In fact, many Black Americans I've met have preconceived notions of Africa as a continent filled with safari animals and jungles, and distance themselves from Black Africans as "lower" beings not only because we are migrants, but because they imagine we've arrived in the U.S. straight from the jungle. I discuss the Black Lives Matter movement in the context of history and my own experiences in this country.

In these discussions, I highlight the fact that many Black Americans are astonished to hear that Africans are trying to flee the Continent, since they are currently struggling against systemic racism in the U.S. and demanding reparations, and I reflect on the reparations debate currently underway in the U.S. I also tackle the news here of Africans giving up their freedom to be slaves in Libya; in late 2017, the U.S. media outlet Cable News Network (CNN) aired reports of West African migrants in the latter stages of their journey to Europe, who had been sold openly in slave markets in Libya. The reports generated widespread condemnation as audiences watched footage of Arab slave traders selling individual people—who were to be used as farm workers—for as little as $400. The CNN revelations suggested that some Africans were so desperate for freedom that they knowingly accepted the risks of entering slavery, and even American rapper Kanye West publicly speculated that the ancient practice of slavery always was predicated as a choice.

3G   Education and Skilled Migration 2 [BG 5/6]

Chair: Lan Lo, University of Nottingham, UK

170   Types of Learning Promoted though Volunteer Non-Formal and Informal Educational Projects in Contemporary Greece: Educational, Cultural, Economic and Political Dimensions

Dionysios Gouvias and Marianthi Oikonomakou

This paper explores the various dimensions relating to the implementation of non-formal and informal educational projects for refugees, which that have been taking place in the last seven years at various locations on certain Greek islands in the North and South Aegean Sea. Some of those lessons have been designed to safeguard the survival and adaptation of refugees to the existing socio-economic settings, where learners are living in conditions of uncertainty and often coping with painful traumatic experiences. Some other lessons aim –at least in principle– to transformative learning and social empowerment.

The field research attempts to generate a self-reflection of various stakeholders in refugee (non-formal & informal) learning: from academics to students, from volunteer teachers to various solidarity collectivities and/or NGOs). The main aim of the study is to raise issues regarding the type of learning that takes place in these education environments, according to various theoretical schemes of LLL (eg. if it is "learner-centred", "knowledge-centred", "assessment-centred", or "community-centred" [Anderson, 2008]), as well as the entanglement of education, culture, economy and politics in the process of offering learning opportunities for refugees.

The tools used for the purpose of the study are teacher and volunteer written reflections and the implementation of focus-groups.

188   The source of trust and vulnerability: Association of Turkish immigrants to the healthcare system in Poland during the pandemic

Gizem Karaköse and Filiz Göktuna Yaylacı

Immigrants and their association with the healthcare system have been a big question in homogeneous countries, especially with the need for official language proficiency in many cases. Immigrants have been considered one of the most vulnerable to inadequate health care. With the pandemic, the risks that immigrants face increased to a high level. Remarkably, the access to the proper treatment, testing, vaccines and psychological support due to the lockdown which have resulted in a negative impact on the health care and adaptation process. In previous studies, Turkish immigrants have been considered one of the well-integrated groups in Poland. In this respect, our research examines the factors that are affecting the accessibility to the system including the socioeconomic, language and cultural aspects of the Turkish immigrants during the Covid-19 pandemic in Poland to understand their experiences in adaptation and systematic participation. The research is based on a preliminary study that focuses on migration and health in Poland. It is planned according to the qualitative methodology based on participatory observation and semi-structured interviews with 11 Turkish immigrants in Warsaw, Poznan, Wroclaw, Bydgoszcz and Torun between January 2021 and June 2021. The results indicate that despite the factors that have a positive effect on social adaptation and communication, not evolving trust in the healthcare system, is related to the deeper concerns that rely on general public opinion and it creates a vulnerability for both immigrants and host society members.

132   Brain circulation? The mobility of Chinese students studying in Taiwan

Yumiko Nakahara

In this study, we analyze the mobility factors, policies, and possible problems of Chinese students in Taiwan, in the context of the brain circulation framework stylized by Saxenian (1999).

In 2010, in attempt to fill expanded enrollment capacity due to higher education reforms and promote mutual cross-strait understanding, the Taiwanese government lifted the ban on Chinese students to study in universities in Taiwan.

Having examined the fields of study selected by Chinese students in Taiwan, we found that business and administration ranked highest. Chinese students may be impressed by Taiwanese businesspersons in China, and are thereby inspired to learn business and administration in Taiwan. The art is the second most popular field. The third is engineering. Chinese students may consider Taiwan's worldwide reputation for advanced technology when choosing where to study abroad.

However, this study found that the policy prohibiting Chinese students from working in Taiwan, part-time and after graduation, is the one that needs the most improvement. The impossibilities of earning tuition money by working part-time jobs and gaining work experience in Taiwan even after graduation may detract some Chinese students from coming to Taiwan to study. If Chinese students can gain work experience in Taiwan after graduation, they may contribute more to China as returnees, in a "brain circulation" scenario.

The policy modification that would allow Chinese students to work can be expected to increase the number of Chinese students studying in Taiwan, which is currently less than expected. In addition, it is important for non-prestigious universities to engage in public relations activities to fill their enrollment capacities.

Chinese students in Taiwan ultimately encourage mutual understanding among the younger generation, which can lead to peaceful cross-strait relations. For this, the policy should be modified.

Reference

Saxenian, Annalee, 1999. Silicon Valley's New Immigrant Entrepreneurs. San Francisco: Public Policy Institute of California.

116   Skills dimension of Pakistani international Migrant workers

Syed Imran Haider, Muhammad Ali Awan, Shahzad Ahmed Shiz

International labour migration plays an important role and a tool to provide human resources to the countries having smaller populations and experiencing shortage of labour. Those countries receive human resources from low-income countries like Pakistan. Bureau of Emigration and Overseas Employment (BE&OE) estimates since 1971 more than 12 million Pakistani workers went abroad for foreign employment including 96% in Gulf Cooperation Countries (GCC). This specific migration corridor to the GCC countries is dominated by temporary labour migration schemes, governed by the sponsorship system (kafala) which de facto ties the migrant worker's emigration status to an individual employer or sponsor (Kafeel) for their contract period. In 2022, BE&OE reported an estimate 832.339 Pakistanis went abroad which is highest number reported after the Covid pandemic. These workers are divided in different categories e.g., highly qualified, highly skilled, skilled, semi-skilled and unskilled workers. The low skilled and unskilled labour migrants' workers are outreached by Overseas Employment Promotors (OPEs) and their networks of sub agents particularly in rural areas working across the country. The present study is an assessment of; how low & unskilled workers using different channels to access foreign employment; what types of skills development opportunities are available for aspiring migrant workers; how better skills can provide fair recruitment and decent work to a migrant. For this purpose, 15 Key Informant interviews were conducted during March to May 2022 with the ILO, BE&OE, and OEPs relevant officials. Findings show that due consideration is required to the new skills development programs designed by human resource sending countries to create job opportunities in local as well international labour markets. Trained and professional workers are attracted by new destinations. The highly qualified and skilled labour has to pay least cost of the migration as they are well aware about the migration process as compared to the semi-skilled or unskilled workers. The more trained and professional migrant workers can be in better position to access decent work opportunity and equal wages in international labour market resulting better remittances to country of origin and more likelihood of assimilation in new culture.

10:30-10:45 BREAK

Day Two 24 August 2023 - 10:45-12:15

4A   Youth, Children and Families 1 [EG17]

Chair: Paulette Schuster, Reichman University, Israel

347   Irregular Migration Among Nigerian Youth: Stemming the Tide

Gloria Anetor and Nathaniel Omotoba

Irregular migration (unauthorized, or undocumented migration) has been on the increase globally for almost four decades. Unarguably, this rise in Nigeria has been particularly among the youths in the past one decade. The practice of crossing an international border without official permission from the authorities has been unacceptable to many countries, because they see the migrants as intruders and additional burden to their economy. This makes the people in the host countries treat them in the most inhuman ways. In this report, drivers of migration are examined, and approaches to stemming the tide were explored in-dept.   In this study, search engines (Google, Mozilla) were used to search the internet, journals and textbooks were used to retrieve information on irregular migration among Nigerian youth. Information was obtained on the causes of migration, countries mostly migrated to and the challenges faced by the migrants in their host countries. The information gathered from different sources pointing to some of the causes of irregular migration such as the traditional determinants of migration including poverty, food insecurity, climate change among others were examined. Additionally, the countries most migrated to and the challenges   faced in their destination countries were also examined, and this information was used to proffer solutions to irregular migration problems among the youths in Nigeria. In conclusion, despite the inhuman treatment meted out   to Nigerian youth who migrate through many dangerous routes including the Mediterranean sea, ironically, the youths are still risking their lives to escape from Nigeria because of untold hardships and insecurity experienced at home. Safe migration awareness should be conducted in rural areas of home countries targeting the most vulnerable groups, – school-age, and youth. They need to be given the required and sustained attention by stakeholders.

211   Music as a catalyst for bio-psycho-social transformation for refugee youth

Eva Marija Vukich and Hala Hamdan

The experience of migration can have a significant impact on the physical, emotional, and psychological well-being of children and adolescents. The challenges of adapting to a new environment, culture shock, prior conflict exposures, and the loss of familiar relationships can create trauma, depression, and anxiety, especially for those who have fled conflict and persecution. For refugee youth, music can offer a powerful tool for overcoming these difficulties, fostering a sense of belonging, and promoting resilience.

This presentation explores the benefits of music for refugee youth as a means of bio-psycho-social transformation, focusing on its potential to enhance mental health, promote social cohesion, and facilitate identity formation (Almedom, Baker and Jones). By engaging in music experiences, young people can develop their emotional processing skills, learn to regulate their emotions, create opportunities for cultural integration, and build positive relationships with others.

Moreover, music can play a crucial role in promoting post-traumatic growth (Almedom, Papadopoulos), helping refugee youth to find meaning and purpose in their lives despite the challenges they face. It can also serve as a means of integration, allowing them to connect with their new communities and feel a sense of belonging (Bergh, A., Sloboda).

Drawing on research from child development, psychology, and music therapy, this presentation highlights the importance of music in promoting transnational social resilience and fostering positive outcomes for refugee youth. The presenters will share short vignettes of clinical music therapy groups with refugee youth in Palestine and UK, and provide a brief music experience for attendees.

In conclusion, it is seen that music can serve as a bridge between the former life and the new life, and support the bio-psycho-social needs of refugee youth (Vukich, Zharinova-Sandersons). By creating opportunities for music experiences and creative expression, refugee youth can explore their multicultural identities, internal resources, and create strong bonds in their emerging communities.

115   Court-To-Court Dialogue: Challenges for the Protection of Children in Migration Processes

Laila Roxina Moliterno Abi Cheble

This paper aims to explore the role of supranational courts in guaranteeing the rights of children in processes of human mobility. Thus, it is important to take into account the context in which children live and "differentiate in order to protect", as law as a social science cannot remain oblivious. The number of children in processes of human mobility is growing significantly and therefore modifying the debates surrounding migration previously understood in terms of adults and men. The issue becomes relevant as thousands of children are crossing international borders both in Europe and the Americas, such as the war situation in Ukraine and Syria, as well as the mobility processes in the Central American region. During these movements, which entail risks and opportunities, situations arise that place them in a situation of increased vulnerability, as some are separated from their families or migrate alone. This calls for an adequate study and an enriched or reinforced protection by understanding the various key actors (families, children and States themselves through public policies). This study highlights the value of soft law instruments and the role of supranational courts in guaranteeing children's rights. To this end, international law instruments (treaties) that contain references to the terms "children" or "children" are taken up, specifically the Convention on the Rights of the Child, additional protocols drawn up by the Committee on the Rights of the Child, the International Convention on the Protection of the Rights of All Migrant Workers and Members of Their Families, etc. In addition, soft law documents (which allow for the constant evolution of the law) such as the New York Declaration, the 2030 Agenda for Sustainable Development, the Global Compact for Safe, Orderly and Regular Migration are analysed. These instruments are used as a framework for the study of cases in the Inter-American Court of Human Rights (IACHR) and the European Court of Human Rights (ECHR), the highest guarantors of law in the respective regions. Based on the cases, points of coincidence and divergence between the understandings developed and the interpretation of the courts are pointed out. While recognising the sovereignty of states over the control of their borders, the importance of international cooperation in border management is highlighted. It is concluded that the term vulnerability(ies) is a point of convergence between the two Courts, as well as references to the best interests of the child, the need for context analysis, detention as a measure of last resort. However, divergences are noted (for this purpose, the standards indicated by the IACHR and the ECHR are demarcated) and the lack of a fluid dialogue between the courts. Finally, dialogues for the construction of a new legal framework for the protection of human rights are pointed out as a valuable tool.

251   Youth Labor Migration vs Youth Bulge in the Central Asia Region

Liudmila Konstants

We find it very difficult to understand and describe the Kahramanmaraş earthquake disaster that shook the society deeply. On the second day of the earthquake, we, as the Esenyurt Youth movement, participated in the aid campaign and formed a team with our friends to distribute them to the earthquake zone. What happened there wasn't a disaster, it was total apocalypse. The earthquake is not a new thing, but when we consider the destructiveness of the earthquake, which is recorded in history as the Kahramanmaraş earthquake, as well as the number of people affected and the breadth of geography (Eda Esma EYÜBAGİL1, 2023), and the human error factor that causes it, we face terrible facts. What's going on here with technology could be overcome.

4B   Insecurities and Migration 2 [UG14]

Chair: Anas Karzai, Laurentian University, Canada

247   Perpetual War-Logic and Global Refugees

Anas Karzai

The imperial war games of the last century have re-emerged, but this time as a nightmare. From the invasion of Afghanistan, Iraq and Syria by the US-NATO war machine since 9/11 to the invasion of Ukraine by Russia in the last year, the world has not seen such a mass displacement of ordinary, mostly poor and disenfranchised people since the WWII. Thus the cold war talk of 'good' vs 'evil'

89

which had divided the world for most of the last century has re-emerged in the political and media echo-chambers of the West. The West is once again on a collision course with a nuclear armed Russia. All reason and sensibility that humans have acquired so far have once again been suspended. In the last year, the warnings and threats coming out of both Moscow and Washington, including its vassal that is the EU are devastating for the future of the planet. However, the perpetual war economy is the engine generating this new cold war. Today, the United Nations High Commission for Refugees (UNHCR) reports that 68.5 million people have been forcibly displaced worldwide, of which 40 million are internally displaced, and 25.4 million are refugees and 3.1 million are asylum seekers.

This paper argues that war-logic is not the product of 'human nature' as is commonly rationalized and culturally understood nor does it belong to the anatomical character of the human brain. Rather, it is the historically specific and culturally produced by-product of the political economy of capitalism. By following a sociological argument, this presentation asks the following questions and proceeds to examine them: Who benefits from the war economy? And what are the cultural and historical forces that normalize and legitimate the perpetual war logic even when it is an existential threat to the human species?

454   Twofold migration: The Story of Awiwi Town in Niger Republic

Maryam Liman

Temporary labour migration has been a cause of concern and is widespread across India. While migration is a complex issue affected by many different factors, climate factor assumes significant importance among them as a risk in the rural areas of developing countries. In this context, the main objective of the present study is to assess the spatiotemporal livelihood vulnerability to climate change for migrant- and non-migrant households for selected regions of Andhra Pradesh and Maharashtra for 2005-14 by employing two waves of ICRISAT data: (i) second generation Village Level Survey (VLS2): 2005-2008 and (ii) Village Dynamic South Asia (VDSA) dataset: 2009-14. In addition, household vulnerability index was constructed to identify climate vulnerability between migrant and non-migrant households; among different farming households as well as map the intertemporal and interspatial vulnerability. Based on the household vulnerability index, it shows that non-migrant households are more vulnerable as compared to migrant households. In this regard, we argue that migrant households adapt extreme weather events through receiving remittances, non-farm income and social networks to counter attack extreme weather shocks. In this background, we infer migration as an adaptation measure to climate change. Further, it is observed that marginal-farm households are most vulnerable, followed by small-farm, large-farm and medium-farm households. The comparison among six semi-arid villages in terms of climate change vulnerability shows that Maharashtra villages were more vulnerable to climate extremes than the villages of Andhra Pradesh in the alternative years of the study periods. Surprisingly, this study found that household vulnerability to climate change has declined from 2005-2014.

282   Perpetrators' Trauma: Emotional State of Immigrants from Russia who Disapprove of the Invasion of Ukraine

Mukhina Varvara

On 24 February 2022, Russia invaded Ukraine and up to 8,104,606 refugees from Ukraine had to leave their homes (UNHCR, 08 March 2023). Undoubtedly, these aggressive actions have affected the emotional state of all Ukrainians around the world. However, these actions have also affected many Russians who disapprove of them. The Russian legislation that came into force in early March 2022 (Russian Criminal Code, Article 207.3, Article 280.3, Article 284.2) prohibits the expression of any position condemning Russian aggression, however, public opinion polls suggest that at least 23% of Russians disapprove of the invasion (Levada-Center, 2023). The 48% increase in the use of antidepressants in the first nine months of 2022 is indirect evidence of how the invasion has affected the emotional state of Russians (TASS, 28 October 2022). According to official statistics, which usually tend to underestimate the number of emigrants, at least 622 thousand of Russians left Russia in January-November 2022 (Federal State Statistics Service, 2022). I suggest that the proportion of those who disapprove of the Russian government's actions is even higher among those who have left. The aim of this study is to show how the invasion has affected the emotional state of Russians abroad, who are able to express their attitudes more openly than those in Russia. I use the theoretical framework of group-based emotions, which are based on an individual's social identity and sense of belonging to a particular group (Yefremova and Grigoryan, 2014). A previous study of Russian immigrants in Japan showed that those who disapproved of the invasion identified with the perpetrator group and experienced group-based guilt, shame, fear, and ingroup-directed anger and contempt (Mukhina, 2023). In this study I use the sample of 511 Russian immigrants (male: 41.10%; female: 57.73%) who disapproved of the invasion of Ukraine to determine whether and to what extent they experienced such emotions. I conducted an online survey that consisted of 34 questions, including basic demographics (gender, age, education, income, etc.), respondents' emotional state, and others. Participants were approached through anti-war Russian immigrant groups on social networking sites and online groups that help new immigrants from Russia move and settle abroad. The results of the survey showed that most respondents experienced shock, helplessness, problems experiencing joy, apathy, and sleep problems in the first days of the invasion. Many respondents experienced varying degrees of group-based guilt, shame, fear, ingroup-directed anger and contempt. The intensity of emotions differed according to gender, age, level of education, income and length of stay abroad. The results of this study showed that Russians abroad experienced acute group-based emotions due to their sense of belonging to the perpetrator group. Although the proportion of those who have experienced such emotions may be over-represented in this study due to the research method, it does help to provide a more comprehensive picture of the overall impact of this invasion.

4C   Remittances 2 [UG11]

Chair: Ahmad Walid Barlas, Greifswald University, Germany

268   International standards of Migrant Domestic Workers and the Kafala System in Lebanon

Nadine El-Dekmak

The kafala system (sponsorship system) is the legal basis of the work relationship between the migrant domestic worker (MDW) and the employer also known as the sponsor. It is a restrictive immigration regime mixed with customary practices which ties the residency of the worker to their employer. This system has been implemented in many countries of the Gulf Cooperation Council (GCC) and the Middle East through a set of bureaucratic and legal procedures that regulate the relationship between the sponsor, the expatriate, and the state. Amongst these countries, Lebanon hosts over 250,000 MDWs, most of whom are women from Ethiopia, Sri Lanka, Nepal, the Philippines, and other African countries, who are recruited through private recruitment agencies to work under the sponsorship system and live under the roof of their employer. Although domestic work is highly demanded in Lebanon, these women face daily exploitation and human rights violations as their working and living conditions are contestable. There, some workers don't get paid, have a day off, have normal working hours, or have the freedom of movement and are unable to travel to their home country, and the majority have their identity papers confiscated by the employer or the recruitment agency. While it has been speculated that the kafala system results in labor exploitation of migrant domestic workers, research has yet to explore whether this national system contradicts migrant workers' international standards. In other words, does the Kafala system fulfill the international standards of migrant workers? In answering this research question, we will start from the hypothesis that the Kafala system facilitates domestic servitude and therefore violates the human rights of the migrant worker. In order to confirm or dismiss our hypothesis, we will conduct a literature review and a comparative analysis between the Lebanese kafala system and international standards of migrant workers in mainly three areas often neglected: the right to freedom of movement, decent work, and the right to free choice of employment. In this context, the paper will be concluded with a set of recommendations on the relevant topics.

377   Differences in Rural Investment Climates for Remittances: Mixed Methods Results and Findings from The Philippines

Jeremaiah Opiniano

Rural areas frequently receive foreign remittances from international migrants, thanks to the incomes wired by townmates from abroad. Rural areas thus become a natural direction for remittances, which thus provide development potential. Those potentials arise especially if rural investment climates favor them. This mixed methods research shares findings from a mixed methods tool, called the Remittance Investment Climate Analysis in Rural Hometowns (RICART), to see if rural municipalities are investment-friendly, and if migrants and their families from those rural hometowns are financially capable and literate to make those investments. Implemented in two rural hometowns in the Philippines, mixed methods results and findings show that rural birthplaces provide heterogenous conditions that see these places either having more or less investments from overseas migrant townmates. At the same time, migrant households exhibit financial capabilities that are nuanced to the conditions of their localities and their levels of financial aptitude. RICART contributes a methodological tool to determine specific contributions of remittances to rural birthplaces while identifying investment climate and local governance-related barriers to rural hometown investing by overseas Filipinos.

483   Political Change and Poverty among Rural Households in Afghanistan: Evidence from Marmul District, Balkh Province

Ahmad Walid Barlas

It has been over eighteen months since the Taliban resumed leadership in Afghanistan and people are struggling with severe issues including insecurity, human rights violations, unemployment, poverty and hunger. This research mainly focuses on poverty status among rural households before and after the political change, using the Marmul district of Balkh province as a case study. The primary data was collected in two phases. In the first phase, 280 households were surveyed in Marmul district before the collapse with assistance of an administrated questionnaire. In the second phase, we attempted to survey the same households after the fall, but only 100 households took part in our study. Poverty headcounts, poverty gap and poverty squared gap were estimated to analyze the status of poverty in the study area. Our findings show that the average household monthly income declined by 30%, from AFG 12,807 to AFG 8,930. Poverty indexes indicate that the severity of poverty increased in addition to the number of people living below the poverty line. This implies that people are becoming poorer and losing their economic power daily. In addition, our logit coefficients exposed that gender and employment status of household head, number of male employed, literacy ratio, remittances, access to banking service and land size are negative correlated with poverty. While the number of males and females (household size) increase the possibility of becoming poor.

4D   Migration, Law and Policy 4   [EG15/16]

Chair: Lilach Lev Ari, Oranim Academic College of Education, Israel

161   Challenges of Legal Clinics in the Context of Immigration Detention: An Assessment of the Current Situation between (Political) Activism and Voluntary Legal Advice in Germany

Hannah Franz

Student run legal refugee clinics occupy an important role in the German legal landscape. Most law clinics were established in response to the so-called "refugee crisis" in 2014, when the number of asylum applications started to rise immensely. The German legal system was not and still is not prepared for this influx: Since migration law is not anchored in legal education, correspondingly there is a shortage of appropriateley trained law professionals. Hence, a discrepancy between needed and available legal advice exists. By providing a low-threshold possibility for refugees seeking information and legal advice without a cost risk, refugee law clinics aim to fill this gap. However, they are confronted with a number of challenges: Besides financial instability, they find themselves in a dilemma between the requirement to provide legal advice within the applicable legal framework but at the same time being confronted with structural deficits within the law. The latter leads to questions regarding the limits of legal clinics.

This conflict gains crucial relevance, when student counselling is provided in an area of law where a variety of elementary rule of law gaps can be observed; such as the area of immigration detention.

Although immigration detention is not a penal sentence, the placement conditions are similar to those of a criminal detention. Furthermore, 50-90% of the judicial detention orders are unlawful; leaving those affected unjustly imprisoned. The reasons include lack of expertise among judges as well as legal peculiarities of procedural detention law. Thus, detainees awaiting deportation are not entitled to a public defense attorney.

Against this background, the question arises whether it is reasonable and expectable for clinical students to expand their volunteer work into the area of political and social influence? Is it their duty to inform the public about experienced grievances and to advocate for changes in law? What problems can arise for the core work of the legal clinics from such an expanded activity?

Especially in the area of immigration detention, public and widespread criticism of detention procedures can significantly complicate the counseling situation and thus have a negative impact on the possibility of offering legal counselling. This is due to the fact that the legal status of voluntary counselling in detention is not comprehensively secured. If volunteer legal counselors are – due to (political) activism – perceived as unpleasant by the actors involved in detention, this can hamper their position as independent legal counselors and thus lead to aggravated conditions in accessing the people in need.

In my paper, I would like to address this conflict between the need for reporting the experienced injustice, acting upon the results of critical examination of the law and the requirement not to restrict the possibility for providing legal advice by doing so. In that regard, structural problems of immigration detention law will be discussed.

458   Estimating the Shocks of the Irregular Migration Phenomenon on Public Spending by using time series models

Iliuta Cumpanasu

Estimating the Shocks of the Irregular Migration Phenomenon on Public Spending by using time series models

Over recent years, the irregular migration has experienced a significant increase worldwide. This reality has caught the attention of the scientific community and practitioners responsible with how to deal with this phenomenon, seeing it at different angles.

The proposed study brings about a major contribution to Academia by providing a fresh viewpoint and research approach regarding the impact of the irregular migration on welfare and public expenditures in the Balkans, its findings being able to capture an area which has not yet benefitted from a comprehensive approach in the scientific community.

Furthermore, this is the first research that captures the most recent international migration phenomenon in the Covid-19 Pandemic crisis or similar lockdowns and the impact on public expenditures, by using the mediation of secondary drivers. The study finally tests the resilience of the public actors to the budgetary burden caused by irregular migration, emphasizes how shocks change their behaviour and core values, providing valuable data as a support in designing effective policies regarding challenges which are hot spots on the world's agenda as well.

Moreover, as a novelty, the study offers an already tested, innovative and ambitious model for estimating of public expenditure due to irregular migration by using border management time series, being able also to forecast important variables (e.g., seasonality, stationarity of the series) that can be leveraged by interested decision-makers.

Specifically, a mixed method of data collection and analysis (Triangulation) is used by leveraging the official databases (e.g., Border Police Organisations, UN, FRONTEX, Word Bank, Eurostat, etc) followed by testing the time series components, got in the process of using adequate statistical methods (i.e., scaling, components, stationarity). Complementary data were obtained by conducting of semi-structured interviews with experts in the field and desk research.

For testing of the research hypothesis, some multi-factorial, auto-regressive, econometric models, or panel models (static and dynamic) were used, all these results being supported by qualitative analysis of the data collected through interviews.

293   Legal aid platform Linking Help z.s.: UA.SUPPORT

Kateryna Balaban and Jana Schneider

Pro bono legal aid refers to the provision of legal services for free to individuals who cannot afford to pay for legal representation. It is a critical aspect of the justice system that ensures access to justice for all, irrespective of their financial status. Legal aid plays a vital role in protecting the rights of vulnerable communities, promoting equality, and advancing the rule of law. Without pro bono assistance, many people would be unable to navigate the legal system and assert their rights, leading to injustices and inequality.

The process of integrating migrants into a new society can be challenging, particularly when it comes to legal matters. In many cases, migrants face difficulties in accessing legal resources due to language barriers, cultural differences, and financial constraints. Pro bono legal aid can assist migrants in understanding their rights and responsibilities, which can help them to integrate better into their new community. In this way, pro bono legal aid can have a positive impact on the integration of migrants and contribute to building more inclusive and cohesive communities.

Linking Help z.s.[1] is an international legal aid platform with its major focus on supporting Ukrainian refugees with the project UA.SUPPORT[2]. The platform facilitates pro bono legal advice and connects people in need with volunteer lawyers from around the world.

Brief overview of the project so far:

3000+ cases solved

290+ volunteer lawyers worldwide

30+ predominantly European countries covered

UA.SUPPORT - Linking Help z.s. is officially supported by a number of European bar associations, global legal institutions and NGOs. The Ukrainian Bar Association lists UA.SUPPORT as a reputable partner to help Ukrainian refugees get legal advice.

The heart of the project is a platform, which was made with the help of artificial intelligence as a clever solution. People in need fill in the request form on the project's website and the request will be processed by one of the Ukrainian Helpdesk associates. Afterwards, volunteer lawyers can then take the cases in the system which are connected to their jurisdiction and field of expertise. After the person in need and a lawyer are connected, the lawyer can handle the case independently or in cooperation with Helpdesk associates, which are supporting the communication. At the moment the platform is receiving a constant number of 100 requests per week.

The impact of the legal aid project has been significant, having helped over 3,000 cases of migrants. However, there are still many more migrants who require legal assistance but cannot afford it. Pro bono legal aid remains a critical resource for these individuals, and supporting the project that provides such aid can have a significant impact on the lives of those who need it. Therefore, it is important to continue supporting the pro bono legal aid project, both financially and through volunteering. We can help to build more inclusive and cohesive communities that benefit everyone, regardless of their background or circumstances.

More information:

https://www.linking.help/

https://www.ua.support/

[1] https://www.linking.help

[2] https://www.ua.support

214   Is it just because of anti-migration border fences? Why Israel's Border Barriers Worked?

Lilach Lev Ari and Arnon Medzini

A generation ago, globalization "shrank" the world: It was supposed to tear down barriers, but security considerations and a widespread refusal to help migrants and refugees have fueled a new wave of wall-building across the world. In recent years, fence-making has become a booming business, pushed by waves of migration, ongoing conflicts, and the growing threat of terrorism. The numbers are clear: Since 2015 work started on more physical barriers around the world than at any other point in modern history. All these barriers have one thing in common: They do not shield nation-states against the traditional military threat at borders, but instead target new challenges including massive migration movements. However, it turns out that walls do not really block migration flow. In spite of the aggressive symbolism, it is not clear that walls are truly effective.   Migrants do not give up. They bypass, using longer migratory routes, more dangerous, on which mortality is much higher.

Israel serves as a good case study of barriers and walls, since it has invested heavily in securing its borders. Between 2005 and 2013 over 60,000 African asylum seekers, mainly from Darfur, Sudan and Eritrea, immigrated to Israel via Egypt. Their motives for leaving their countries of origin include ongoing bloody wars on the African continent as well as corruption, severe conditions of poverty and hunger, economic and political disintegration. Israel has been forced to cope with these migration waves. Its first attempt was to build a massive security fence along its border with Egypt to prevent forced migrants from entering the country. The government of Israel was not enthusiastic about building a border barrier, mainly for financial reasons. Yet ultimately, political and public pressure generated a negative image of a government incapable of overcoming the forced migrants problem. The government of Israel offered a number of justifications for blocking asylum seekers from crossing its border with Egypt: Sovereign rights, security considerations, and national identity. However, in contrast to the failure of border fences erected in many parts of the world to prevent the passage of immigrants, the impact of the Sinai barrier has been significant. Since the fence was first erected, the number of illegal migrants from Africa to Israel has significantly dropped, and from 2017 no asylum seekers crossed the border. Few borders on earth are as secure as Israel's.

The purpose of this presentation is to analyze the multiple aspects of the separation barrier built by Israel and evaluate its effectivenessIs it the separation barrier that prevents immigrants from crossing, or a combination of a massive border fence, an increased military presence, an increase in the danger of life along the migration route and a new set of laws enacted against immigrants, together created a situation where Israel has become an unattractive country for immigrants.

Examine why countries continue to build new walls - especially when, as history shows, the old ones rarely did what they set out to do?

Walls between countries are nothing new.

4E   Theory and Methods in Migration Studies 1 [BG3/4]

Chair: H. Yaprak Civelek, Anadolu University, Turkey

420   "There is no freedom anymore". The impact of Canada's Covid policies on migrants' return intentions and strategies. A case study of Poles living in Toronto

Agnieszka Malek

All over the world the pandemic resulted in unprecedented socio-political consequences and severely impacted the life of migrants. Some of them were forced to return to their countries of origin, many faced economic difficulties due to limited access to work and income, and still others tried to find new ways to adapt and cope with unstable situation. The government of Canada implemented emergency legislation such as lockdowns, social distancing, travel restrictions, vaccine requirement, household quarantine, closure of workplaces, schools, and places of worship. On the one hand, these measurements upset the daily routines of individuals and families and, in case of immigrants, disrupted their transnational ties, but on the other hand, effected a change in the ways people think, allowing to redefine their goals and values.

Drawing from 40 in-depth interviews conducted with Polish immigrants in Great Toronto Area (GTA) on 2022 and 2023, this presentation aims to explore how the pandemic itself and legislation introduced by federal and/or provincial governments have affected the mobility intentions and life strategies of Polish long-settled immigrants living in Toronto. The research participants expressed dissatisfaction with public-health restrictions and general distrust towards the PM Justin Trudeau and his liberal government. A significant number of Poles living in GTA supported the so called Freedom Convoy protests, that were aimed at forcing the government to revoke COVID-19 measures and mandates. Immigrants' engagement and positive attitude towards protest actions were even called the biggest political mobilization of Polish migrant community in Toronto in the last two decades. The presentation will discuss the role of the pandemic policies and distrust towards public authorities and institutions, on the long-settled migrants' intensions and decisions, especially in terms of possible return to Poland. The migrant own narratives will be analysed in relation to their social trajectories and life histories. As such, the research contributes to the literature on return migration and decision-making process. Although migration scholars have increasingly paid attention to the various aspects of return migration, new issues have been emerging, especially in the context of pandemic and post-pandemic reality.

287   Understanding the Determinants of Migration Intentions - An Individual and Spatial Perspective

Fares Ben Youssef and Mohamed Kriaa

Migration is a complex phenomenon that has been a defining aspect of human history for thousands of years and continues to be of great importance today. Understanding the reasons that drive people to leave their homes and seek a better life elsewhere is crucial to comprehending the causes of migration. This research aims to explore and understand the determinants of migration intentions from both an individual and spatial perspective in the context of Tunisia, a country that experiences significant migration stocks and flows.

Socio-Economic theories such as the neoclassical theory, the new economics of migration, and the network theory have contributed greatly to our understanding of the dynamics and trends of the phenomenon in a world where migration has become an inexorable pillar of social and economic life.

The study is designed to examine the determinants of migration intentions through a multidisciplinary lens, drawing on insights from economics and sociology, specifically; the research uses econometric modelling to explore the determinants of migration intentions from a sociodemographic and economic perspective, while also conducting spatial analysis to detect the impact of regional characteristics on migration intentions.

The first part of the study involves using econometric modelling to understand the determinants of migration intentions from a sociodemographic and economic perspective through survey data (Tunisia-HIMS*, General Census of Population and Housing, consumption survey, and the national survey on population and employment).

In the second part of our research, exploratory spatial data analysis and modelling through spatial econometrics are employed with a dual perspective aimed at describing the spatial characteristics of the studied population, as well as their impacts on the intention to migrate.

By providing a comprehensive understanding of the determinants of migration intentions from both individual and spatial perspectives, this research aims to contribute to the development of effective policies that can better govern migration flows in Tunisia and beyond.

562   A Critical Perspective on "Online" Research Practice in Population Studies

H. Yaprak Civelek

Demographers technically use objective data, and accept the truths exposed to any interpretation as "hung in the air". Today, digital surveys are based on collecting data from the internet and that kind of scientific act doubles the "distance" to human life. This study brings forward how social demographers especially those who choose "online" field research cause a loss of the dialogic interaction between the researcher, participant, and the effect of the contextual environment. They mostly think that the questionnaire is doing its job because the senses are at work during the whole interview, which is true to some extent. Demography is mainly located on a positivist side: seeking out the frequencies and trends in population is quite a job. One can suggest that demographers focused on fertility or mortality, or migration, thanks to demography training, have a "numeric" background they do not care about empathy enough as needed for an anthropologist for the very reason. Most of social demographic studies employ qualitative methods as complementary. For instance, while studying fertility, it is possible to see that some remarkable and significant statistical indicators can disturb a demographer's mind and push her/his to do qualitative research to understand the issue deeply. The deepest point always presents the covered truths; the ideological facts. Reaching such a point is not possible with an online face-to-face interview because it perfectly needs to be stepped on the mugged ground; observations, senses, emotions, sociability, and empathy. Moreover, some scientists dare to construct a "theoretical framework" by connecting online practice to explanatory or explicative theories without discussing the limitations of losing observation and context. But being humanist and the power of context is important and valid for both methodological perspectives. As we know the famous "warning" about the relationship between those perspectives and field studies comes from Bourdieu: "Theory without practice is empty; practice without theory is blind". It puts a moral responsibility as an excellent social demographer must have the ability to explain the "numeric" or "scientific" matter in front of her/his according to the related theory to create a new "discussible" one; every research has the potential for constructing a new theory or giving a push to the conventional one. Digital practices in social sciences do not care about the importance of attending to a field anymore and apparently, the Covid-19 pandemic has increased the tendency. The researcher needs to know the participants' social demographic characteristics like age, sexual identity, place of residence, and income level. Then what we see is a researcher connecting from one city to another or from one neighborhood to another and a half-body participant looks like an object with nothing influencing him/her while speaking. This means the blue screen built its own -meta- context and demographers, even some who say that the blue screen is already progressing on the same line with their understanding of research, must discuss the limitations of this kind of construction. The argument of this paper is supported by the interviews with demographers and free researchers.

223 Mobility governance and ambivalent humanitarian protection in Brazil: continuities and changes during the COVID-19 pandemic

Gisela P. Zapata

The Brazilian migration landscape radically changed in the last two decades, both in quantitative and qualitative terms, given the increase in volume and the diversification in the origins and motives of international migrants. For instance, the number of people seeking international protection – primarily from other countries of the region such as Venezuela, Haiti and Cuba – grew five-fold between 2011 and 2019 (Silva et al., 2020). A direct and well-documented consequence of the pandemic is the threat to the security and protection of the rights of migrants, with several governments around the world having used the pandemic as an excuse to redouble border control measures, carry out summary deportations and limit access to those in need of international protection (Crawley, 2021; Hennebry & KC, 2020; The Lancet, 2020). Although Brazil has recently undergone a normative transition from a security-oriented to a human rights-based migration legislation and has a long tradition regarding refugee law and protection (Jubilut, 2006; Zapata & Tapia Wenderoth, 2022) the pandemic provoked a radical change in the governance of international mobility in the country. This paper explores the ways in which the pandemic has been used to increase mobility controls and limit access to asylum, particularly for Venezuelan nationals, (re)signifying the border as a stage for the subordinate reproduction of the global, securitised control and management of migrant and displaced populations. More broadly, it reflects on the symbiotic, often ambivalent, relationship between spatial control and humanitarian assistance practices, and the contradictions of these policy changes vis-à-vis the country's progressive mobility framework. These type of political-institutional responses to 'crises' speak to the ever-present threats to the global refugee protection system widely documented in the North (De Lucas, 2016; Mountz, 2020). The paper draws on a systematic review of migration and refugee-related laws, decrees, and administrative acts before and during the COVID-19 pandemic and 11 semi structured interviews with key actors such as government officials, civil society, and international organisations, conducted between June and July 2020.

References

Crawley, H. (2021). How Covid-19 Became a Cover to Reduce Refugee Rights. The Conversation. https://theconversation.com/how-covid-19-became-a-cover-to-reduce-refugee-rights-156247

De Lucas, J. (2016). Sobre el proceso de vaciamiento del derecho de asilo por parte de los Estados de la UE. AIS: Revista Europea e Iberoamericana de Pensamiento y Análisis de Derecho, Ciencia Política y Criminología, 4(1), 21–27.

Hennebry, J., & KC, H. (2020). Quarantined! Xenophobia and Migrant Workers During the Covid-19 Pandemic. International Organization for Migration (IOM): Geneva. https://publications.iom.int/system/files/pdf/quarantined.pdf

Jubilut, L. (2006). Refugee Law and Protection in Brazil: a Model in South America? Journal of Refugee Studies, 19(1), 22–44.

Mountz, A. (2020). The Death of Asylum. Hidden Geographies of the Enforcement Archipielago. University of Minnesota Press.

Silva, G. J., Cavalcanti, L., Oliveira, T., & Macedo, M. (2020). Refúgio em Números - 5a Edição. https://www.justica.gov.br/seus-direitos/refugio/refugio-em-numeros

The Lancet. (2020). Editorial: COVID-19 will not leave behind refugees and migrants. The Lancet, 395(April 4, 2020), 1090.

Zapata, G. P., & Tapia Wenderoth, V. (2022). Progressive Legislation but Lukewarm Policies: The Brazilian Response to Venezuelan Displacement. International Migration, 60(1), 132–151.

4F   Migration and Integration 4 [UG13]

Chair: Gökay Özerim, Yasar University, Turkey

518   Occupational Attainment of Second Generation of Ethnic Minority Immigrants in the UK: An Analysis Using Labour Force Survey 2014-2018

Rukhsana Kausar and Issam Malki

The integration and assimilation of ethnic minority immigrants (EMIs) and their subsequent generations remains a serious unsettled issue in most of the host countries. This study conducts a labour market gender analysis to investigate specifically whether second generation of ethnic minority immigrants in the UK is gaining access to professional and managerial employment and advantaged occupational positions on par with their native counterparts. In contrast to existing literature, we distinguish between first- and second-generation natives.

The data used to examine the labour market achievements of EMIs is taken from Labour Force Survey (LFS) for the period 2014-2018. We apply potential outcome model with a multivalued treatment to estimate the differential in career attainments across generations, gender and ethnicities. We report estimates of Average Treatment Effect (ATE), and Average Treatment Effect on the Treated (ATET) of four categories: first generation immigrants, second generation immigrants, first generation natives, and second-generation natives for both male and female respondents.

Our findings suggest that the estimated probabilities and differences across groups are consistently similar and highly significant. As expected, first generation natives have the highest probability for higher career attainment among both men and women. The findings also suggest that first generation immigrants perform better than the remaining two groups including the second-generation natives and immigrants. Furthermore, second generation immigrants have higher probability to attain higher professional career but are less likely to succeed in managerial attainment. Our findings coincide with Migration Policy Index (MIPEX 2020) results that UK's integration policies encourage temporary integration- Halfway favourable with average score of 57/100 indicating provision of basic rights and equal opportunities, where public sees immigrants as their equals and neighbours but also as foreigner rather than potential citizens.

316   The Transnational Generations and Education: The models of Integration in Qatari Schools

Abdullah Arbabi

GCC countries as it hosts a huge community of migrants with diverse backgrounds and cultures, developed relevant models and experiences of the social integration. And to narrowing this geographical part of the world and dealing with a specific case like Qatar, with a majority population of migrants "residents", looking at the manifestations of the Social integration are more demanding. This article tries to get a closer look into the integration models that adopted by the transnational generations in Qatari schools, as is sphere for social interacting a engaging.

The paper will give a data about the schools environment and the kind of inclusion and integration approaches.

501   Excercises in Estrangement: Experiments in an Italian School at the Border

Giulia Zanfabro

In the field of second language acquisition, the prevailing approach is communicative, functional and situated. This approach, at the very basis of contemporary glottodidactics, finds its institutional expression in the Common European Framework of Reference for Languages. Unlike other approaches, the communicative approach requires the learner of a target language to achieve various degrees of 'communicative competence' (Diadori 2019; Cohen 2011; Doughty, Long 2005). Knowing a language means being able to use it, "to do things with words".

The emphasis on usability is crucial, but highly problematic. The first risk is that of reducing teaching to the learning of a language that only serves to carry out a certain job, often a poorly qualified one, and which thus precludes any possibility of emancipation, while maintaining the various situations of exclusion (Zoletto 2007, p. 84). The second risk is that of supporting, even 'only' implicitly, the neo-liberal ideology underlying so many of the discourses surrounding adults education, in which, as Mayo points out, the focus is placed on the technical-rational aspect and on 'what works'. According to Mayo, this focus reflects an interest in 'marketability' to the detriment of, for example, social justice, and also supports the creation of programmes aimed at providing a 'flexible' and 'adaptable' workforce (Mayo 2007, p. 19).

"Doing things with words", however, can also mean something else. Following Freire, literacy is not simply a technical skill to be acquired, but is the necessary foundation for the cultural action that has freedom as its goal (Freire, Macedo 1987, p. 5). Learning a language and knowing how to use it means, in this sense, becoming aware of the reality, the context and the ways in which that language is used (Zoletto 2007, pp. 83-84). The goal is emancipatory: for Freire, literacy is a political project aimed at creating possibilities; the starting point of literacy is thus the understanding of one's own existence as part of socially constructed practices within specific power relations of which both students and teachers are part (Freire, Macedo 1987, p. 5).

These are two very different perspectives on language teaching/learning. Yet, it is not so difficult to slip - sometimes actually fall! - in the attempt to provide emancipatory tools to students towards practices, choices, and actions that, on the contrary, contribute to their marginalisation and exclusion.In this paper, I bring into play the notion of estrangement in teaching Italian as a Second Language to MSNA (minori stranieri non accompagnati - unaccompanied foreign minors). The aim is to realize exercises of estrangement to ceate interculturally inclusive contexts and make it possible to imagine spaces of agency, possibility and resistance for/of the young adults who are the target of the classes within which these exercises have been experimented. The exercises I refer to have been tried out at the Centro provinciale per l'Istruzone degli Adulti (CPIA) of Trieste, within various Italian classes for unaccompanied foreign minors and/or in the curricular classes ("terza media") with a high presence of foreign minors.

380   Social Farming for the Integration of Refugees and Asylum Seekers: An Italian Case Study

Giuseppe Gambazza

Asylum seekers and refugees are often employed in Italian agriculture both in rural and urban areas, where they may be victims of labor exploitation and caporalato.

Along with these episodes, virtuous forms of agriculture are spreading. Since 2022, in fact, migrants and refugees can be included, by law, in social agriculture activities (the so-called DL Aiuti).

This research explores how social farming can promote good practices of social and labour inclusion for asylum seekers and refugees. After a short contextualization of the phenomenon in Italy, the paper focuses on a specific case study, from which it will analyze how environmental sustainability strategies are combined with processes of social integration, training, and employment.

4G   Special Panel: Universidad Iberoamericana's research and advocacy actions in the field of Human Mobility [BG 5/6]

Panelists: Carla Pederzini, Karla Valenzuela, Andrea Margarita Nuñez

In 2020, scholars and professionals committed to study and advocate for Human Rights of migrants, asylum seekers and refugees at Universidad Iberoamericana, got together to reflect upon the most important issues concerning migration in Mexico and suggest public policy actions to improve the conditions of people on the move in Mexico. The results of these gatherings are two documents that serve as a Statement of Purpose concerning migration policy in the country.

The purpose of this panel is to present our most recent Statement of Purpose, issued in May 2023, which analyzes the following topics: Government, State and law in contemporary migrations; The role of the media and government narratives; Migrant integration and Mexico as a destination and origin country; Mobility and its consequences on mental and emotional health; and Climate migration.

View full document in Spanish here

12:15-13:15 LUNCH BREAK

Day Two 24 August 2023 - 13:15-14:45

5A   Wellbeing and Migration 2 [EG17]

Chair Adi Binhas, Beit-Berl College, Israel

35   English "I'm like a chameleon": Coping Strategies Used by Haredi Women Doctoral Students Reconciling Their Religious and Academic Identities: Haredi Women

Adi Binhas

The study dealt with the cultural, not physical, immigration of ultra-Orthodox women in Israel who entered academia and studied for a Ph.D. In Israel there are less than 100 ultra-Orthodox with a doctor's degree and no comprehensive research has yet been conducted on this population. This population migrates between two different value systems - ultra-orthodox society and academia. The study focused on the unique challenges of ultra-Orthodox women in academia.

This study examined Jewish ultra-Orthodox (Haredi) women doctoral students and ordered them to analyze the shaping of their religious and academic identities, and particularly the coping strategies they use to reconcile them. Theories inform it on the definition of social and collective identities and the way individuals assimilate upon encountering a new collective, as well as by actual processes of Haredi integration in Israeli academia over the years. The study concludes that in their academic development, these women challenge their traditional social worlds and enter the world of learning, which is exclusively preserved for men in their community.

*Binhas, A. "I'm Like a Chameleon": Coping Strategies Used by Haredi Women Doctoral Students Reconciling Their Religious and Academic Identities. Cont Jewry (2022). https://doi.org/10.1007/s12397-022-09466-7,Q1

174   A study on mental and physical well-being of immigrant women during the post COVID-19 time – an overview of changing workplaces

Khadijah Kainat

Post COVID time has brought a lot of changes in our working lives, especially with the greater reliance on digital platforms and social media during 2021 and onward (Alheneidi et al., 2021; Liu et al., 2021). In this study, I intend to understand the challenges of immigrant working women living in Finland towards the use of digital platforms and social media in post COVID time in their working lives. The main research questions are: How immigrant working women deal with highly digitalized working environments in the Finnish companies? How changing nature of work (especially #workfromhome culture) has influenced their working and personal lives? And, how they deal with the problem of "information overload" on digital platforms/social media in this changing work environments? It is important to study this particular study subject i.e., the immigrant working women, who are often ignored during the integration process and are mostly struggling with work-related challenges (Nardon et al., 2022). Most of the previous studies mainly focus on the male immigrants and their employment issues while ignoring the fact that the women immigrant might have different nature of working issues along with the responsibility of parenting, other family responsibilities and their physical and mental health. In this study, I am using qualitative research method (interviews and workshop for discussion group) with 15 or more volunteer immigrant women from different countries (Pakistan, India, Bangladesh, Iran, United Kingdom) living in Finland for 3 or more years. So far, I have conducted 10 interviews and more interviews are in progress. Some of the main findings so far show that post COVID time has brought many challenges in participants' working lives such as, information overload on digital platforms and social media (Instagram, Facebook) has caused physical and mental stress. Long sitting hours in front of computers has caused muscles pain, poor posters, weight gain and stomach issues. Additionally, mental health is one of the most important areas of our working lives. The results indicate the risk of poor mental wellbeing of immigrant women in their working and personal lives due to too much information on websites, digital platforms, and social media accounts. This has somehow lead to intentional information avoidance and information fatigue for some participants.

258   A Study of The Detrimental Impact of Covid 19: With Special Emphasis on Female Migrant Workers in New Delhi, India

Niimisha Kaul

Introduction

The migrant workers in India encountered loss on many fronts including financial, social, and emotional as well. The situation was so grave that they were more apprehensive about having food for survival than fearing an alien virus which was so deathly that people were dying.

Owing to such an uncontrollable situation, a huge percentage of these migrant workers decided to go back to their respective hometowns. But the condition was such owing to the lockdown that barely any public transport was available. So, a lot of them with their families walked back on foot to their native places.

The researcher took over a study with female migrant workers in New Delhi, India, which is the capital city of the country. The researcher interacted in person with around 500 such female migrant workers to understand the issues faced at the grassroots level by them. The researcher has made a special attempt to highlight the plight of the women migrant workers and to gauge the intensity of their socio-economic status during the pandemic.

Objective

To evaluate the economic condition of female migrant workers amidst the pandemic Covid 19 in Delhi, India.

To evaluate the hardships faced by these female migrant workers because of Covid 19 and the lockdown in New Delhi, India.

To understand the impact of the pandemic on female migrant workers in New Delhi, India.

Research Methodology

The researcher adopted a mixed approach to evaluate the qualitative and quantitative dimensions of the living conditions of these female migrant workers during Covid 19. These female workers were reached through NGOs, Resident or Associations of various locations where they work and these female workers introduced the researcher to her peers. New Delhi comprises 11 districts in total. Thus, the researcher interviewed around 500 female migrant workers from all 11 different districts of New Delhi, India with good representation from each district for the collection of data. The data has been collected through primary sources and secondary sources.

Findings and Conclusion

This paper contributes immensely towards showing a realistic overview at the grass root level of the concerns of these female migrant workers. Further, some of the major findings in the study as to the hardships faced by female migrant workers during Covid 19 are enlisted below:

Out of 148 respondents, over 25% said that they walked on foot to go back to their native place from New Delhi as there was no public transport available owing to the lockdown.

Out of 500 respondents, over 60% said that they migrated to Delhi to earn money as it was a challenge to earn money in their native place.

Out of 500 respondents, over 50% said that they did not have money to survive during the lockdown.

Out of 500 respondents, over 75% said that they lost their job during the lockdown.

Out of 500 respondents, over 70% said that they had to borrow money to survive during the lockdown period.

175   Trauma Exposure among Central American Immigrants   Seeking Asylum at the U.S.-Mexico Border

Alfonso Mercado and Frances Morales

Central American immigrants, particularly families seeking asylum in the United States, report significant trauma exposure and mental health concerns upon arrival at the U.S.-Mexico Border (Venta, 2019; Venta & Mercado, 2019). These forced migrants are severely affected by the excessive violence in their home countries and exposure to other forms of trauma (Mercado et al., 2019). Migration itself poses risk of further trauma exposure. Many report experiencing assaults and sexual violence along their journey. Recent U.S. migration policies, such as the Zero Tolerance and Remain in Mexico policies, have also added new sources of trauma exacerbating the risk for mental health problems in migrant children and families (Mercado et al., 2021; Mercado et al., 2022). Due to the unpreparedness and inefficacy of federal agencies to respond to this humanitarian crisis, asylum seekers encounter precarious circumstances while awaiting processing. Knowing the implications associated with cumulative life adversities, the experiences of this population deserve much attention.

The main objective of the present study was to measure the frequency of traumatic events to evaluate the level of trauma experienced by asylum seekers who have recently fled the Northern Triangle region of Central America. The study sample consisted of 51 adult asylum seekers primarily from the Northern Triangle region of Central America which encompasses the countries of Guatemala, Honduras, and El Salvador. The sample included 15 males and 36 females ranging from 18 to 51 years of age ($M = 28.02$, $SD = 7.193$). Quantitative analyses measured trauma exposure using a Spanish translation of the Harvard Trauma Questionnaire Revised (Mollica et al., 2004). A key feature of this study is the recency of the experiences as the participants were interviewed within 24 hours of being processed by U.S. immigration officials for seeking asylum, making their experiences quite recent. Results indicate that all participants experienced some form of traumatic event either in the country of origin, during the travel through Mexico, and/or in a detention center. The most traumatic events experienced by a single participant were 18 out of the 27 possible traumatic events. On average, the participants reported experiencing approximately 8 traumatic events ($M = 8.19$, $SD = 4.24$). The most common traumatic experiences reported included experiencing extortion or robbery, living through a natural disaster, witnessing someone get hit, having been in a shooting, and witnessing the torture or death of someone.

The observed high frequency of traumatic events endorsed by the participants supports previous findings that adults migrating from Central America are experiencing alarmingly stressful and traumatic events during migration (Keller et al., 2017; Mercado et al., 2019; Venta & Mercado, 2019; Mercado et al., 2022; Venta, 2019;). It is clear that asylum seekers constitute a vulnerable population that faces immense hardship not only before leaving their home country, but also during and after their migratory journey. Psychologists and other mental health providers who engage with this community are uniquely poised to educate and spread awareness about the needs of this population and influence policy that has the potential to impact their welfare.

5B   Migraciones and Transnacionalismo 2 [BG3/4]

Chair: José Salvador Cueto-Calderón, Universidad Autónoma de Sinaloa, Mexico

148   El Régimen de Refugiados en Chile: Un análisis al desarrollo institucional entre 2010 y 2022

Byron Duhalde y Adriana Palomera

Chile is a country that is characterized by recognizing a very low percentage of people as refugees, compared to the total number of applications it receives annually, unlike other countries in the region. The present work is structured as a case study of the management of the refuge in Chile from the year 2010 in which Law 20,430 of Refugees is promulgated. Through the conceptual tools of Historical Institutionalism, the institutional development of the refuge and the way in which Chile applies and manages the International Regime are analyzed. It is shown that in the agency space elements are developed that hinder access to due process, as well as the process of recognition of refugee status, generating a detrimental impact on the Chilean refuge institutionality.

147   Entre la permanencia y la reemigración: factores asociados a las intenciones migratorias de la población venezolana en Montevideo

Martín Koolhaas y Julieta Bengochea

Este trabajo contribuye a la literatura que estudia las intenciones y decisiones migratorias de las personas migrantes, examinando para el caso de la población migrante venezolana residente en la ciudad capital de Uruguay (Montevideo) los factores asociados a sus planes de permanencia o reemigración.

Para ello se realiza un análisis estadístico tanto transversal como longitudinal con base en la Etnoencuesta de Inmigración Reciente (ENIR). La ENIR fue realizada en 2018 y obtuvo la respuesta de un total de 371 personas migrantes de origen venezolano. En 2021 se realizó un seguimiento a esta población y se obtuvo un panel de 236 informantes. Por último, mediante un análisis de regresión logística, se exploran factores asociados a las intenciones migratorias, examinando aspectos vinculados a motivaciones de la migración, trayectorias de inclusión socioeconómica, configuraciones familiares y nacionalidad de parejas, itinerarios documentales y efectos derivados de la pandemia de COVID-19.

Los resultados obtenidos identifican cuatro aspectos importantes.

Primero, un incremento de diez puntos porcentuales en las intenciones de permanencia de la población venezolana en 2021 respecto a 2018, siendo mayoritaria la preferencia por la permanencia en Uruguay frente a la reemigración a un tercer país o Venezuela.

Segundo, un alto nivel de estabilidad respecto a los planes de migración declarados tres años atrás, a pesar de los cambios acaecidos entre 2018 y 2021 (con la pandemia por COVID-19 de por medio).

Tercero, entre quienes tienen un plan de reemigración en ambas olas se verifica una alta volatilidad en las preferencias de los países mencionados como eventuales destinos, dado que en 2121 la gran mayoría declaran estar pensando en reemigrar a un país diferente al mencionado tres años atrás.

Cuarto, se destaca que la existencia de planes de reemigración no se asocia a intenciones de retorno a Venezuela, sino a reemigraciones a terceros países en general situados en el Norte global (sobre todo, en Norteamérica y Europa; en particular, Estados Unidos y España), explícitamente motivadas por razones económicas y/o laborales.

451   Migración de tránsito en México: el papel del Estado y la política de contención migratoria en la Ruta del Pacífico

José Salvador Cueto Calderón

El pasado 12 de marzo de 2023, más de dos mil migrantes en tránsito, principalmente de origen venezolano, intentaron cruzar la frontera norte de México a través del puente internacional Paso del Norte que conecta a Ciudad Juárez, Chihuahua, con El Paso, Texas. La estampida humana logró romper el cerco de elementos de la Guardia Nacional que les impedía cruzar las casetas mexicanas, sin embargo, fueron detenidos por las fuerzas estadounidenses a mitad del puente. Este acontecimiento se suma a la actual crisis migratoria que se vive en la región, que inicia con el éxodo masivo de migrantes provenientes de diferentes países latinoamericanos y que se enfrentan a las adversidades de cruzar fronteras y transitar territorios hostiles.

Esta crisis se presenta en México bajo el contexto de una política de contención migratoria que se ejecuta en todo el territorio mexicano por presión de los Estados Unidos, que se traduce en amenazas arancelarias a diversos productos mexicanos, y que a su vez son dictaminadas por ellos mismos. En este sentido, el Estado mexicano vigila e impone políticas en una frontera vertical a lo largo del país, donde se han establecido 50 centros de detención o estaciones migratorias para las personas migrantes donde se replica -al igual que en Estados Unidos- un modelo criminalizante y punitivo de la migración, de hecho, México es el país con más centros de detención para migrantes en toda América Latina.

En las decenas de centros de detención en México, resalta a la vista la escasez que se presenta en el Noroeste de México -donde se encuentra la Ruta del Pacífico-, reducidos casi por completo a uno por entidad federativa -salvo en las excepciones de aquellos con más de un cruce fronterizo-, comparada con la saturación en las otras áreas geográficas del país, sobre todo en el Sur, Sur-Este; obedeciendo, pues, a un mayor flujo de la población en tránsito en estas zonas. Sin embargo, podemos observar que el flujo de migrantes en tránsito por la Ruta del Pacífico ha aumentado desde el inicio de las caravanas migrantes en 2018, siendo su presencia cada vez más notoria en las ciudades que se encuentran en la ruta. A pesar de la escaza presencia de las instituciones del Estado en materia de migración en la Ruta del Pacífico, sus políticas se manifiestan a través de la violación a sus derechos humanos por parte de diversos agentes del Estado.

En este sentido, desde la óptica de la antropología del Estado, que busca analizar las prácticas cotidianas en las burocracias y la construcción discursiva del Estado en la cultura pública, la propuesta pretende realizar una etnografía a estas instituciones del Estado, particularmente a las oficinas de representación del INM en Sinaloa, así como en la estación migratoria ubicada en Mazatlán, Sinaloa, con la finalidad de observar cómo el discurso sobre la criminalización de la migración va creando una cultura pública que se manifiesta en la subjetividad y en el actuar de los agentes migratorios.

5C   Insecurities and Migration 3 [UG14]

Chair: Olga Gulina, +Benefit Research, Germany

274   The interrelationship between the war in Ukraine and the precarization of Central Asian migrant workers in the Russian labor market

Anastasia Blouchoutzi

The Russian Federation has been an attractive destination for Central Asian labor force that emigrated from their countries of origin to search for employment. As a result, Russia hosts 76% of all Kyrgyz migrants, 73% of Tajiks, 65% of Kazakhs, 72% of Turkmens and 55% of Uzbek migrants (World Bank, 2017; Author's calculations Author's calculations). Language, proximity, ties, mindset, freedom of entry and the prospect of citizenship are possible reasons for such a superior position of Russia as a host country (Khramova et al., 2020). Bilateral economic remittances' estimates for 2017 from the Russian Federation reached 63,8% of the total remittances flows in Kazakhstan and 77,3% in Kyrgyz Republic, 76,4% in Tajikistan, almost 100% in Turkmenistan and Uzbekistan accordingly (World Bank, 2017; Author's calculations). Remittances have been a channel to transmit economic growth from the Russian Federation to these countries (Brownbridge and Canagarajah, 2010). These financial flows have the potential to ease foreign exchange constraints, finance external deficits, increase savings and capital formation, facilitate human capital formation, raise the standard of living of the recipients and even reduce poverty and inequalities (De Zwager et al., 2005). However, the downturn in remittances flows to these countries during the Russian economic crises affected their macroeconomic indicators. This research draws upon the concept of migration interdependence between the countries of migrants' origin and destination (Tsourapas, 2018) as developed due to the importance of economic remittances for the developing countries. The research question we intend to answer is whether and in which ways Russia's war in Ukraine affects the labor market integration of Central Asian migrants in the Russian Federation and consequently their remittances. Our research begins by reviewing the literature on the importance of migrant remittances, we continue with an overview of key economic factors of the Central Asian countries and we map the migration flows from Central Asia to the Russian Federation and their demographic and socio-economic characteristics. Afterwards, we relate them with the occupation of Central Asian migrant workers in Russia and the remittances they send to their countries of origin and we seek to identify the vulnerability and/or resilience of the Central Asian countries to migration through their international partnerships. Last but not least, we investigate the policies implemented for the migrant workers' residence permit and the naturalization process in the Russian Federation before and after the beginning of the war.

References

Brownbridge, M. and S. Canagarajah (2010) Remittances and the Macroeconomic Impact of the Global Economic Crisis in the Kyrgyz Republic and Tajikistan, China and Eurasia Forum Quarterly, 8(4), pp. 3-9.

De Zwager N., I. Gedeshi, E. Germenji and C. Nikas (2005) Competing for Remittances. Tirana, Albania: IOM.

Khramova, M., S. Ryazantsev, A. Rakhmonov, O. Kasymov (2020) The impact of remittances from abroad on socioeconomic development in Tajikistan, Central Asia and the Caucasus, 21(4).

Tsourapas, G. (2018) Labor migrants as political leverage: migration interdependence and coercion in the Mediterranean, International Studies Quarterly, 62(2), 383-395.

World Bank Group (2017) Migration and Remittances Data. Available at: https://www.worldbank.org/en/topic/migrationremittancesdiasporaissues/brief/migration-remittances-data Accessed 19 October 2022.

164   Displaced Security: Understanding refugees' sense of safety through their resettlement experiences in Montreal, Canada

Krystal Tennessee

The concept of safety/security speaks to the notions of being safe, being saved, being protected and being in a safe haven. Canada presents itself as a safe resettlement site for refugees (Government of Canada, 2019) although it has been suggested that refugees may be welcomed with suspicions of criminality, terrorism, and aggression. In this climate of fear, refugees are subjected to stereotypes and cultural misunderstandings or miscommunications in receiving societies (Rousseau, 2002), even though in legal discourses at a local/global level, refugees are legitimized by the United Nations Convention Relating to the Status of Refugees. Therefore, the legal definition of a refugee in Canada is linked to the sociopolitical definition that contributes to the national discourse on refugees. Notwithstanding, the legal acceptance of refugees does not mean social/political acceptance (Razack, 2002).

This paper presents the results of a master's thesis that explored accepted refugees' sense of "safety" in Montreal, Canada and how the intersections of their experiences influenced their conceptualization of the dimensions of safety. Data collected from semi-structured interviews highlighted how political, legal and social categorization of the label "refugee", contributed positively and/or negatively to refugees' construction of safety. This paper raises questions about resettlement policies, the social manifestation of what/where/when a refugee is supposed to be and problematizes the normative discourse of safety/security in Canada.

29   Scapegoated *or* Reality? Undocumented Migration, Poverty, inequality, and the Struggle for Jobs: Reflections from South Africa

Victor H. Mlambo

A World Bank report titled: Inequality in Southern Africa: An Assessment of the Southern African Customs Union revealed that South Africa, the largest country in the Southern African Customs Union, is the most unequal country in the world, ranking first among 164 countries in the World Bank's global poverty database. Ever since the demise of apartheid, South Africa has witnessed an increase in the inflow of undocumented migrants from Africa in search of economic opportunities. While migration has been at times viewed as a catalyst for development, in South Africa, undocumented migrants have become an instigator of societal tension between locals and foreigners. Between 2000 and March 2008, at least 67 people died in what were identified as xenophobic attacks. In May 2008, a series of attacks left 62 people dead, although 21 of those killed were South African citizens. South Africans argue that the rate at which the inflow of undocumented migration is taking place in SA has left them no choice but to take the law into their own hands. The central argument is that migrants are stealing jobs, are involved in drugs and human trafficking, and do not pay taxes, thus South Africans feel their presence is an additional strain on government resources. Over the years, rather than addressing the issue through legal channels, South Africans have opted to (out of the boundaries of law) address the issue themselves, by shutting down foreign-owned shops, calling for the government to increase border security, and the forming of pressure groups. This has resulted in strained relations between South Africa and her neighbors. This paper, employing a qualitative research approach using relevant literature seeks to understand whether the allegations leveled against undocumented migrants are a reality or they are being scapegoated. It seeks to examine if foreign nationals are indeed stealing jobs, involved in drugs and human trafficking, or rather South Africans are taking out their frustration on migrants because of government policy failure. The following questions will guide this paper? Has government policy failure concerning addressing poverty, inequality, and unemployment contributed to the xenophobic sentiments directed at undocumented migrants and how can the South African government address the increasing inflow of undocumented migrants to reduce societal tensions?

232   A new Russia's Emigres in Berlin

Olga Gulina

Over centuries and decades, people left Russia, and the presence of Russia´s émigrés in the capitals of Western Europe remained a source of the continual question. While the October revolution of 1917 was one of the major reasons among the push factors leaving Russia – it is by far not the only one. After Bolsheviks came into power, thousands of Russians were forced to leave the country. The country´s military and civil best heads, crème de la crème of a nation, its writers, painters, philosophers, musicians, and many others were exiled and tried re-building Russia they lost.

In Soviet time ethnic Germans, Jews and Poles left Russia for their ethic homelands, because representatives of these groups were discriminated by a Soviet law. Admission of Jews, Poles and Germans to some universities or state-relevant positions was limited. After the collapse of the Soviet Union, a mass exodus took place. Russian nationals, including intellectuals en mass left country in search for better paid jobs and positions in the West (Naumova 2005). Throughout all these extensive historical periods, diverse factors pushing Russians to emigrate were political instability, economic challenges, and ever search for a better life and of knowledge.

Modern emigration from Russia has its own specifics, albeit it emerges the same phenomenon of "no-returns", that was well known in Soviet and Tsarist Russia, usually because of current Russia´s invasion of Ukraine, harmful political persecution, human rights violation, religious/sexual intolerance, and fear to be oppressed and persecuted at home. Nowadays the question to leave or not to leave Russia remains an urgent issue for diverse social groups in the country.

Current research examines today´s Russian émigré in German metropolis, in particular in Berlin. Berlin was and remains to be "the first capital of Russian emigration" (Marten-Finnis 2021), one of the centers of Russia´s exile activity (Williams 1966), and the place where "… everyone met each traveler toured between Moscow and the West" (Roditi 1961).

Modern Russian émigrés in Berlin can be roughly divided into five groups by their legal status within the country: (1) Russia´s emigres residing with a Schengen visa (type C) or with a German national visa (type "D"); (2) newcomers submitting an asylum application within the territory of Germany; (3) high qualified Russians with blue card status; (4) those with a legal permit according § 19-21 Immigration Law (AufenthG), i.e. specialists from creative industries and freelancers, and (5) their family members

5D   Migration and Gender 2 [UG11]

Chair: H. Yaprak Civelek, Anadolu University, Turkey

423   Queer Compassion: A phenomenological exploration of LGBT+ participation in migration activism

Valentina Massone

Homophobia and transphobia contribute to the displacement of thousands each year (Vance et al., 2018; ILGA Europe, 2023). While refugee grievances and LGBT+ rights are top priorities on Europe's human rights agenda (Slootmaeckers, 2020; Ayoub & Paternotte, 2014), many EU countries struggle to reconcile universalists pro-LGBT+ inclinations with nationalist anti-immigration policies (Raboin, 2017; Andreassen, 2020; Lunau, 2019). This contradiction has created a gap within the protection system, prompting civil society organisations (CSOs) to participate in the process. This paper explores the particular forms of organised solidarity practised by LGBT+ CSOs. Specifically, it focuses on the contested relationship between queer mobilization and the commodification of LGBT+ narratives and identities to investigate how activists recognize, navigate, and make use of homonormative structures while actively working towards their disruption.

It does so through the in-depth case study of LGBT Asylum, an organization catering to the vulnerabilities of queer asylum seekers and refugees in Denmark. Their primary aim is to help LGBT+ asylum seekers gain a footing in the country of destination by providing legal assistance, a safe space and a social network. The study is built on six months of ethnographic fieldwork, including participant observation within the organization and nine semi-structured interviews with members of the group involved at the different organizational levels.

Rooted in Sarah Ahmed's philosophical approach, this paper explores queer participation in migration activism through phenomenological (2006) and affective lenses (2014). Reflecting on the concepts of orientation and disorientation examines the relationship between the activist body and political mobilization. Then, by looking at emotions such as discomfort, pain and anger, it engages with the participants' life experiences to investigate how they understand and utilize LGBT+ categories, relate to each other and ultimately shape humanitarian action.

This framework emphasizes the affective dimension of aid, pushing citizen engagement in direct relation with global politics. Furthermore, by placing LGBT+ individuals at the centre of the inquiry, the analysis shifts the emphasis from queer victimization to queer participation, reaching beyond the management of queer asylum seekers and highlighting their role as agents of change. It joins a growing but still fragmented body of scholarship expanding the scope of what constitutes "the humanitarianism worthy of study" (Richey, 2018).

This approach allows me to contest widespread assumptions (Richey, 218; Aly, 2020), framing queer activists as both helpers and beneficiaries, challenging the separation between formal/informal aid spaces and including hybrid, transnational and non-hegemonic configurations of assistance in the broader humanitarian network. Finally, this paper demonstrates how the combination of queer theory and humanitarian studies is conducive to the in-depth analysis of civil society groups involved in aid, both within and beyond the scope of LGBT+ realities.

242   Queer, Iranian and in exile: Comparing the experiences of Iranian queer refugees living in Turkey, the UK and Canada

Nuno Ferreira

In this presentation, I will discuss some provisional findings of the project 'Negotiating Queer Identities Following Forced Migration' (NQIfFM, https://iranqueerefugee.net/). NQIfFM is a project that explores the experiences of people who have left Iran to escape persecution or discrimination on grounds of their sexual orientation or gender identity (SOGI). Building on a mixed-methods approach – including semi-structured interviews and poetry workshops with refugees and other stakeholders – the project investigates the processes of identity transition of Iranian diasporic queers seeking international protection in countries generally seen as being of transition, destination or resettlement. The empirical work and data analysis is being carried out against the background of literature on postcolonial sexual identities, life histories of exile, and trauma-based cultural politics. In particular, the project explores the hypothesis that rigid Western categories of LGBTQ+ are imposed by immigration structures (immigration offices, UNHCR, UK Home Office, NGOs) on those seeking asylum, to show how migrant subjects may be misrecognised, retraumatised, or silenced by the constraints of such classification. After briefly discussing the project's aims and methodology, I will present the project's theoretical framework and a selection of themes emerging from the data analysis so far, including in relation to agency, stereotyping, trauma, silencing, discrimination, integration, and identity.

153   A shift towards positivity through migration in Japan: New Chapter in South Asian Masculinities

Afsana Begum

The research looks into the causes of behavioral changes among migrant South Asian men after migration; especially changes in roles that they always considered are closely related to their gender identity. Masculinities inspire men to endure gender inequalities in the society. Therefore, one of the most significant causes of the research is to trace out the innate reasons of such changes, to plan some conscious actions that can be applied back in migrants native country to challenge and change the prevailing constructs of masculinities to ensure a gender sensitive socio-cultural environment. The study reveals migrant South Asian men's support to the perceived positive masculinity of Japanese culture and their will to follow such practice. This study finally argues that migrant South Asian men in the Japan adopt a new kind of masculinities that doesn't have serious clash with the masculine ideologies that they had before migration and doesn't challenge their hegemonic position in the family.

396   LGBTIQ+ refugees vs. refugees who are LGBTIQ+

Annamari Vitikainen

This paper develops a conceptual framework for analyzing debates on LGBTIQ+ refugeehood, admission, and integration, by identifying the morally salient features of the discussed group of refugees (LGBTIQ+) and the kinds of harms that LGBTIQ+ persons may be fleeing from and/or have a right to be protected against. The paper makes an important distinction between the commonly used category of LGBTIQ+ refugees (e.g. in international law) and a broader category of refugees who are LGBTIQ+, and provides a preliminary argument for utilizing the latter, more expansive definition in debates on LGBTIQ+ refugeehood, admission, and integration. Some exemptions to the rule of utilizing the broader category are provided. These relate to instances where the causes of one's fleeing (e.g. SOGI -based persecution vs. persecution based on religion) are morally significant for the assessment of the case at hand. Such instances may arise, for example, in relation to the questions of refugee status determination, and some (albeit not all or even very many) questions relating to the appropriate means of integrating refugees into the social fabric of the host society.

5E   Migration, Law and Policy 5 [EG15/16]

Chair: Styliani Christoforidou, Hellenic Open University, Greece

130   Dichotomy at the Curzon Line: Legal and Political Aspects of the Differential Treatment of Migrants at Poland's Borders with Belarus and Ukraine

Magdalena Bogucewicz and Julia Kienast

In the last two years, Poland has become one of the most interesting sites of European asylum policy. Many of the weaknesses of this system, but also its strengths, have been exposed by the dichotomy on Poland's borders with Belarus and Ukraine.On the one hand, Poland's border with Belarus was closed to irregular migrants and the EU was asked to help fend off the Lukashenko regime's "hybrid attack", i.e. the organised arrival of thousands of people from the Middle East and North Africa. On the other hand, Poland willingly accepted millions of refugees fleeing Russia's invasion of Ukraine.These different approaches are also reflected in the responses at the EU level, including a proposal for an "instrumentalization" regulation to deal with the influx of refugees from Belarus and the first application of the Temporary Protection Directive in response to the war in Ukraine.The proposed paper examines these different approaches at the two Polish border sections. By combining a political analysis of Polish domestic and foreign policy with an analysis of the legal situation at the Polish and European levels, the paper aims to answer the question of 1) why these contrasting responses occurred at the same time and place and 2) what the advantages and disadvantages of the two governance strategies are.

1122   Time as a governance tool and case workers' perceptions of processing times in the Swedish immigration system

Hilda Gustafsson

Despite international and national regulations stipulating time goals regarding case processing, immigrants wait for extended periods, sometimes years, for their applications to be evaluated. For families waiting for reunification, the wait often entails being forced to live in separate countries, an experience which has been drawn attention to in an increasing number of studies. Less attention has been directed at the executing side of these waiting experiences: the role of time as a tool to deter migrants and case workers' perceptions of the process. This study examines a) how Sweden's increasingly restrictive immigration policy reveals time tools (e.g. temporariness, biological time limits, deadlines) as a way to regulate unwanted immigration and b) the experiences of employees at the Swedish Migration Agency regarding the long case handling times. Using a mixed method with document analysis and qualitative interviews, the study provides a nuanced image of on the one hand strict policies and rules followed by case workers, and on the other hand the case workers' attempt to both justify the execution of these policies while catering to the requests from frustrated families wishing for their wait to end. The study contributes to several areas of migration studies: migration policy and practice, street-level bureaucrats' attitudes, and the increasing field of waiting and time in migration governance.

162   Critical examination of repatriation programmes in the EU periphery (The case of Kosovo)

Valon Junuzi

Repatriation programmes have received attention only in recent years, mainly due to some arbitrary imposed preconceptions on migration studies which have erroneously considered that with the physical return of the deportee to the country of origin comes the end of the migration cycle. This sedentarist bias has been criticized increasingly by scholars that reject the reified equation 'repatriation=homecoming', and instead have urged for a scientific engagement that examines what happens beyond the act of deportation, and document hardships and unsettling truths of the repatriated. However, these contributions have been parsimonious in both opening new avenues of research and interrogating the rising policing techniques of repatriation. More specifically, the accounts of what happens to the repatriated tend to consider deportation as a conclusive act of 'taking out' from the territory the undesirable migrants, failing to take into consideration ways through which the deporting state stretches its expulsionary practices beyond its national territory through financing repatriation programs in countries of origin. Similarly, the role of countries of origin in shaping subjectivities have been largely undertheorized, rendering repatriation a neutral state enterprise. The research aims to address these theoretical gaps by situating repatriation programmes within exigencies of global mobility regimes that enact and reproduce forced immobility in a world of flows and perpetual motion. It does so by examining repatriation programmes as techniques of extended expulsion that ensure that those that have been deported are demotivated to initiate a new migratory cycle. It also critically interrogates the content of these programmes and how they are utilized to push forward the neoliberal agenda of 'crafting' risk-taking, self-interested, entrepreneurial, and apolitical citizens. To this end, the project relies on ethnographic fieldwork in Kosovo, as an interesting case in the EU's periphery where the successful repatriation of irregular migrants has been prioritized by state institutions in order to get a free visa regime by the EU. Interviews have been conducted with state institutions, NGOs, EU officials responsible to implement these programs, but also with the recipients of the reintegration assistance. Based on these empirical findings, the analysis aims to understand not only the rationale behind these interventions but also the subjectivities that emerge from these interventions.

47   Decent living conditions for asylum seekers and refugees. The problem of protection in Greece

Styliani Christoforidou

German jurisprudence highlighted the significance of the same protection between citizens and non-citizens regarding their Existenzminimum, i.e. the decent living. The right to a minimum level of subsistence arises a universal right and as an obligation of the state to act for its protection. Under this framework, It will be analyzed critically the care of the Greek law to offer such kind of protection to immigrants at the same quality level comparing with the Greek citizens in line with the equality principle. Comparing with other legal orders, it will emphasized the inadequacy of the Greek social system to treat the non-citizens equally safeguarding a decent standard of living.

5F   Migration and Integration 5 [UG13]

Chair: Pascual Garcia, Universidad Técnica Particular de Loja, Ecuador

496   Intercultural Mediators in Healthcare Settings: Vulnerability and Empowerment

Marianna Ginocchietti

Effective communication and mutual understanding between healthcare providers and patients are crucial to the effectiveness and the quality of care (Olani et al. 2023; Schyve 2007). Moreover, studies show that the healthcare providers' ability to listen, explain, and understand patients' emotional status may play a significant role in disease outcomes and patients' experience of care (Olani et al. 2023; Charlton et al. 2008).

Migrants with a lower socio-economic position and with no social and linguistic support often experience a multifaceted kind of vulnerability during medical encounters and, even more seriously, in the early access to healthcare services. I propose to distinguish and analyse the above-mentioned vulnerability as linguistic vulnerability, epistemic vulnerability (see Peled 2018) and interactional/social vulnerability.

It is recognized that intercultural mediators in healthcare settings may play a significant role in improving accessibility and quality of care for migrants (Schyve 2007; Ruiz-Lozano 2015; Verrept 2019), but what about their role in supporting healthcare providers to understand patients' vulnerability, and consequently, in empowering patients position in the social medical interactions?

The aim of the paper is twofold. Firstly, to distinguish and analyse the multifaceted vulnerability experienced by migrants with a lower socio-economic position and with no social and linguistic support in their interactions with healthcare institutions.

Secondly, to propose a frame where intercultural mediators play a crucial role in understanding, distinguishing and decoding patients' vulnerability in social-medical interactions, and consequently in enhancing migrants' empowerment during social medical interactions with healthcare institutions.

Within this frame, intercultural mediators are not only "linguistic facilitators", but rather they are understood as part of the health staff, with specific competencies, roles, and responsibilities (see Esposito, Vezzadini 2011). Moreover, both healthcare providers and intercultural mediators need to be the target of proper transdisciplinary training programmes to understand their particular role and their responsibilities in interpersonal medical interactions within the healthcare institutions.

The paper is structured in three parts. In the first part, I analyse and distinguish the multifaceted kind of vulnerability experienced by migrants with a lower socio-economic position. In the second part, I discuss the role of intercultural mediators in supporting healthcare providers to understand patient's specific vulnerabilities and in empowering patients' position in the social medical interaction. In doing that, I refer to 10 ethnographic interviews conducted with intercultural mediators working in the healthcare context in the city of Trieste (Italy). In the third part, I draw the frame where intercultural mediators act as linguistic facilitators and as part of the health staff responsible for the social medical interaction with patients.

285   "The House that Jack Built:" DIY Housing Renovations and Integration-through-Materiality by Russian-speaking Migrants in Japan

Ksenia Golovina

Migrant homemaking and engagement with material objects has received considerable attention in the literature to date. In terms of housing construction and renovation, much of the focus has been on the activities of transnational and returning migrants in their sending communities, where migrant actions have served to revitalize and develop areas of origin. While studies have begun to examine the external and internal architecture and architectural aesthetics of migrant housing, there is a need to trace how migrants engage in the immediate practice of housing (re)construction and arrive at decisions to build or adapt their housing in particular ways. Such an approach has the potential to reveal the embodied processes through which migrants self-integrate into the host society. Based on anthropological fieldwork consisting of in-depth interviews, home visits (including construction sites), and participant observation, this study responds to this agenda by examining how Russian-speaking migrants (re)construct their housing through DIY activities. In order to provide the necessary context, the study first investigates situations and strategies surrounding the choice of location and housing for purchase and rent, including negotiations with agents. The study then presents three close-up cases in which migrants (re)construct the buildings or significantly alter the interiors of their dwellings. Curiously, the three migrants share an artistic background, so the study contributes not only to the discussion of migration and housing, but also to the discussion of migrant art. The aim of the study is to reveal the process by which these migrants (re)build their homes or parts of them, focusing on the imaginings that guide the migrants' choices of design and materials, their visions and actual practices regarding the use of the renovated spaces, the negotiations with their Japanese spouses regarding the DIY work, and the interactions with the local community surrounding the renovation practices. The paper also examines how migrants obtain construction materials that may not be available in the local market and negotiate affordable prices through various person-to-person networks and e-commerce sites. Building on these findings, as well as on previous literature that has highlighted the link between homemaking, belonging, and identity, this study suggests the need to develop a framework of "integration-through-materiality," in which DIY practices serve to provide migrants with an integrative rootedness in the host society. It is argued that in the absence of robust integration programs, as is the case in Japan, material practices surrounding housing may provide migrants with the missing links to establish meaningful, tangible connections to their new home country.

279   The Symbolic Violence against Minority group in Korean society: Focusing on the Moderated Effect of Multicultural Activities between Multicultural Acceptability and Perceived Risk towards immigrants

Youn-young Lee

*This work was supported by the National Research Foundation of Korea (NRF) grant funded by the Korea government (Ministry of

Education) (No.2022S1A5A8055727)

Objective

Recently, the number of foreign residents including unregistered foreigners living in South Korea has surpassed 2.5 millions. Also the National Statistical Office predicts that the number of migrants expected until 2040 will reach 3.2 million, 6.4% of the total population. Since 2008, Korean government has formulated and implemented "the basic plan for foreigners" every five years to support foreign residents and integrate the Korean societies with a high level of ethnic diversity. Nevertheless, the level of multicultural awareness is not very high and the problem of expanding negative cognitions toward them is emerging as a social issue because Korea is traditionally homogenous society. Therefore, the purpose of this study is to analyze the relationship between "perceived risk toward foreign migrants" and "multicultural acceptability" of the Korean people and to find the moderating effect as multicultural activities.

Literature review

This paper is based on the 'symbolic violence theory' and 'contact theory'. Bourdieu explains the concept of symbolic violence as the mechanism used by upper-class groups that dominate the social structure of society. Contact theory explains about the access to outside communities as an important factor influencing discrimination between different groups.

Research Methods

This study empirically analyzes the 2021 National Multicultural Acceptance Survey data collected by the Ministry of Gender Equality and Family. Data are responses from 5,000 people between the ages 20 to 75 selected by the multi-level stratified cluster sampling collected in 2021 on a national scale. The dependent variable consists of the perceived risk toward immigrants as a kind of symbolic violence. The independent variable is the multicultural acceptability and it is composed of three levels: culture openness, national identity and discrimination. The multicultural activities are analyzed as a moderating variable between the relationships. Based on this, the research model is constructed and the statistical analysis was performed using by Statistical program.

Research Results

Major findings are as follows. First, while many Koreans generally have open-mined and tolerable attitudes to foreigners, but also show negative attitude toward immigrants. Second, culture openness has proved a strong effect on the decrease of perceived risk toward immigrants, but in contrast, national identity and discrimination have an opposite effect on those tendencies. Third, multicultural activities are significantly related to reduce the perceived risk toward immigrants.

Last, multicultural activities are found to moderate the relationship between cultural openness and discrimination except national identity and perceived risk toward immigrants.

Conclusions

The result shows that respondents with the higher level of participation to multicultural programs are tended to have the lower level of perceived risks toward immigrants. Therefore, this study will support the Korean policy makers by suggesting the directions of multicultural programs for diversity and inclusion in Korean society to increase the understanding of multiculturalism and foreign residents.

References

Bourdieu, P. (1989). "Social Space and Symbolic power". Sociological theory, 7(1), 14-25. https://doi.org/10.2307/202060

Kim, I. S. (2022). "2021 National Multicultural Acceptance". Ministry of Gender Equality and Family.

Lee, Y. Y. (2019). "Effect of the victimization experience of school violence on Acculturative Stress: Focused on Moderated Effect of Social Support". Journal of Korean Criminological Association, 13(1), 27-48.

Pettigrew, T. F. (1998). "Intergroup Contact Theory". Annual review of psychology, 49(1), 65-85. https://doi.org/10.1146/annurev.psych.49.1.65

Doo. Y. S. & Kim. K.K.(2022). "The Relationship between Immigrant Contact and Multicultural Acceptance among Korean Adolescents". Journal of Education & Culture, 28(5), 529-550. http://dx.doi.org/10.24159/joec.2022.28.5.529

*Youn-Young Lee, Halla University, Ph. D of Sociology, Assistant Professor, younyoung.lee@halla.ac.kr

100x "We're constantly fighting for that opportunity": A Qualitative Study of Access Barriers to Sexual and Reproductive Health for Hispanic Immigrant Women in the United States

Jessica Merone, Rossella De Falco, Paola Degani

Immigrant women in the United States face overlapping difficulties when seeking sexual and reproductive healthcare. A large amount of literature has demonstrated the significant barriers undocumented immigrant women have encountered in accessing this type of healthcare, but little research has explored the uses of services and outcomes among different groups of immigrant women. Therefore, to help in part close the gap in the literature, this study examines how Hispanic immigrant women in Philadelphia, Pennsylvania, with various immigration statuses and conditions, access and utilize sexual and reproductive services and describe the obstacles they face. An exploratory qualitative study was designed with 18 in-depth interviews with Hispanic women with the following immigration statuses: first- and second-generation immigrants, lawful permanent residents, naturalized citizens, and undocumented immigrants. The barriers were understood in terms of discrimination and inequitable access to healthcare under international human rights law. To detect the root causes of healthcare inequalities and lack of human rights fulfilment, we relied on an intersectionality perspective to analyse and understand the multiple sources of discrimination and how they overlap and create multiple levels of social injustices in the lives of the women. The research yielded four key themes: historical cultural beliefs, practices, and languages; fear, stigma, and negative self-perception; the role of community and social services; and influence of socioeconomic status. The results showed that while a woman's immigration status impacted their access to healthcare, other interconnected barriers were present that were mutually reinforcing sources of marginalisation.

5G   Migration Policy

Chair: Jara Al Ali, Hamburg University, Germany

81 Compatibility of the EU-Turkey Statement to EU Law and International Human Rights Law

Havva Yesil

The EU-Turkey Statement was released on March 18, via the Council of the European Union. Immediate and intensive negotiations began in October 2015, leading to the Statement delivered on the grounds of the European Council meeting on 17-18 March 2016. This problematic and controversial statement has been consistently proclaimed by the European Council. This paper focuses on the legal flaws and implementation challenges of the EU-Turkey deal. Regarding the procedure, EU norms for negotiating with third parties are laid forth in Article 218 of the Treaty on the Functioning of the European Union. It refers to collaboration between the EU and a non-EU country. I analyse the General Court orders which are the first rulings on the EU-Turkey Statement and evaluate these decisions in light of EU legal regulations and literature in law. Also, the EU-Turkey Statement violates the principle of non-refoulement, as the EU has committed to taking back one Syrian from Turkey for every Syrian that Turkey accepts from the Greek islands. The EU-Turkey deal violates the ban on collective expulsion under Article

19 of the EU Charter of Fundamental Rights, Article 13 of the ECHR, and Article 4 of Protocol no. 4 to the ECHR since it can result in the deportation of asylum seekers without examination of their asylum claims. This paper also assess the statement's compatibility with the EU Law and International human rights law.

252   Nature-Based Belongings in the UK: National and Local Policies

Azadeh Fatehrad

The natural environment can play a valuable role in shaping migrant belongings in the UK. However, despite parks, woodlands, gardens, beaches, rivers and other blue/green spaces being places where migrants and non-migrants often come together, the benefits of nature are not recognized in UK integration policy. This paper draws on 'Nature-based integration: connecting communities with/in nature', a research project funded by the Nuffield Foundation and the British Academy.

This paper, reflects on local and national policy making in our three case studies urban (London Borough of Harringay), peri-urban (Blackburn with Darwen) and rural (Stornoway) integration sites across the UK, to support the realisation of the natural environment as a resource for migrant integration.

Overall, this paper will argue that the definition of nature-based integration should be seen as a never-ending and multidisciplinary process, and that it should respond to the specificity and subjectivity of geographical, social and historical contexts. Looking at strategies of local and national policies, this paper will also explore how nature based integration can be problematize, renegotiate and counter notions of historical erasure, cultural fusion and otherness embedded in land- and waterscapes.

186   Public universities in Poland as actors helping forced migrants from Ukraine: case study of SGH Warsaw School of Economics

Jan Misiuna, Pawel Kubicki, Marta Pachocka, Dominik Wach

After the full-scale Russian aggression against Ukraine on 24th February 2022, Poland became the default destination and transit country for millions of Ukrainians seeking a safe haven. Among the public institutions rushing with the humanitarian response to the crisis, universities turned out to be particularly well equipped to fulfill this task, thanks to their administrative resources. Firstly, dormitories and other facilities that usually serve students became good solution to provide shelter for the forced migrants. Moreover, public universities often have their own medical staff and labour market services designed to assist students. Also, a sizeable group of Ukrainian students already studying in Poland turned out to be an important asset in the process of accommodating forced migrants from that country.

This paper aims to present how a public university in Warsaw (Poland) used its resources to help forced migrants from Ukraine in the first period after their influx in 2022. It focuses on the analysis of initiatives taken by the universities as institutions but also shows the attitudes and insights of the hosted migrants. The paper is based on desk research, IDIs conducted at the SGH Warsaw School of Economics within the project "SGH in Warsaw as center of support for forced migrants from Ukraine", as well as participatory observation.

58   The Return Emigrants of Kerala Amid COVID 19: Role of Institutional Governance in The Rehabilitation Efforts

Shibinu S

Return migration is an integral and significant element in the cycle of international migration. In recent years, it has received increased focus from host and origin countries because both groups are interested in leveraging return migration to their economic advantage. Recent researches have increased the pressure on developing countries to adopt good governance as a strategy has been increasing enormously. It necessitates new discourses on the translation of the abstract theoretical notions on the role of institutional governance into more practical terms. Migrants were beset with innumerable difficulties while they were abroad during the pandemic. By the finish of July 2020, nearly six lakh Indians were reported to own back to India from different countries with the help of the Vande Bharath Mission, and among them, a third were migrant employees. Now Kerala has been confronted with two unprecedented situations- large scale return emigration from the Middle East is the first aspect and the second is the demographic dividend of a large number of the youth population. The paper aims to identify the consequences of the fast-growing reverse emigration to Kerala from the Middle East and examined the possibility of suggesting efficient institutional policies to be adopted to uplift and reintegrate the migrants returned due to the economic chaos created by the spread of the virus.

14:45-15:00 BREAK

6A   Youth, Children and Families 2 [BG3/4]

Chair: Liat Yakhnich, Beit Berl College, Israel

17   Parent-Child Relationships and Future Parenting among Immigrant Young Adults in Israel

Liat Yakhnich and Rinat Michael

Background: Immigration is a multifaceted process that affects the stability and continuity of family roles (Foner, 1997). The loss of resources and support systems may increase family reliance on their children and lead to parentification and role-reversal (Kosner et al., 2014). Children often become language and culture brokers for their parents, translating the new language and interpreting cultural practices (Oznobishin & Kurman, 2016; Suarez-Orozco & Suarez-Orozco, 2001). Such changes may alter parent-child relationships and impact immigrant children's development and adaptation (Suárez-Orozco et al., 2018). While scholars have investigated changes in the roles of immigrant parents, few studies have examined how children from different cultural groups experience these changes. In addition, little is known regarding the long-term implications these changes may have on immigrant children when they reach adulthood.

Objectives: This study aimed to explore parent-child relations in the context of immigration and its contribution to future parenting perceptions. To understand the impact of both immigration and culture, we focused on the two largest and culturally different immigrant groups in Israel: immigrants from the former Soviet Union (FSU) and from Ethiopia (Walsh et al., 2015). Although largely diverse (Kacen, 2006; Remennick, 2007; Yakhnich, 2016), these groups often live in close proximity and consume educational and social services provided by the same professionals. In order to provide them with services and treatment that best suit their needs, an understanding of the ways in which their culture, as well as immigration experiences, impact parent-child relations and future perspectives is required.

Methods: The study applied a qualitative phenomenological approach (Creswell & Poth, 2017). Twenty-five young adults who immigrated to Israel from Ethiopia (n=14) and from the former Soviet Union (n=11) were interviewed for this study. All were 1.5 generation immigrants who immigrated between the ages 6-12 (Rumbaut, 2012). The data was analyzed in line with the phenomenological approach to data analysis (Creswell & Poth, 2017)

Results: Analysis indicated that the participants' experiences of relations with their parents may be organized into three main domains: shifting relations in the context of immigration, relations in the context of long-term adaptation and maturation, and relations in cultural context (e.g., cultural perceptions about family life and culture-related immigration challenges). Participants' perceptions of their own parenting incorporated culture-specific factors (e.g., family hierarchy and cohesiveness, child-rearing practices, and respect given to parents) as well as difficulties and strengths experienced by their families during immigration. Although most participants wished to be different from their parents (not wanting their children to work so hard) they hoped to preserve some of their culture of origin's child-rearing practices.

Conclusions: Research findings have implications for professionals who work with immigrant families and for policymakers. Considering a family's specific cultural background and helping parents integrate diverse parental practices may assist immigrant families in coping with challenges of immigration and help young adults who immigrated as children in creating a coherent parenthood.

225   The topic of migration and tolerance among the younger generation: on the example of the students at al-Farabu KazNU Faculty of Journalism

Marlan Negizbayeva

The necessity for scrutinized research on issues related to migration and tolerance is determined by the presence of paradigms and negative stereotypes in society. Certain problems arise from the fact that the migration issue is over-politicized. Some politicians and journalists see this situation as a cause for the pressurization of the tense situation.

A research Club for students operates at the faculty of journalism, the aim of which is to shape effective communication and science-based problem-solving skills among students.

Within the Club, students identify hostile language and hate speech in the journalistic texts, put them up for discussion, and propose their examples of texts. Among members of the Club, besides local students, are students from Uzbekistan, Tajikistan, Turkmenistan, Afghanistan, and China. The Club fosters the establishment of moral values, tolerance, and guidelines among young people.

A survey was conducted among the members of the Club to check the Club's work efficiency and determine the tendencies in the development of interethnic and cross-cultural dialogue. Creative works of students and texts of their articles have also been studied for civil solidarity and the nature of dialogue and compromise.

Experience of the Club can serve as a good example of ensuring an objective public perception of migration issues: understanding the global nature of the topic, assessing objectively the migration processes, and explaining laws and rules of labor migration.

238   Mobilities Among Marginalized Youth in Morocco: Precariousness, Agency and Networks

Boutaina Idrissi and Rachid Touhtou

The Mediterranean migration flows are considered sometimes a threat and sometimes a capital. Our paper is situated in the current juncture to understand the new migration trends in Morocco as a sending country in the southern Mediterranean basin. The paper aims at understanding the dynamic processes of mobilities in the Mediterranean basin from the perspective of youth in Morocco. We aim to shed light on marginalized youth migratory tendencies focusing on the post-Arab Spring generations and the COVID19 impacts on mobilities. This paper is based on a current ethnographic fieldwork among young people in the city of Sale, Twin city of Rabat the Capital. It is a qualitative research based on life narratives among 22 young people who dream of migration. The goal of the life narrative is to construct young people's lives and highlight the influencing factors pushing them to think of migration. Through analyzing these life narratives, focusing on biographies, practices and discursive imaginaries of youth, we attempt at highlighting the interrelatedness of various and conflicting categories of the migratory trajectories in order to highlight the role of agency in the production of the migration culture, its sustainability and its alterations.

471   Growing Together with Your Pregnancy: A Space Where Newly Arrived Immigrant Pregnant Mothers Belong

Silvia Juarez-Marazzo

Groups interventions are culturally responsive modalities that offer a space where families from collective cultures, such as the immigrant Latino and Latinix families we serve, feel that "they belong." United States helping systems are profoundly influenced by Medical Models, pregnant parents' groups are typically offered to address specific topics such as breastfeeding and psychoeducation on the baby's care and development. If newly arrived immigrant pregnant parents struggled finding places where they that it was safe to explore the emotional complexity of their experience prior to the COVID-19 pandemic, where would they find a safe space to process the terrors of the unexpected brought by the unthinkable combination of the Trump years and the COVID-19 pandemic?

As the COVID-19 pandemic gradually and effectively took hold of families' ways of living and making life possible, the Bronx, one of the five boroughs in the City of New York, in the United States, scrambled for creating ways to reach and support immigrant families with pregnant mothers, babies and very young children. Prior to the pandemic, immigrant families with babies and very young children welcomed Infant Mental Health clinical services; yet that was not the experience with pregnant mothers. To our surprise a number of newly arrived immigrant pregnant mothers reached out for help, most of them self-referred, a few of them were referred by other providers. These mothers shared experiencing overwhelming feelings of fear, anxiety, isolation, and in a few cases, detachment from the baby-to-be in spite of the advanced gestational stage. We decided to create what at the time seem to be impossible: a virtual space where immigrant pregnant mothers could feel that they belong. Would a virtual group like this be possible? Could carefully thought interventions that "kept in mind" the mothers' history of immigration and their cultural ways of protecting and nurturing pregnant mothers and babies restore a sense of connectedness to themselves and to their pregnancy and the baby-to-be? Our brave pregnant mothers sat the course and taught us, that a group like this, is not only possible but is the answer to making accessible a space of healing, support, hope and repair for them and for their babies-to-be.

6B   Migraciones and Transnacionalismo 3 [UG11]

Chair: Pascual Garcia, Universidad Técnica Particular de Loja, Ecuador

215   Una aproximación sociocultural al sufrimiento de mujeres latinoamericanas migrantes en trabajo doméstico, en Alemania y en España, durante la pandemia de COVID-19

Ivette Alejandra Abanto Ramos, Ximena Pamela Claudia Díaz Bermúdez, Alejandro Goldberg

Este trabajo es un proyecto de investigación de Doctorado en Salud Colectiva de la Universidad de Brasilia (Brasil). Busca realizar una aproximación sociocultural del sufrimiento social de mujeres latinoamericanas migrantes que se desempeñan en trabajo doméstico en Alemania y en España durante la pandemia de COVID-19, considerando las interseccionalidades de género, raza/etnia, clase y nacionalidad. La metodología es la etnografía virtual y análisis de contenido, e incluye técnicas cualitativas de recolección de información. La importancia de este estudio se basa en el déficit de investigación sobre el tema, pues todavía hay pocos estudios sobre salud mental en migrantes de países de bajos y medianos ingresos (como Latinoamérica), en comparación con países de altos ingresos, e incluso menos estudios específicos sobre la salud mental de las mujeres migrantes latinoamericanas. Esto permitirá visibilizar particularidades de la pandemia, de las mujeres migrantes latinoamericanas que se desempeñan en el trabajo doméstico, características de los sistemas de salud, sistemas de trabajo, entre otros aspectos de la sociedad receptora en relación a mujeres migrantes latinoamericanas, así como aspectos de los países de origen de las participantes. Tal visibilidad permitirá pensar en acciones de prevención colectiva, e incluso futuras intervenciones en la salud mental de las participantes y mujeres con perfiles similares.

14   Experiencias de integración y motivaciones de retorno de uruguayos retornados de España en el contexto de la Gran Recesión

Martín Koolhaas

La presente comunicación se propone ahondar en la comprensión del proceso migratorio reciente de uruguayos a España, incorporando la perspectiva de los actores involucrados en el mismo. Para ello en primer lugar realiza un análisis de las valoraciones que plantean las propias personas migrantes sobre sus respectivos procesos de integración en España, contrastando las mismas con la descripción más objetiva sobre las condiciones de inclusión que surge de las narrativas de los entrevistados. En segundo lugar, se describen la diversidad de motivaciones asociadas a las decisiones de retorno y se examinan cómo influyen aspectos al género y a la experiencia migratoria en el mosaico de motivaciones para retornar.Desde una perspectiva retrospectiva se recurre al análisis de 37 entrevistas en profundidad realizadas a varones y mujeres trabajadores/as migrantes que vivieron en España y han retornado a Uruguay a partir de 2008. Los resultados identifican un conjunto de factores asociados a trayectorias de inclusión propicias o deficitarias, sugiriendo que la integración laboral es condición necesaria pero no suficiente para una integración plena al país de acogida, en la medida que no existe una relación unívoca entre las diferentes dimensiones de la integración. El análisis de las motivaciones para retornar corrobora el carácter multifacético de las razones para el retorno y la interrelación entre las mismas, así como la plausibilidad de los enfoques que adhieren a la literatura que postula la importancia de las dimensiones emocionales en las decisiones que los migrantes toman sobre sus vidas y sus trayectorias de movilidad (Erdal, 2014; Carling y Collins, 2017; Martínez Buján, 2015). Asociado a esto, se encuentra que las razones del retorno están menos ligadas a aspectos económicos y más a aspectos familiares que la primera migración (King, 2000; Constant, 2020; Rivera Sánchez, 2015; Parella y Petroff, 2019; Rivero, 2019), aún en contextos económicos del país de acogida y de origen excepcionalmente inversos a los que dieron origen a los flujos migratorios, pautados por el grave deterioro de las condiciones de empleo en España y por condiciones extraordinariamente favorables en Uruguay. Asimismo, se identifican diferentes niveles de voluntariedad asociados a las decisiones de retorno, con consecuencias en los procesos de reintegración posteriores, que contribuyen a problematizar la noción de retorno "voluntario", reafirmando la importancia de considerar el contexto de las decisiones de retorno y de evaluar las alternativas existentes al curso de acción tomado (Erdal y Oeppen, 2022).

230 Las migraciones centroamericanas por México durante el gobierno de López Obrador (2018-2022) caracterizado por la militarización de las políticas migratorias, la mayor subordinación a Estados Unidos y un enorme costo social para los migrantes

Rodolfo García Zamora y Selene Gaspar Olver

El gobierno de López Obrador inicia en diciembre de 2018 enfrentando la llegada masiva de las caravanas migrantes de Centroamérica rumbo a Estados Unidos sin tener una política migratoria integral con visión de desarrollo económico y derechos humanos, luego de una breve etapa de apoyo solidario hacia los migrantes de esa región, las presiones de Trump para frenar esa movilidad humana a su país, se profundiza la militarización de las fronteras sur y norte y en los principales corredores migratorios, la subordinación a Estados Unidos con la aceptación del Titulo 42 en marzo de 2020 y ratificado en la Cumbre de los Líderes de América del Norte en enero de 2023 en que se informa que México acepta recibir 360 deportados centroamericanos de ese país sin ninguna contraprestación financiera, ni de legalización de los 5 millones de indocumentados mexicanos en aquel país. Los costos han sido una violencia creciente y mayor costo social para los migrantes y la aplicación de las políticas migratorias militarizadas, de control de fronteras y seguridad regional del gobierno de Estados Unidos por parte del gobierno mexicano actual.

6C   Migration, Religion, and Religious Groups [UG14]

Chair: Deniz Cosan Eke, University of Vienna, Austria

399 Civil Society in defense of religious rights: the Islamic Civil Society in France and its strategies in achieving Muslims' rights

Enrico Maria la Forgia

Since the 80ies, in specific situations, France's Muslims (whether citizens or foreigners) have enacted political actions to reply to attacks on their identity or assimilation attempts (Alicino, 2016), using their religious affiliation as a resource for the organization and expression of collective claims (Mandelbaum 2000). Indeed, despite Islam's internal sectarian and ethnic differences (Zibou, 2019), religion may be politicized when minorities' cultural and religious rights are under attack (Ralpin, 1979; Cohen, 1992). French Civil Society organizations, in this specific case those with an Islamic background (ICSO - Islamic Civil Society Organizations), play an essential role in defending Muslims' rights and their identitarian specificities. As a matter of fact, Civil Society organized on an ethnic or religious base is a way to strengthen minoritarian communities and their role as political actors (Cinalli, 2013), especially in multicultural contexts (Habermas,

1999). Since the first 1983's "Marche des Beurs" (slang word referring to French citizens with foreign origins), the development of ICSO contributed to the defense of Muslim minorities' rights and attempted to change the perception of Islam itself in the national society (Talpin, 2018).

However, since representing a visible and stigmatized minority, ICSO do not relate only to protests as a strategy to achieve their goals (Fregosi, 2017): on several occasions, pressure on authorities through personal networks, or the introduction of bargaining into public debates through the exploitation of national or international crisis, might appear as more successfully strategies (Kastoryano 2002; Tilly & Tarrow, 2006). In the same way, it appeared that ICSO prefer to participate in demonstrations and actions that catalyze several grievances (not only those concerning Muslims' religious rights) instead of boosting accusations of communitarianism advanced by authorities through their participation in actions that focus only on Muslims' requests (Talpin, 2017)

Therefore, the proposed abstract, based on a literary review and a theoretical/methodological reflection on the state of knowledge on the topic, aims to open a new branch of studies and analysis of Civil Society and Social Movements in Europe. In order to do so, we aim to answer questions such as:

-What are the relations developed by ICSO with authorities?

-What are the relations established by ICSO between them? And those established with secular Civil Society organizations?

-What relations can be observed between ICSO, French Muslims, and Muslim migrants?

Hence, the opted methodology relies, on one hand, on a qualitative approach based on ethnography and face-to-face interviews addressing heads and middle-high level activists from ICSO, in an attempt to individuate the strategies enacted by ICSO in bringing their requests to authorities. On the other hand, the paper relies on a quantitative approach based on a Network Analysis to analyze how ICSO builds relations with local and national authorities and other actors belonging to the Civil Society/political sphere.

171   Reversion/Religious Conversion and Networks: Overseas Filipino Workers in Saudi Arabia: Filipino converts and social networks

Simeon Magliveras

Over Seas Workers (OFW's) come to the Kingdom of Saudi Arabia (KSA) with the intension to better the lives of their extended families back in the Philippines. However, their sojourn exposes them to new ideas and new ways of life. In KSA religious practice is embedded in everyday life. As a result, Filipinos are (in)advertently exposed to Islam. For many who find their faith lacking, they find Islam fills this gap. This paper tests the perception that if one converts to another religion then they reject old beliefs and abandon old social ties resulting from adoption of a new a cosmology. Their family and old cohorts may socially reject them and their new belief system. This study will not focus on the reasons why they convert, or revert- as Muslims refer to adopting Islam-, however, the reason why they revert maybe referred to, to so some degree. This study examines what reverting entails. It uses ego-centric social network analysis to understand whether the hypothesis that people who reject their old religion is a moment where they must establish an entirely new network or does reversion create a space where new networks and old networks are created, strengthening their position both in Saudi Arabia and in the Philippines. To conclude this study will visualize through social network analyses the effects reversion has on their personal networks and if these effects are even visible.

385   Crafting Muslim Selves: Understanding the Authority of Mosques among Pakistani Muslim Diaspora in Australia

Tasmia Jahangir

Australia's reverential connection with Islam is time-honoured, however, September 11 attacks followed by the Bali bombings, signalled a major shift portraying militarisation, Shariatisation, and resurgent movements such as the Taliban as representative imaginings of Islam. Consequently, the common Muslim's long-standing practises of ordinary Islam forming religious subjectivities and intimate dimensions of their lives became marginalised in the scholarship of Islamic revivalism. Against this backdrop, the authority of mosques and their imams (clerics) in the Muslim diaspora is a topic of critical importance, as it shapes the way in which community members navigate their religious and cultural identities in a foreign land. The current research while focusing on Pakistani Muslims - a sizeable and well-established Pakistan-originated Muslim diaspora in Australia - asks how mosques and imams in relation to the worship practises influence everyday social structure? The study employs participant observation and in-depth interviews among first and second-generation Pakistani migrants living in Sydney. By examining the authority of mosques in the Pakistani diaspora, this study aims to shed light on the complexities of religious and cultural identity formation in a diasporic context.

555   The Politics of Emotion in Interfaith Dialogue in the Time of Migration

Deniz Cosan Eke

Migration often leads to the encounter of diverse cultural and religious communities, which can create both opportunities and challenges for interfaith dialogue. The emotions experienced by migrants and members of host communities can play a critical role in shaping their attitudes and behaviors towards one another. Therefore, it is important to build bridges between different communities, and to investigate the feelings of people of different faiths about each other in order to develop interfaith dialogue. Emotions play a crucial role in interfaith dialogue as they can either facilitate or hinder communication and understanding between different faith communities. For instance, fear can lead to defensiveness, mistrust, and suspicion, making it difficult for individuals to engage in open and honest dialogue. On the other hand, empathy can create a sense of shared humanity and promote mutual respect and understanding. However, emotions can also be used as a political tool to manipulate and control the dialogue. For example, politicians or religious leaders may use emotional appeals to mobilize their followers or to discredit their opponents. This can lead to a polarization of the dialogue and make it more difficult to find common ground. The politics of emotion in interfaith dialogue refers to the ways in which emotions and affective states such as fear, anger, anxiety, hope, and compassion can shape and influence the communication, attitudes, and actions of individuals and groups in interfaith encounters. However, there are limited research about how emotions, which play a significant role in interfaith dialogue, influence migrants' participation in such dialogues and promote social cohesion among migrants of different backgrounds. In the current study, the main research Question is how emotions influence the interfaith dialogue in promoting peaceful coexistence among immigrants and non-immigrants. The aim of this research is to investigate the role of emotions in shaping the attitudes and behaviors of them towards one another in the context of interfaith dialogue.

6D   Migration, Law and Policy 6   [EG15/16]

Chair: Olivia Joseph-Aluko, RADET, UK

382   1.5 and 2nd generation diaspora engagement in complex humanitarian crises: Case Studies from Haiti, Syria, and Sudan

Kirstie Kwarteng

As more nations are experiencing complex humanitarian crises, diaspora populations are working to provide humanitarian assistance to impacted people and communities in their countries of origin. Examples of this include the response of Haitian diaspora organisations to the August 2021 earthquake in Haiti, Ukrainian diaspora responses to the conflict in Ukraine from 2014, and Pakistani diaspora responses to the 2022 floods in Pakistan. When discussing the role of diaspora communities in humanitarian crises, the contributions of first-generation immigrants are often the most highlighted. The contributions of younger generations in diaspora communities, specifically 1.5 and 2nd generation diaspora, are underacknowledged. While some scholars previously assumed 1.5 and 2nd generation diaspora would be less engaged with their countries of origin (Portes, 2009), evidence proves otherwise. Motivated by their parents' trauma, critical geopolitical events, and their own lived experiences (Ahmed, 2019), 1.5 and 2nd generation diaspora are engaging in various forms of transnational action, including supporting their countries of origin in humanitarian crises as well as crisis advocacy and political engagement. As such, this paper will highlight the important role 1.5 and 2nd generation diaspora have in supporting humanitarian efforts in their countries of origin. Drawing on Shabaka's research and learning from recent projects, this paper will demonstrate how 1.5 and 2nd generation diaspora are supporting their countries of origin during complex humanitarian crises using examples from Haiti, Syria, and Sudan. Findings from these projects show that 1.5 and 2nd generation diaspora are supporting humanitarian efforts in a variety of ways including, but not limited to, fundraising events, social media advocacy, creating humanitarian organisations, and relocating to their country of origin to support humanitarian efforts directly. They also draw on and deploy different yet complementary sets of resources, skills, knowledge, and networks to first generation diaspora. However, there remains a lack of structured pathways for 1.5, second, and subsequent generation diaspora to engage in humanitarian activities in origin countries.

References

Ahmed, B. (2019). Reasons for Giving Back?: Motivations for Engaging in Transnational Political Activism by Adult Children of Migrants from the Horn of Africa. [Unpublished Doctoral Dissertation]. University of Sussex.

Portes, A. (2009). Migration and Development. Ethnic and Racial Studies, 32(1), 5-22. doi:10.1080/01419870802483668

444   Weaponizing public health policies to exclude and expel the unwelcomed migrants: The Use of Title 42 in the US

William Arrocha

If xenophobia was to find its perfect scapegoat, Covid 19 and its massive impacts on public health could not have come at a better time. States have been securitizing migration and criminalizing irregular migration to keep out of their borders those migrants considered a a burden or a threat. Regardless of the erection of walls and barbed-wired fences, those fleeing from conflict, extreme poverty, or natural disasters continue to find ways to reach to a safe place. However, many anti-immigrant pundits consider migration flows as "invasions," as was the case with US President Trump in 2019, or even "poison," as with Hungarian Prime Minister Viktor Orban in 2016. This paper will explore from a discursive and political-legal analysis the use of Title 42, a section of the United States Code that deals with public health and welfare used to prevent the introduction, transmission, and spread of infectious diseases into the United States. In March 2020, the Trump administration would introduce it to control immigration but, most notably, to stop and expel at their borders the flow of irregular migrants, including those seeking asylum. Although Title 42 has been contested in the courts, it is still in place, causing unnecessary harm to those forced to migrate and, in many cases, violating the principle of non-rafoulment. This paper will contend that the use of measure like Title 42 sets a dangerous precedent as other states could follow suit in weaponizing public health measures to exclude those migrants considered undesirable, putting at risk the fundamental international legal protections for immigrants, irregular or forced migrations, including refugees or those seeking asylum.

291   Freedom of movement in the "Mercado Común del Sur" (Mercosur): A human rights approach and its conflictual implementation

Zoé Maja Perko

Many regional integration projects attempt to implement freedom of movement frameworks in macroterritorialization processes, therefore facilitating intra-regional cross border movements (Mau, 2021). Yet, even though these visions and goals exist, regions still struggle to implement such measures and thus, in some cases, barriers to intra-regional mobility remain. To this day, the phenomenon remains understudied (Nita, 2017).

This paper examines the barriers to freedom of movement in the "Mercado Común del Sur" (Mercosur), a common market that follows a striking human rights approach to migration after a "social turn", distancing itself from a solely economic perspective and gradually viewing migrants as citizens (Brumat, 2020, p. 7). The existing literature provides valuable information on problems and conflicts while implementing the framework in Mercosur and the subsequent barriers to free movement, pointing to a contradiction between the humanitarian discourse and the actual rejection of migrants (Acosta Arcarazo & Freier, 2015). However, to the best of my knowledge, there is no study focused specifically on implementation difficulties, barriers mostly being mentioned either as a side-note in an analysis focusing on another topic or relating to region building and not specifically to freedom of movement of persons (see e.g. Brumat, 2020; Granja & Villareal Villamar, 2017). Therefore, more research has to be conducted on the discrepancy between the vision and the actual implementation of free movement policies in Mercosur. My systematization of implementation issues will therefore help to assess, whether citizens can actually move freely in the region.

In this paper, the discrepancy between the project - goal and vision for the regional mobility - and product – whether there is freedom of movement in the region – (based on Van Langenhove, 2012) is assessed through a document analysis and interviews with stakeholders from regional institutions (Mercosur), national institutions (member states), civil society actors (NGO's and migrant organizations) and academics conducted in Argentina, Uruguay, Brazil and online.

Even though freedom of movement and border integration are important pillars to regionalization and Mercosur has an advanced and dedicated approach on paper, human mobility still faces many barriers in practice. These include the lack of resources and general capacities to implement agreements, restrictive tendencies of member states depending on their current government, the intergovernmental structure and the perceived weakness of Mercosur institutions and barriers within nation states such as the chaotic overlap of different institutions managing migration. These difficulties during or after the implementation process of Mercosur's freedom of movement framework results in the lack of implementation of certain agreements and breaches of already implemented policies, such as arbitrary rejections at intra-Mercosur borders or difficulties for Mercosur residents to access their rights in host countries. However, punctual bottom-up approaches and the informal nature of Mercosur borders partly still enables cross-border movements, leading to a partial compensation of breaches and complementation of the regional framework.

146   International Migration and Human Trafficking

Olivia Joseph-Aluko

Purpose

Human trafficking is the second largest and fastest growing crime in the world to identify victims and stop traffickers

The crime of human trafficking is currently occurring on a scale unprecedented since the trans-Atlantic Slave Trade. Human trafficking represents a significant challenge to all involved countries, presenting obstacles to social and economic development and the rule of law as well as posing a severe threat to human security. This study examines forms of human trafficking and the links to forced and labour migration. The topic of migration is evidently closely associated with human trafficking. It describes antecedents and factors that facilitate human trafficking, as well as its economic, social, and human impacts.

Method/Approach

This study analyses primary data regarding human trafficking and migration collected by intergovernmental organisations such as the United Nations (UN) Office on Drugs and Crime, the UN High Commissioner for Refugees, and the International Organization for Migration, as well as dedicated databases such as the Migration Data Portal. It also examines data on the human impacts of migration collected by groups such as Caritas and Anti-Slavery International.

Findings

Human trafficking is considered as a modern form of slavery representing a serious threat to human dignity. The 2021 Global Report on Trafficking in Persons estimates that about 49.6 million people are in modern day slavery on any given day, either forced to work against their will or in other perennial circumstances.

Forced and labour migration are the primary mechanisms for victimisation by human trafficking. Men are commonly employed in sectors such as mining and construction, whereas women and children are trafficked for purposes of sexual exploitation, hospitality services, domestic work, and forced begging. Trafficking victims are often relegated to the informal economy, and therefore endure harsh working conditions, limited government regulations, and no benefits. Moreover, inhospitable migration rules prevent most victims from accessing basic health care or legal protections.

Conclusions

It is critical that global governments collaborate to strengthen existing legislative and policy frameworks and develop new mechanisms to combat human trafficking and protect migrants from exploitation. Governments and international organisations also must work to increase data on the nature and scale of human trafficking and migrant smuggling. Migration and immigration laws must be adjusted to treat migrants more humanely and reduce draconian policies that hinder trafficking victims' ability to seek aid.

References

Caritas (2019, 25 July). Forced migration is one root cause of human trafficking. Retrieved from https://www.caritas.org/2019/07/forced-migration-and-human-trafficking/

David, F., Bryant, K., & Larsen, J.J. (2019). Migrants and their vulnerability to human trafficking, modern slavery and forced labour. International Organization for Migration. Retrieved from https://publications.iom.int/system/files/pdf/migrants_and_their_vulnerability.pdf

Migration Data Portal (2019, 4 June). Human trafficking. Retrieved from https://migrationdataportal.org/themes/human-trafficking

United Nations Office on Drugs and Crime (2019). Human trafficking and smuggling of migrants. Retrieved from https://www.unodc.org/westandcentralafrica/en/newrosen website/TIPSOM/Human-trafficking-and-smuggling-of-migrants.html

Yousaf, F.N. (2018). Forced migration, human trafficking, and human security. Current Sociology, 66(2), 209–225. https://doi.org/10.1177/0011392117736309

6E   Theory and Methods in Migration Studies 2 [BG 5/6]

Chair: H. Yaprak Civelek, Anadolu University, Turkey

319   Working with a range of under-served disability and migrant communities using innovative and inclusive participatory methods - the CICADA study

Carol Rivas, Kusha Anand, Amanda P Moore

We need to be more attentive to the practices we utilise in data collection to avoid exacerbating perceptions of discrimination and distrust, to ensure minoritised groups are more successfully represented in research. This is especially important with the widening of inequalities caused by the COVID-19 pandemic.

The strengths-based CICADA study has explored the impact of the last three years on health conditions, service access, social support and mental well-being for people from minoritised ethnic groups with disabilities living in the UK. One important component of this study is the use of methods that include, engage, collaborate with and give voice to diverse migrants of different migration status and different types of disability. Specifically, we deployed a range of asset-based participatory approaches - interviews, workshops and disseminations and knowledge exchange (including theatre). These successfully involved migrants from communities across England as lay co-researchers, and participants as the co-designers of pragmatic interventions to improve their health and wellbeing.

Our approach enabled the collection of rich data, including from groups often excluded from health research, such as disabled migrants arriving in the UK since the pandemic or without documents. Data show the extent, diversity and intersecting nature of various determinants of health and inequalities, discrimination (ableism, disablism, racism) and also successful coping strategies used. Co-design work with migrants and disabled people based on these findings has resulted in practical solutions to some of the issues we found. We have also produced a toolkit designed to help future researchers to engage productively with a range of vulnerable communities. We intend this to contribute to enhanced social, health and wellbeing outcomes for migrants.

Feedback from our participants and lay researchers and the success of our study shows that our easily implemented approaches are effective in in giving voice to the under-served and also in problem-solving from a position of community empowerment to improve the quality of health and social care.

This study is funded by the National Institute for Health and Care Research (NIHR) [NIHR132914, HS&DR]. The views expressed are those of the author(s) and not necessarily those of the NIHR or the Department of Health and Social Care.

391   The Legal Regulations on Migrant Women Working in Domestic Services in Türkiye from the Perspective of Feminization of Migration

Zeynep Banu Dalaman and Deniz Bade Akkoyun

One of the trends that have come to the fore with globalization is the increased visibility of women in migration. As the rate of women's participation in the labor force through paid work has increased, their mobility from rural to urban areas or from one part of the world to another has also increased. In this process, also known as the feminization of migration, women have become geographically more mobile than ever before in history. With this process, women started to migrate independently from their family members across national borders to work in a variety of jobs, particularly domestic work and sex work. The diversion of domestic work (caring for the sick, children and elderly, cleaning, etc.) to women in poorer countries through the global division of labor has played an important role in this change. This division of labor, which arises from the combination of the gendered character of domestic work and cheap female labor, has necessitated the geographical mobility of poorer women from all over the world. As a result, women have also begun to engage in geographical mobility on a global scale. In addition to these reasons that push women to migrate, developments in destination countries that create demand for migrant women's labor are also important.

Today, almost every part of the world has become a destination point for women migrating for domestic work. Especially after the collapse of the Soviet Union, Türkiye has also become one of these target countries. However, migrant women have faced various problems in Türkiye, both due to deficiencies in existing regulations and political attitudes towards migrants. These women, most of whom work as domestic workers, have been at the center of problems arising from both the migration system and the specific conditions of domestic work.

In this study, the problems faced by female migrant domestic workers in Türkiye are discussed within the aforementioned framework. In particular, the main axis of the discussion is how domestic workers are affected by legal regulations in Türkiye. The study interrogates how women's migration to Türkiye has developed within the existing migration system and examines the migration experience of migrant women working as domestic workers in Türkiye.

191   Defection and human rights activism by North Korean refugee women in the UK: through the lens of hermeneutic phenomenology

Hyun-Joo Lim

The paper aims to highlight the voices of North Korean defector women and activists, using hermeneutic phenomenology. It seeks to demonstrate that the Heideggerian phenomenology can be an effective tool for feminist research on female migrants and refugees, using the experiences of North Korean women and their activism as an example. As such, this paper applies feminist interpretations of hermeneutic phenomenology (Holland and Huntington 2001), as originated from the work of Martin Heidegger (2005 [1994], 2019 [1962]). The data is drawn from 13 life history interviews with North Korean defector women living in the UK. The paper argues that Heideggerian phenomenology enables the analysts to shed light onto the lived experiences of women migrants and refugees in their pathways from invisible victims to vocal activists, together with human rights violations faced by them in the process of their journeys. Thus, it has a huge potential as a feminist philosophical and methodological tool that critically examines the subjective experiences of displaced women and their transnational activism in depth, as illustrated by the examples of North Korean women defectors and activists.

265   Presumed (Illegal) Migration Trajectories of Serbian Youth in the Context of the Culture of Migration

Mirjana Stanojević

This contribution examines the narratives that young people in the Pomoravlje region of Serbia create around their plans to emigrate illegally. The region has a culture of migration that evolved around the Gastarbeiter emigration in the 1960s, and contemporary youth is still strongly motivated to emigrate to the imagined West while existing on the „immediate outside" of the EU (Jansen, 2009). Qualitative data, used in this contribution, was gathered through interviews, focus groups, and native ethnography in the Pomoravlje region in 2021.

Due to the long history of outward international migration and many success stories of the Gastarbeiter, emigration seems to be a very straightforward and simple process involving many illegal practices. The acquisition of financial and material wealth through irregular emigration without evident consequences has made it attractive to many young people. Members of the Serbian diaspora, that are themselves participating in irregular migration, often encourage aspiring migrants to follow their path by employing them illegally or inviting them as alleged family members.

The perceived social anomie reflected in the non-existence of laws and order in Serbia is often described as a strong push factor. At the same time, aspiring migrants are often willing to partake in illegal practices like fictive marriages or illegal labor in order to "get the papers" or legalize their residence abroad. Illegal migratory practices of Serbian emigrants have been so widespread that they have been carved in the minds of young people as legitimate. Having social networks abroad is considered to be crucial in the migratory process, and fictive marriages are often casually mentioned as one of the possible mediums for achieving this goal.

Greenberg (2011) explains this proneness to illegal movement as a consequence of decades-long state crisis, moral decay, international isolation, and people's belief, "that they are no longer normal agents capable of moral action in the world" (p. 89). She also explains it as a consequence of the inability of Serbians to participate in "good travel" while being forced to take part in "bad travel" or immobility. The decline of state institutions made Serbians rely on social networks instead, which also reflects in outward migration. In other words, the Serbian diaspora has been institutionalized in the migratory process, and aspiring migrants have more confidence in it than the state institutions in both Serbia and abroad. Petrović (2017), on the other hand, describes illegal emigration as a way to "both legitimize and challenge internal European hierarchy that places Serbia in a subordinated position". Hence, illegality can be seen as a response and aversion to seemingly never-ending transition and European integration processes. Strong occidental images in Serbian society also help justify the moralities of irregular mobility.

To conclude, this contribution will delve into potential illegal migratory trajectories and the narratives that Serbian youth creates to justify them. I would also like to reformulate Kandel's and Massey's statement that "successful illegal migration causes more illegal migration" in the context of the culture of migration (2002).

6F   Economics, Work and Migration 2 [UG13]

Chair: Gökay Özerim, Yaşar University, Turkey

88   'Xenophobia on all fronts': The case of South Africa

   Amanuel Isak Tewolde

Theoretical conversations on xenophobia have largely focused on the ways in which the general public or some extremist right-wing groups express and enact their xenophobic attitudes against recent immigrants. How ever there is little theoretical debate on expressions of xenophobic attitudes and actual violence on all fronts in a host society such as on the streets in everyday life, government agencies, politicians, anti-immigrant radical groups and other settings and social encounters. I draw on my auto-ethnographic experiences as an African refugee with visible foreign physical and cultural/symbolic markers and secondary literature to argue that xenophobic expressions in South Africa tend to be fairly pervasive and embedded within a wide range of entities such as the media, public officials, political figures, the everyday public, private and public agencies and organizations, and numerous other social encounters and interactions. Where refugees and migrants experience xenophobic attitudes and violence on all fronts in a host country, they find themselves in extremely volatile and unsafe socio-cultural environment prone to psychological trauma, physical harm and even death. In a context of a highly xenophobic environment such as South Africa the primary and urgent resolution to the ongoing predicament of refugees appears to be resettlement to relatively safer countries or repatriation if the conditions at home have improved significantly.

309   Analyzing the Vulnerability of Overseas Filipino Workers to Radicalization and Violent Extremism: Basis for the Development of a New PDOS Module for Prevention

Renante David

This study aimed to analyze the push and pull factors that lead to the vulnerability of OFWs to radicalization and VE as well as the prevention of Overseas Filipino Workers (OFWs) towards violent extremism (VE), to educate/teach outbound OFWs by introducing and/or integrating a new module to the PDOS curricula towards preventing and countering exposures to radicalization and violent extremism. The vulnerability of OFWs to radicalization and VE has never been implausible as millions work in areas where conflict proliferates, and the prominence of terrorist and extremist groups thrive. Based on the 2018 Philippine Statistics Authority data, of the 2.3 million OFWs working abroad, 54.9 percent or about 1.3 million OFWs work and reside in the Middle East and one out of four OFWs work in Saudi Arabia, making them evident prime targets for recruitment for radicalization and VE. This study used mixed methods combining quantitative and qualitative approaches employing a triangulation method that used (1) survey questionnaire, (2) focused group discussion, and (3) a key informant interview, along with secondary sources. Results revealed that the pull factors that affect the vulnerability of OFWs to radicalization and violent extremism, namely: socio-economic opportunities; potential status on marginalization and discrimination; and governance, human rights, and the rule of law are influential. In a similar way, the pull factors that affect the vulnerability of OFWs to radicalization and violent extremism, including individual backgrounds and motivations; collective grievances and victimization; beliefs, political ideologies, and ethnic and cultural differences; and leadership and social network are also influential. As a result, these identified push and pull factors are found to contribute to the vulnerability of OFWs to radicalization and VE. This study also revealed that the development of a separate module on preventing radicalization and violent extremism for OFWs is necessary and essential. The study also discovered that having National/Local Action Plans and establishing good practices in cooperation with the religious sector are significant interventions in creating awareness among OFWs to counter the vulnerability towards radicalization and VE.

Keywords: vulnerability; radicalization; violent extremism; OFWs; push factors; pull factors; prevention; raising awareness

138   The Global Ethiopian Diaspora: An Historical, Geographic and Thematic Overview

Hewan Girma, Mulugeta Dinbabo, and Shimelis Gulema

Ethiopia is one of the largest African sources of transnational migrants with an estimated 1-2 million Ethiopians living outside of the home country. Given the extent of the diaspora, this presentation gives an historic, geographic and thematic overview of Ethiopian migration mapping out its scale, scope and destinations. We discuss the state of knowledge and current debates on the diaspora and suggest alternative frameworks for interrogating and understanding the Ethiopian migration and diasporic experiences. From a historical perspective, we identify key time periods and literatures to examine Ethiopian transnational migration starting from a survey of patterns in pre-twentieth century Ethiopia, followed by the imperial period, and under succeeding post-revolutionary regimes. Geographically, we outline the contours of the Ethiopian diaspora, identifying key destinations and patterns of return and correcting the traditional tendency to conflate the Ethiopian diaspora with North America and Europe to include areas that have thus far been marginalized, such as inter-Africa, Asia, and the Middle East. The objective is not to construct a simple cartography of migration but an analysis of national and global issues, policies, trends, and processes that shape the roots and routes of the migration dynamic. Thematically, this project aims to challenge the existing boundaries of Ethiopian migration and diaspora studies and raise familiar yet important concerns about representation, ghettoization and perpetuation of inequalities. Employing a trans-disciplinary approach, this study proposes to rethink Ethiopian migration and diaspora studies and provide a much needed historical and geographic context and depth. Furthermore, we interrogate the future of Ethiopian migration and diaspora studies and identify new avenues for expanding research. We argue that we cannot move forward in our understanding of this multifaceted phenomenon without a retrospective analysis, identifying lacunas and theoretical contributions that go beyond the specific case study. These discussions emerge from a forthcoming book project titled The Global Ethiopian Diaspora with implications for questions of nation-state building, ethno-national identity, socio-economic development, gendered interactions, social stratification and so forth.

117   Migration and violence experiences: exploratory study

Syed Imran Haider

The migration has a relationship with experience of violence

6G   Migration and Integration 6 [EG17]

Chair: Mónica Ibáñez Angulo, University of Burgos, Spain

469   Informal Microfinancing Systems and Networks: Transnational Senegalese Tontines in the Migratory Context

Mónica Ibáñez Angulo

Also known as Rosca, a tontine is a very popular type of informal microfinance strategy in the form of a rotating credit system consisting of several people, usually women, who pool their money together and distribute the savings on a monthly/yearly basis, with each of the participants taking her turn to receive the money collected from the group. Tontines constitute a very popular form of informal microfinance initiative among small-scale networks of women in different West African countries (Senegal, Togo, Cameroon, Côte d'Ivoire, Mali, Niger), where they play an essential role in the domestic and national economies, in the creation, diversification and strengthening of women's networks, and in the reproduction of traditional forms of women's solidarity and reciprocity.

In the migratory context of the European Union, many West African women, especially Senegalese women, have created and/or participate in tontines, usually in more than one. Drawing upon ethnographic research among West African women living in Burgos, in this paper I will analyze the economic, social, and cultural dimensions of tontines in the migratory context by exploring on the following issues:

The genealogy of Senegalese tontines in the municipality of Burgos (Spain): the relevance of kinship, vicinity, origin, ethnic group, or language spoken in the configuration and consolidation of the network; women's motivations to participate in a tontine, which may be different from those experienced by women in rural Senegal where they may face serious difficulties to access to formal banking institutions, although research has found that, regardless of their access to formal banking, women who participate in tontines prefer this kind of informal savings and financing to obtaining credits from the bank.

The organization and structure of the tontine: patterns of redistribution; the amount pooled in a weekly/monthly basis; where do they meet and how often, what are other non-economic activities developed by these women that strengthen mutual trust (e.g. dancing, sharing of food, of information).

The diversification of tontines according to different types of needs: the traditional Tontine Mutuelle which is a mutual aid fund, or the Financial Tontine, which is a fund where people put in money which is then lent to outsiders as well as insiders for interest.

The transnational character of tontines: the savings obtained through tontines initiated in the migratory context can become remittances, while at the same time, these remittances can serve to initiate other tontines in the country of origin and/or in another country by means, for instance, of transnational networks of kin members who have migrated to different European states.

The main aim of the paper is twofold. On the one hand, it aims to contribute to academic literature on gender and migration by exploring new avenues of research that highlight empowering strategies developed by women in the migratory context, and to show their contribution to the family (even national) economies; and, on the other hand, the paper aims to reveal the economic value and social significance of traditional practices, such as informal microfinancing, in transnational urban capitalist settings.

395   Unresolved ambiguities – Unaccompanied minor refugees experience with integration as a false promise of belonging in Norway

Hans Aksel Choudhari

This paper examines how unaccompanied minor refugees (UMR) experience and navigate their transition into adulthood in Norway. Eide et.al (2020) highlights the importance of understanding ambiguities related to care, agency and resettlement as central themes when doing research on UMR early years in a new host country. Expounding on this, we argue that certain ambiguities stay unresolved deep into their adult lives in Norway, and that understanding how these affect them long term is of great academic and political importance.

Unaccompanied minor refugees are by their categorization as both children and refugees, victims and burdens, caught in two separate discursive regimes. As children they are seen as especially vulnerable and deserving of the care and compassion underpinning the Western idea of childhood, but concurrently as refugees, they fall into the logic of control and national interests. This become more precarious as they reach adulthood where their only viable path to deservedness is through socio-economic integration. The aim of this study is twofold: it examines how and if successfully integrating in a socio-economic sense create a feeling of inclusion and belonging, and furthermore, it explores the ambiguity that rests in UMR making sense of and navigating the vague concepts of integration and belonging.

Drawing on in-depth unstructured interviews with six UMR, we explore their experiences with integration, participation and belonging and to what extent a successful socio-economic integration translates into a feeling of actual societal inclusion. Using a narrative approach their stories guide our inquiry and in doing so their perspectives is our primary source of knowledge. The data shows that the participants experience an ambiguous relationship with the Norwegian society. They are well integrated in a socio-economic sense; they are settled and expect to live out their lives in Norway, but at the same time they feel as outsiders whose efforts to integrate is not rewarded with belonging. This can be framed as a false promise inherent in the host societies expectations of integration, and paradoxically that – by being the sole avenue to deservedness without facilitating a proper societal inclusion – a successful socio-economic integration may come to reinforce feelings of exclusion rather than negate them.

Navigating these ambiguities and striving for a sense of coherence in incoherent circumstances seems to be integral aspects of UMR transition into adulthood in Norway. I conclude by reflecting on how UMR living many of their formative years in a foreign culture seem to be particularly sensitive to socially exclusionary mechanisms. This insight puts an onus on us as researchers to focus on previous UMR as a key field in itself, rather than simply treating it as an auxiliary aspect of generalized studies of 'immigrant integration'.

Reference

Ketil Eide, Hilde Lidén, Bergit Haugland, Torunn Fladstad & Hans A. Hauge (2020) Trajectories of ambivalence and trust: experiences of unaccompanied refugee minors resettling in Norway, European Journal of Social Work, 23:4, 554-565, DOI: 10.1080/13691457.2018.1504752

558   The Migration, Integration and Territorial/Spatial Context: The Case of Inner (isolated) Areas in Italy

Hilde Caroli Casavola

The growing awareness of the structural character of migration, combined with the serious negative consequences of demographic decline and the presence of inner (isolated) areas (two thirds of the country's surface area is inner areas), mostly overlapping with rural ones, make Italy a unique case-study of migrant's integration. That is the basis to understand how to adapt the legal framework in connection with spatial dynamics, local core-periphery patterns and the emerging of a number of institutional and socio-political tools, including collaborative pacts for the management of common goods, co-programming and co-planning of public and social services, useful to implement integration policy. The paper aims at analysing the issue in the perspective of the National Strategy for Inner Areas (2021-2027), the collaborative governance (of public goods) approach, the innovations of municipal and participatory welfare and in comparison, with similar experiences and related regulatory solutions eventually defined in other EU countries.

16:30-17:00 BREAK

Day Two 24 August 2023 - 17:00-19:00

ROUNDTABLE: "Digitalisation and Artificial Intelligence in Migration and Asylum" [Rechtshaus Hörsaal]

Convener: *Prof. Dr. Markus Kotzur, Universität Hamburg [Conference Chair]*

Panellists:

- Prof. Dr. Daniel Thym, Universität Konstanz
- Prof. Dr. Mario Savino, University of Tuscia
- Prof. Dr. Gabriele Buchholtz, Universität Hamburg
- Dr. Derya Ozkul Kusoglu, University of Oxford, UK

END OF DAY TWO

Day Three 25 August 2023 - 09:30-11:00

7A   Theory and Methods in Migration Studies 3 [UG14]

Chair: H. Yaprak Civelek, Anadolu University, Turkey

340   Partnering with youth and families in the service of education justice: Insights from community-based research

Maria Paula Ghiso and Hans Gerald Campano

Youth from immigrant backgrounds often enter schools that hew to unexamined monolingual, colonial norms and devalue their transnational funds of knowledge and community cultural wealth (Mignolo, 2011; Yosso, 2005). When schools do focus on equity and inclusion, many initiatives become depoliticized, with a proliferation of race-evasive practices that homogenize student experiences (Ladson-Billings, 2014). Within and against these challenges, educators have sought to remake classrooms to learn from and honor students' knowledge and community legacies of activism and resistance (e.g., Authors, 2016; de los Ríos & Molina, 2020). These efforts raise questions regarding what notions of (im)migration circulate in schools, existing educational barriers for transnational communities, and how we might affirm youth and family legacies while also inviting inquiry into broader socio-political histories that shape the complexities and contradictions of (im)migrant identities.

This paper draws from a long-term community-based partnership that brings together members across racial, linguistic, and migration backgrounds to co-investigate issues of education justice through multimodal forms of inquiry. Grounded in feminist of color epistemologies (e.g., Alcoff et al., 2006; Anzaldúa, 1987/2015), we focus on the border as a productive space and also "as part of historic and contemporary imperial relations" (Walia, 2021, p. 3). The partnership—including literacy researchers from multiple academic institutions and adults, youth, and children from Vietnamese, Cambodian, Filipino/a, Indonesian, and various Latin American communities— has generated original research about inequalities across the education system. The work is guided by methodological traditions that seek to democratize knowledge generation and make research a participatory and community-based endeavor (e.g. Authors, 2022; Cochran-Smith & Lytle, 2009; Rappaport, 2020). We strive to adopt a shared culture that honors individual and collective experiences and the identities of youth and families of color, and which explicitly breaks down divides between the "researcher" and the "researched."

For this presentation, we analyze youth and family inquiries from across the partnership, driven by community priorities and co-planned by youth and families themselves. Data sources included transcripts of inquiry meetings, planning notes, and artifacts, which were reviewed independently and alongside community partners in an iterative process (Charmaz, 2014). We highlight three findings: (1) how research across borders of nationality, language, age, and institutional roles can foster what we refer to as a local intellectual commons; (2) the intersections of educational justice with other forms of oppression – such as economic displacement, neighborhood gentrification, and policing of migratory status – as well as local activist movements of resistance; and (3) equitable practices of partnering in community-based research. In our findings, we argue that our research team's varied transnational histories uniquely position the group to examine linkages across global phenomena and the ways in which all human beings have a relationship, for example, to white supremacy, class exploitation, the prison industrial complex, and colonization. We spotlight youth and families as makers who, in dialogue with each other, authored counter narratives of migration as linked to broader "crises of displacement and immobility" (Walia, 2021, p. 3).

125   Migration without movement: Arrival, Immobility and Edo Identity Formation

Osarugue Otebele

Discourses of migration often figure the migrant and those who stay behind as separable identities marked by locational difference. However, what is often the case, specifically for Edo women migrants from Nigeria is that migrant mobility is inextricable from immobility and that those who stay behind also perform culturally specific form of migration. The possibility of migration without movement and movement without migration is central to Sudabeh Mortezai's 2018 Joy, where the sexual labor, physical and psychology immobility of Edo Women migrants captures viewers within the constructive structures of irregular migration. This paper examines the confinement and sexual labor of said women as instrumental in the construction and tethering of an Edo cultural identity to migration. The formation of this national identity emerges through the Nigerian concept of arrival, which suggests that the families of those who migrate to European countries, through the migrant's body, experience migration without leaving their home country. As the film demonstrates for Edo women, migration and sex work produce an identity constrained within a double that renders them legible for migration but illegible for mobility yet simultaneously secures the societal legibility of those left behind. In other words, while the women engage in sex work and attempt to secure legal status in migrant country, those left behind also enter a process of securing their own identity tied to their violently formed connections to Europe.

120   Growths in-between places: Identity formation process and authentic self(s) of transnational migrants

Dilvin Dilara Usta

This paper explores the implications of migration on transnational migrants' identity formation process concerning self-exploration and self-expression. Recent migration studies approach these identities by illustrating connections between the social landscape and migrant identities (Elliott and Urry, 2010; Beck and Beck-Gernsheim, 2014) and investigating the impact of globalisation on migrant identity presentations in different places (Brah, 1996). In particular, recent studies on Turkish transnational migrants focus on how some Turkish migrants establish their identity representation and belonging while they accommodate themselves into host countries. Although these studies successfully examine the identity representation of Turkish migrants within migration processes, they are limited in their investigations of how migrants' transnational everyday practices and interactions, including economic, cultural and intimate ties and connections, play a role in their identity formation process. This paper provides empirical discussions on this issue, drawing from qualitative interviews with transnational Turkish migrants. This paper (i) explores how migration can influence transnational Turkish migrants to constitute their identity while interacting with different everyday practices, emotions, and relationships, and (ii) investigates the resolution of the tension between participants' authentic self and presentational self affecting their identity-formation in between Turkish and English transnational spaces.

356   The fluidity of return: Changes of (im-)mobility aspirations by returnees in the Casamance, Senegal

Philipp Roman Jung and Amadou Mballo

For long return migration has been understood as a relatively straightforward process, in which migrants return to the place where they "belong" to, without encountering any major obstacles for their "reintegration" there. However, more recent studies have shown that return is neither a linear process nor is a successful post return "reintegration" guaranteed. The latter often depends on how migrants return, but also on how they left in the first place, and what they carry in their "baggage" (e.g. financial means for future project, the support of the family or the repayment of debts related to the migration etc.) (Kleist, 2020). In other words, the entirety of the migration cycle influences the way how returnees manage to reintegrate socially and economically at their place of origin (Kuschminder, 2022). Furthermore, return decisions should be conceptualised as open and fluid. In the literature on migration aspirations/intentions and migrant trajectories, the non-linearity of migration processes and the dynamic nature of migration decisions has been well documented. With the exception of work on transnationalism and return (Carling & Erdal, 2014; Sinatti, 2011), little is known about the fluidity of return. However, the reasons for the development of re-emigration aspirations by returnees cannot be found only in transnationalism. Unsuccessful reintegration or difficulties to readapt to the circumstances, or the sudden appearance of opportunities for international movement may trigger aspirations to migrate again. Furthermore, the circumstances within which aspirations and intention to move or to stay develop may change gradually over time or suddenly due to specific events. The same counts for individual characteristics and social relations that interact with the structural forces in the development of aspirations.

For this article, we analyse how and why (im-)mobility aspirations by return migrants in the Casamance region, Senegal, may change over time. Using longitudinal data from qualitative interviews with returnees and their family members conducted during two periods of fieldwork, 2019 and 2022/23, we compare their situation with regards to their social and economic reintegration, and seek to determine how possible changes have impacted their aspirations. Furthermore, we analyse how important developments of the last years like the COVID 19 pandemic, high inflation, and the rise of the cost of living, as well as the peace treaty between the Senegalese government and the Movement of Democratic Forces of Casamance from 2021, have influenced their projects and aspirations.

References

Carling, J., & Erdal, M. B. (2014). Return Migration and Transnationalism: How Are the Two Connected? International Migration, 52(6), 2-12. doi:https://doi.org/10.1111/imig.12180

Kleist, N. (2020). Trajectories of involuntary return migration to Ghana: Forced relocation processes and post-return life. Geoforum, 116, 272-281. doi:https://doi.org/10.1016/j.geoforum.2017.12.005

Kuschminder, K. (2022). Reintegration strategies. In R. King & K. Kuschminder (Eds.), Handbook of Return Migration (pp. 200-211). Cheltenham: Edward Elgar Publishing.

Sinatti, G. (2011). 'Mobile Transmigrants' or 'Unsettled Returnees'? Myth of Return and Permanent Resettlement among Senegalese Migrants. Population, Space and Place, 17, 153-166. doi:10.1002/psp.608

Chair: Suat Dönmez, Istanbul Topkapi University, Turkey

59   Xenophobism a product of jealousy and ignorance? Interrogating the noise surrounding migrants in South Africa using Ubuntu diplomacy

Toyin Adetiba

This paper explores the implications of migration on transnational migrants' identity formation process concerning self-exploration and self-expression. Recent migration studies approach these identities by illustrating connections between the social landscape and migrant identities (Elliott and Urry, 2010; Beck and Beck-Gernsheim, 2014) and investigating the impact of globalisation on migrant identity presentations in different places (Brah, 1996). In particular, recent studies on Turkish transnational migrants focus on how some Turkish migrants establish their identity representation and belonging while they accommodate themselves into host countries. Although these studies successfully examine the identity representation of Turkish migrants within migration processes, they are limited in their investigations of how migrants' transnational everyday practices and interactions, including economic, cultural and intimate ties and connections, play a role in their identity formation process. This paper provides empirical discussions on this issue, drawing from qualitative interviews with transnational Turkish migrants. This paper (i) explores how migration can influence transnational Turkish migrants to constitute their identity while interacting with different everyday practices, emotions, and relationships, and (ii) investigates the resolution of the tension between participants' authentic self and presentational self affecting their identity-formation in between Turkish and English transnational spaces.

552   'They are here only for the short-term' - How the perception of EU nationals as mobile residents influences their political engagement at local level in post-Brexit England.

Michele Zadra

According to the latest Home Office figures (December 2022), 5.6 million EU nationals have obtained a temporary or permanent permit to live and work in the UK through the EU Settlement Scheme, almost doubling pre-Brexit estimates. For the time being, EU nationals who resided in the UK before Brexit still retain the right to vote and run for office at the local level. However, despite representing over 10% of the population in many British towns, little is known about their engagement with local authorities and their participation in local politics. At the same time, the quick rise of grassroots organisations advocating EU citizens' rights, like the 3million or Settled, has shown how in the aftermath of the Brexit referendum EU citizens have made their entrance into the British political arena. This paper reports the preliminary results of a qualitative study that attempts to fill this gap in the literature about migrants' political participation. The analysis of 49 semi-structured interviews of EU residents, migration experts, Council officers and elected Councillors, conducted in four English local governments, has revealed how Councils tend to consider EU citizens as 'transient economic migrants', self-sufficient and disinterested in local politics, hence less worth engaging if compared to non-EU migrant communities, perceived instead as more permanent and committed to their host society. Because of their former status of mobile citizens, EU nationals appear to be lacking the bonding social capital that has helped other migrant communities to self-organise and become vocal political constituencies for British local institutions. These findings raise important questions about the future political integration of European citizens in post-Brexit England and the capacity of local governments to account for their views and needs in their decision-making process.

235   Migration from Ukraine and EU Migration Policies

Suat Dönmez

In the post-Cold War period, different security issues have come to the agenda with the transformation of the security perception. In this context, the waves of irregular migration due to armed conflicts and economic problems, especially in regions living in internally unstable regions, have gradually begun to affect the migration and migration policies of the European Union countries. In this period, when the risk of conventional war has disappeared, the European Union has started to see migration movements as an essential security issue in the context of new security risks and to harden its policies on migration. Because in the contemporary conjuncture, mass migration has started to be seen as the problem that will affect the public order and socio-economic structure in Europe the most. In this period, migration movements originating, especially in African and Asian countries, have become an essential source of concern. This study aims to examine how the migration policies of the European Union have changed in the recent period and to evaluate the approach taken by this change in the context of the Russian-Ukrainian war. Mass migration movement toward European countries from Ukraine is the central focus of this paper. In this context, while the European Union countries adopted a strict stance against the migration waves from different geographies, they did not depict similar harshness against Ukraine's sudden and mass migration movements. The current migration policies of the European Union and the discourses and statements of the leaders of the European Union countries during the Ukrainian war, and the institutional decisions taken by the EU were examined, and the policy change on the subject was observed. The literature on the subject was reviewed to determine the reasons for this change. In this context, basically, several explanations have been identified. Another issue that draws attention in this context is the role of the FRONTEX organization. This organization has been established primarily for the external land and sea border management, supervision, and security of the European Union countries. The EU did not use this organization against Ukrainian migration as it was actively employed on several occasions previously. With this incident, there may be different ways of flexibility based on the situation where there will not be a standard usage concept.

Keywords: Irregular Migration; European Union Migration policies; Russia-Ukraine war; Ukrainian migrants

7C   Youth, Children and Families 3 [EG17]

Chair: Gökay Özerim, Yaşar University, Turkey

489   We did it for your future: Parental work migration and educational trajectories of their descendants in the home country

Tanja Schroot and Georgiana Udrea

Thousands of children are annually left behind by their parents who work abroad (Unicef 2020). Education plays a major but often ambiguous role for migrants' decisional processes. Many depart for a better work that might not valorise their competences but provides an advantageous economic retribution and thus enhanced educational opportunities for their family. Effects of parental work migration on children's educational trajectories may span from positive to detrimental (Cappelloni 2011). However, the ongoing global health emergency has not solely challenged mobility projects on a local and temporal scale but shifted also decisively migration outputs. Often, migrant parents are exposed to an immense pressure from their family and on societal level, through community and research. Building on these premises and the pronounced need for further research (COE 2020), this paper aims to draw a picture of decisional processes and potential educational outcomes along the life course for different actors involved and calls for a shift from judgemental constructions towards a contextual risk and prospect analysis. The case is exemplified by the Romanian context. Whereas most existing works studied the phenomenon in the home context only (Bezzi 2013) this research builds on a qualitative data analysis, rooted in host and home contexts. It represents thus a bi-fold perspective of 15 migrant mothers living without their children in Italy, and 15 youths currently left behind in Romania by parents working in Italy, Spain and UK.

124   Knowledge Construction of Immigrants in The Digital Age: A Case Study of Young Turkish Immigrants in Germany

Salih Günay

This study examines the role of the media in the construction of political knowledge of young Turkish immigrants within their egocentric networks as a part of their integration process in Germany. A modern approach to media ecology theory is applied in this study to explore young immigrants' media environments. In this study, multiple theoretical perspectives on the debated terms of migration, integration, and political knowledge have been comprehensively examined and presented. A qualitative research method with semi-structured interviews was applied to collect the data for this study. In addition, a qualitative egocentric network approach has been applied to collect data for egocentric networks of young immigrants. The study presents several key findings that young immigrants commonly exist in entertainment-oriented, connection-oriented, and information-seeking media environments. Although there are significant changes in the young immigrants' media environments in respect of habitual, platform-based, and practical behavioral changes, the young immigrants' media environments are completely different from their elders.

Moreover, technological changes or specific features of digital technologies impact the young immigrants' lifestyles, shaping their media environments. In terms of political participation and civic engagement activities, this study explores how young immigrants' participatory activities show diversity in an online-centered world as predictors of political knowledge. Young immigrants heavily benefit from digital technologies to obtain, share, and distribute political knowledge within their social networks. This study provides the results of their egocentric network analysis and interaction process concerning young immigrants' social networks. Finally, this study contributes to the field theoretically and empirically by providing new insights into applying media ecology theory to discuss the construction of political knowledge in the immigrants' integration process by applying egocentric network analysis.

1125   Analyzing the Council of Europe Recommendation on Supporting Young Refugees in Transition to Adulthood

Gökay Özerim

Young refugees face difficulties as they enter adulthood in host countries. The Council of Europe has made a significant recommendation for supporting young refugees in their transition to adulthood, realizing the need for all-encompassing support and direction for this vulnerable population. The goal of this essay is to analyze the Council of Europe recommendation and consider how it may affect young refugees' successful integration and empowerment at this pivotal juncture in their lives.

The Council of Europe Recommendation on Supporting Young Refugees in Transition to Adulthood offers member states a thorough framework for developing policies and initiatives that address the particular needs and difficulties faced by young refugees. The major components and clauses of the recommendation, such as those relating to education, legal standing, health care, housing, employment, and participation in decision-making, will be critically examined in this paper. The purpose of this paper is to provide a thorough understanding of the measures required to support young refugees as they make the difficult transition to adulthood by looking at these components.

This study will analyze the Council of Europe Recommendation and look at the opportunities and problems that come with its application. In order to incorporate the Recommendation into their policies and practices, member states need to adopt a variety of contexts and strategies. The goal of the paper is to shed light on the shortcomings and potential areas for improvement in supporting young refugees as they transition to adulthood by identifying implementation challenges like scarce resources, language barriers, and disparate legal frameworks. Additionally, the paper will highlight noteworthy lessons learned and suggestions for successful implementation from initiatives that have been adopted by various member states.

498   Age Assessments: Blurring the Lines of Childhood to Adulthood

Monique Mehmi

In the United Kingdom, there has been an influx of unaccompanied asylum-seeking children (UASC) arriving via many routes. Upon arrival, many people who claim they are children are age disputed and undergo a protracted process, which potentially leaves them with a precarious immigration status. Those children are deemed to be some of the most vulnerable people in society and require appropriate support from the Government, Home Office and Local Authorities. Since the enactment of the Nationality and Borders Act 2022, there has been vast uncertainty for UASC who arrive in the United Kingdom, especially without documentation. This Act introduced the use of scientific methods to be used by the Secretary of State and Local Authorities, which in essence violate the human rights of UASC. This project aims to examine how age assessments are used as instruments to dispute unaccompanied asylum-seeking children's (UASC) ages, when they enter the United Kingdom. This will be achieved by three objectives; To scrutinize the law and policy around age assessments to attempt to show if current law revokes children's rights in this context; To explore how age assessments are used to disrupt children's rights in the social care context; To apply the theory of vulnerability to UASC and age assessments to explore the possibility of blurring the lines of childhood and adulthood.

7D   Migration, Agency and Insecurity [UG13]

Chair: Deniz Yetkin Aker, Tekirdağ Namık Kemal University, Turkey

499   What Hinders Migrant Agency? Policy Implications for Fair Migration within the framework of the Western Balkans Regulation

Miriam Raab and Mariella Falkenhain

Temporary migration programmes (TMP) have been criticised in migration studies for putting migrants at risk of social exclusion and exploitation due to their vulnerable position and restricted rights (Bauböck & Ruhs 2021), while other scholars reject the notion of victimhood and highlight migrants' agency instead (Alberti 2014). Focusing on migration to Germany on the basis of the Western Balkans regulation, we want to discuss how migrant agency is hindered and which policy implications are necessary to both protect and enable labour migrants. Starting out as a TMP, the Western Balkans regulation allows migrants from Albania, Bosnia and Herzegovina, Kosovo, Montenegro, North Macedonia and Serbia to pursue employment in Germany provided they hold a valid work contract. While liberal in its access to the labour market, the regulation causes many administrative insecurities for the migrants. Drawing from qualitative interviews with 42 labour migrants working in Germany on the basis of the Western Balkans regulation, 44 German employers and 21 representatives of the state administration, we encountered a broad spectrum of migrants' information behaviour and agency as well as several barriers they have to face. These can be personal such as low language skills but are generally the consequences of law restrictions regarding job changes, complicated professional recognition procedures, opaque decisions concerning residence statuses and unequal distribution of information. As the regulation is in discussion to be extended indefinitely and to include further states within the framework of a new German migration law, it is crucial to identify shortcomings and provide enhancements such as increasing the monitoring of employers, facilitating job changes and thoroughly informing migrants about their rights and options.

References

Alberti, G. (2014) Mobility strategies, 'mobility differentials' and 'transnational exit': the experiences of precarious migrants in London's hospitality jobs. Work, Employment and Society 28: 1–17.

Baubӧck, R. and Ruhs, M. (2021) The Elusive Triple Win: Can temporary labour migration dilemmas be settled through fair representation? 2021/60.

267   The Gender Dimensions of Human Security of Forcibly Displaced Refugees in Asia: A Literature Review

Monira Ahsan

Purpose- Drawing on the concept of human security, this paper aims to explore the gendered nature of human security along the economic, food, health, environment, personal, community, and political dimensions of forcibly displaced refugees in Asia.

Methodology/Approach- This literature review is based on the document search for primarily qualitative peer-reviewed studies from several multidisciplinary academic bibliographic, including manual search on disciplinary areas such as refugee studies, forced displacement, migration, and critical feminist literature.

Findings: Reframing peace around human security, this transdisciplinary paper argues for reconceptualising the gendered dimensions of peace and sustainability of forcibly displaced refugees in Asia. Four key findings are critical in designing policies and programmes for forcibly displaced refugees. First, both gender-specific needs, as well as the underlying gender relations, are significantly essential, considering that these relations can be changed during displacement and or as a result of humanitarian-development interventions. Second, an intersectional analysis of gender with other indicators such as age, class, education, ability, location, ethnicity, religion, sexuality, and other contextual indicators that cause disadvantages need to be addressed, which requires collecting disaggregated data and structural gender-sensitive analysis of the multilayered human security situation of the subjective experiences and perceptions of forcibly displaced refugees. Third, various dimensions of human security are interconnected and therefore require an analysis of each of the seven dimensions for a holistic understanding of the refugee situations for integrated interventions across the humanitarian-development-peace nexus. Fourth, the rapid improvement of communication technology implies that different actors in virtual spaces can shape many aspects of migrants' or refugees' lives across multiple countries, which requires a critical understanding of the forcibly displaced refugees in light of human security in the expanded and intersecting glocal (global-national-local) terrains.

Originality/Value- Despite significant progress in global evidence on and understanding forced displacement, there has been scanty research and analysis of the gendered dimensions of forced displacement in general and in the refugee situation. Moreover, though there has been increasing attention to both the human security concept and developments in gender equality and gender mainstreaming, there is little research and evidence on the overlap between the two areas, the gendered dimensions of human security. A gendered human security perspective helps us to identify better practical implementation challenges to contribute to policies and programmes for promoting inclusive and improved protection, peace and sustainability of refugees in forced displacement settings.

Keywords: Gender equality; Human security; Forced displacement; Migration; Refugees; Asia

Paper type: Literature review

297   Art-informed Methodologies in Refugee and Forced Migration Research from the perspective of research about and with Iranian queer refugees

Nilofar Shidmehr

Overview

My presentation centres on using art-informed methodologies of research such as poetic/narrative inquiry and research-creation in particular creative writing as auxiliary methods of inquiry while doing research with and about people who have experienced forced migration. I base my presentation on an ongoing research project about queer Iranian forced migrants.

Poetic Inquiry (Poetry Creation) and its Viability as an Auxiliary Methodology of Research

I begin with a short presentation of the NQIfFM project, outlining its objectives and the theoretical and methodological framework for achieving them. Negotiating Queer Identities Following Forced Migration (NQIfFM): A Comparative Study of Iranian Queer Refugees Living in Turkey, the UK and Canada is a research project investigating the processes of identity transition of Iranian diasporic queers seeking international protection in countries generally seen as being of transition, destination or resettlement. Running from 2021-2023, it is funded by the ESRC and based at the University of Sussex, UK. I am a pioneer of poetic inquiry and a creative-writing-research scholar who serves as an external research consultant to this project.

After outlining the project, I focus on demonstrating the benefits of adding poetic inquiry to interview and life history studies as primary methodologies employed in this project. Poetry is produced in the workshops I hold with Iranian queer refugees and immigrants in Turkey, the UK, and Canada. The poems are put together in a booklet as an outcome of the project. They will be also included in the project website and a documentary which is another project's output. Moreover, the poems are used as means of gathering, measuring, weighing, and analyzing data that comes from the interviews. As such, they enable a comparative study that can help with advancing knowledge with regard to human rights research and practice.

I am going to present some examples of poetry produced in the research and show the benefits of using poetry in our research. I will argue that poetry gives direct agency to research subjects (Iranian queer refugees) to participate in research production. It also gives the participants a chance to reveal their subtle feelings that don't come through interviews. It empowers them to express their journeys for 'sexual liberty' in verse. Through imagination and metaphor, poetry enables the queer poet refugees to make a dynamic imagination with their lived lives and the ways in which they aspire to form their new identities and challenge immigration processes that re-stigmatise, silence, and exclude them.

484 The International Protection System and Forced Labor of Asylum Seekers and Refugees. Findings from Italy

Natalia Szulc

The theory of structural injustice (SI) according to I.M Young assumes that it exists when institutional actions place people in a situation of constant threat, depriving them of opportunities for development, rights, and intensifying inequality. In this research, SI serves as a bridge between Refugee and Forced Labor Studies. Focusing on the asylum regime - I go beyond the traditional analysis of the problem guided mostly by the vulnerabilities of asylum seekers and refugees (ARs).

The goal was to examine whether and how the international protection system and its various procedures can affect forced labor of ARs (including trafficking for labor exploitation). I consider registration, identification, and multi-level reception procedures and mechanisms in a host state. I identify how they affect the occurrence and forms of the problem.

The results are based on focus groups conducted in Italy and a survey with representatives of two systems: international protection and anti-trafficking. This was supplemented by a two-stage systematic review, and an analysis of court proceedings.

I will present the first results from Italy. The findings allowed to transform the theory of structural injustice and situate the international protection system and forced labor as its relevant examples. The research also resulted in the development of the "safe host country" concept. Driven by the growing demand for Needs Led Research - the results will build practical solutions for policy makers and representatives of the asylum system, anti-trafficking practitioners and the private sector.

7E   L'émigration [UG11]

Chair: Mohamed Khachani, University of Mohammed V, Rabat, Morocco

103   Perception des élèves immigrants des écarts entre les valeurs entre l'école et leurs parents et l'engagement scolaire au secondaire: effet médiateur du sentiment d'appartenance à l'école

Marie-Laure Rulleau, Kristel Tardif-Grenier, Corinne Hébert, Isabelle Archambault

La présence des élèves issus de l'immigration dans les écoles québécoises est importante et croissante. De nombreuses études se sont attardées aux défis auxquels ces élèves font face. Toutefois, ces jeunes peuvent compter sur plusieurs facteurs de résiliences comme l'engagement scolaire qui est fortement associé à la persévérance scolaire ainsi qu'à un plus grand bien-être psychologique (Gonzales et al., 2014; Motti-Stefanidi et al., 2021). Par ailleurs, on sait que le sentiment d'appartenance est un facteur jouant un rôle crucial dans le maintien de l'engagement scolaire à travers le temps (Gillen-O'Neel et Fuligni, 2013).

Les écarts de valeurs famille-école perçus par l'élève pourraient teinter l'engagement scolaire et le sentiment d'appartenance à l'école chez ses élèves. En effet, la recherche montre de plus grands écarts de valeurs sont associés à un plus faible sentiment d'appartenance (Tyler et al., 2008) et que celui-ci peut varier selon la génération d'immigration (Chiu et al., 2012). Les écarts de valeurs pourraient contribuer à expliquer les différences au niveau du sentiment d'appartenance. En raison des différentes valeurs valorisées par leur culture d'origine, les élèves issus de l'immigration vivraient de plus grands écarts que les autres élèves non issus de l'immigration.

L'étude actuelle a pour objectif de documenter si le sentiment d'appartenance au milieu scolaire constitue un médiateur dans la relation entre les écarts de valeurs famille-école et l'engagement scolaire des élèves issus de l'immigration et d'identifier les types d'écarts de valeurs (ex. l'importance de la religion, les activités pédagogiques utilisées) associés à l'engagement scolaire et au sentiment d'appartenance. Elle s'appuie sur un devis transversal qui a été réalisé auprès de 1 598 élèves (57 % = filles), provenant de huit écoles québécoises (Canada) ayant répondu à un questionnaire en ligne (automne 2017 et printemps 2018).

Des modèles de régressions réalisés à l'aide de PROCESS ont permis de tester l'effet médiateur du sentiment d'appartenance au sein de la relation entre les écarts de valeurs et l'engagement scolaire. Puis, des analyses de régressions hiérarchiques ont été réalisées afin de déterminer la relation les différents types d'écarts de valeurs et l'engagement scolaire ainsi que le sentiment d'appartenance.

Les résultats suggèrent la présence d'un effet médiateur du sentiment d'appartenance sur la relation entre les écarts de valeurs et l'engagement comportemental uniquement. De plus, les analyses ont démontré que certains types d'écarts plutôt que d'autres avaient tendance à être associés à l'engagement et au sentiment d'appartenance. En effet, un écart entre les méthodes pédagogiques utilisées à la maison et à l'école, la perception des différences entre les hommes et les femmes ainsi que la perception de ce qu'est une vie réussie étaient associés à un sentiment d'appartenance moins élevé. Les écarts perçus entre les différences hommes-femmes étaient associés à un moins grand engagement comportemental. Les écarts entre les méthodes pédagogiques utilisées étaient associés à un moins grand engagement affectif des élèves.

Cette étude permet de mieux comprendre la perception qu'ont les élèves issus de l'immigration des relations entre les écoles et les familles et leur association avec leur réussite éducative.

443   La relation entre la migration et le développement

Safae Zbat, Zemmouri Ghita, Hakkou El Mehdi

La migration internationale est un sujet de débat quotidien, puisque les conséquences de cettemigration peuvent contribuer au développement inclusif et durable tant dans les pays d'origineet aussi de destination.Par ailleurs, un ensemble de théoriciens ont pu traiter la thématique migratoire et sa relationavec le développement, en se penchant sur l'intention de migrer des individus et ce quipeuvent apporter en termes de développement pour leur propre pays et aussi de destination.Selon Ehrenberg et Smith (1997), les facteurs à l'origine des inégalités, notamment au seindes sociétés d'origine, montrent que les décisions migratoires s'inscrivent dans un contextesocial, économique et politique.Adams et Richard (2003) montrent que la migration internationale peut avoir un effet négatifsur le développement économique des pays d'origine. De plus, le rapatriement de l'argent desmigrants peut entraîner une augmentation de la demande de biens importés au détriment desbiens produits localement, ce qui n'aurait pas d'effet multiplicateur sur l'économie.En outre, cette relation a fait l'objet d'étude de plusieurs auteurs et plusieurs documentssurtout officiels en parlent, par rapport à un ensemble de facteurs et leurs résultats. Pour cefaire, nous allons nous appuyer d'une part, sur la revue empirique.D'après l'étude d'Abderrahim Saidane dans sa thèse, en se basant sur une enquête menée parla banque mondiale au Burkina Faso en 2010 auprès de 2102 ménages, les transferts de fonds

des migrants burkinabés vers leur pays d'origine ont potentiellement un impact positif sur lacroissance économique à travers l'investissement dans des activités économiques ainsi que laréduction de la pauvreté dans les milieux ruraux plus particulièrement. Toutefois, l'inégalitédes revenus reste intacte étude de Borjas

(2014), intitulée Immigration Economics, à travers des enquêtes auprèsdes ménages et les données fiscales, ainsi que des modèles économiques. Les travailleurs peuqualifiés subissent des pertes de revenus en raison de la concurrence accrue sur le marché dutravail, tandis que les travailleurs hautement qualifiés bénéficient d'une augmentation de lademande de travail dans les secteurs liés à l'immigration. L'impact net de l'immigration surl'économie américaine est positif, mais il est important de mettre en place des politiques pouraider les travailleurs les plus vulnérables.Finalement, cet article consistera à la fin, une étude de cas qui reposera sur une comparaisonde l'impact de la migration sur le développement d'un pays du sud et celui du nord, en sebasant sur des données qui vont être expliquer sous forme d'un modèle économétrique.

567   Le contexte migratoire dans l'espace euro-mediterraneen: pour une gestion concertee des flux

Mohamed Khachani

Depuis 1990, les flux d'émigration légale vers les pays de destination traditionnels en Europe ont fortement régressé, les réseaux clandestins ont pris le relais des circuits légaux. Les dispositions prises à la suite de la convention d'application des accords de Schengen signée en juin 1990 (établissement de visas, contrôles rigoureux aux frontières, système très sélectif de délivrance de permis de travail,…) ont réduit l'émigration légale.

Au vu de ce constat, ne serait–il pas plus humain de définir une autre politique d'immigration moins controversée en pensant à une gestion organisée de «d'ordre migratoire» entre les deux rives de la Méditerranée. Ceci permettrait d'atteindre cet objectif tant souhaitée d' « une migration sûre, ordonnée et régulière », comme le stipule le Pacte Mondial dont la plupart des pays de l'UE sont signataires. Mais cela semble butter contre un certain nombre de paradoxes de la politique migratoire européenne. Plusieurs facteurs militent pour une gestion concertée des flux.

-Les dérapages d'une politique focalisée sur des mesures restrictives et l'externalisation de la question migratoire. Les restrictions réglementaires apportées à la circulation des étrangers ont moins empêché les entrées qu'elles n'ont entravé les déplacements de va et vient.

- Une demande de travail spécifique existe dans les pays de l'Union Européenne, celle-ci répond, pour des raisons de coût et de flexibilité, aux besoins du marché de l'emploi.

-Le manque de canaux légaux stimule l'irrégularité de l'emploi : La migration irrégulière se voit ainsi stimulée par l'excès de demande en Europe de main d'oeuvre non qualifiée et par le manque de canaux légaux pour couvrir ladite demande. En fait, le marché s'est avéré plus fort pour engendrer des flux que les États pour les réguler.

- Le défi démographique Il s'agit ici de rappeler l'apport de la migration face aux perspectives des déficits démographiques dans les pays de la rive nord.

- Cette dialectique du rejet juridique et de l'appel économique a favorisé le développement des réseaux mafieux qui se sont installés de part et d'autre de la Méditerranée et tout au long de l'itinéraire migratoire pour assurer leurs services à des prix exorbitants.

- Cette politique a un coût élevé pour les contribuables européens : D'importants moyens sont mobilisés pour accompagner les politiques de lutte contre la migration irrégulière à travers la création d'institutions dépendant de la commission ou créées par des États de l'Union.

- L'immigration irrégulière engendre un manque à gagner pour les Etats des pays d'accueil La migration légale contribue à la lutte contre le travail au noir, permet à l'Etat de bénéficier de versements d'impôts et accule les entrepreneurs à verser des contributions sociales

- Cette politique a aussi un coût très élevé en vies humaines, car cette aventure est très périlleuse. La Méditerranée est devenue ainsi le plus grand cimetière du monde.

- Enfin, du point de vue géostratégique, l'Union Européenne ne peut pas continuer à prospérer avec à ses flanc Sud et Est des poches de misère. Une attitude solidaire de la part des pays de l'UE est nécessaire.

7F   Migration History [BG3/4]

Chair: Caner Tekin, Ruhr University, Bochum, Germany

261   Refugees Rehabilitation in Pakistan 1947-1961: Process, Policies and Execution

Nayyer Abbas

The research paper sheds light on major contours of the rehabilitation process undertaken by the state during 1947-1961 in Pakistan. Rehabilitation of the refugees after the partition was one of the biggest challenges in front of the nascent state of Pakistan. The general accounts provided a very simple picture of the very complex and varied history of displacement and resettlement of millions of Muslim refugees in Pakistan after the migration from India in 1947. Migration patterns varied from East Bengal to different provinces of West Pakistan, and further complicated by class and gender issues; the 'everyday state' accounts of refugee resettlement and rehabilitation contradicted, at different scale, to the official narrative. The process of settlement was very diverse as compared to uniform as generally perceived. The plans and policies for the settlement of the migrants for this region are covered in this article. This research will not only provide insight into the rehabilitation process but also be helpful to understand socio-economic changes in Pakistan in post-partition period. This research is based on the fresh sources drawn from the Punjab Archive Lahore, the Commissioner office Lahore, British Library, and the National Archives-Kew Gardens, London. Finally, it will link with the literature on the concept of the 'everyday state' and oral history accounts. This raises the issues of citizenship and refugee status, the issue of 'corruption' and highly differentiated experiences of partition-related refugees in west Punjab in general and in Toba Tek Singh in specific.

417   The history of the migration industry – how had the employers been supported in sourcing the workforce

Kamil Matuszczyk and Sara Bojarczuk

As international labour migration accelerated, massified and diversified, migration brokers played an increasingly important role in facilitating mobility. Globally, an organised transnational business, nowadays referred to as the migration industry, emerged at the turn of the 20th century. From the beginning of its development, it was formed by a broad group of profit-oriented actors who, as third parties in labour relations, were responsible for matching workers (would-be migrants) with employers with a demand for foreign labour. For a variety of motives, a significant proportion of migrants chose to use either formal or informal intermediaries who, in both Global North and Global South countries, had an increasing influence on immigrant labour market allocation.

The aim of the presentation will be to show which configurations of the relationship between employers and migration intermediaries occurred in industrial and post-industrial countries. Using and elaborating on the dichotomous classification of these relationships presented by Philip Martin (2017), I will explain their evolution from the one-way provision of workers by migration agents to specialised global corporations offering a range of additional services to clients (employers and workers). During the presentation, I would like to outline the three main positions that intermediaries have taken: agents, partners and allies. Drawing on selected case studies from labour migration, both of low and highly skilled foreign workers, I argue for the professionalisation of intermediary services as well as the creation of lasting relationships with employer-clients. To the best of the authors' knowledge, the paper presented here is one of the first attempts to comprehensively capture the development of the migration industry and is part of the academic discussion on the commercialisation process of international labour migration.

513   Turkish Migrant Activism at Plant Level: Works Council Elections in Ford Cologne

Caner Tekin

Migration and labour history of Turkish workers in Federal Germany is a topic of a large literature, but not much light has been shed on the interplays between guest workers and German trade unions in factories. If anything, the participation of the Turkish workers in works council elections, either on the side of or against trade unions, was an early example of democratic participation. Based on the archive material about the work council elections in the Cologne Ford factory during the 1970s and 1980s, the paper discusses the key attitudes raised within the Turkish unionist and conservative groups towards how to engage German trade unions at companies. In brief, the federal government's migration policy, IG Metall's attitudes towards migrants, as well as mobilisation strategies of the politicised migrant groups at the company underpinned conflicting disputes about the idea of democratic participation through works council elections.

Keywords: Turkish Migrant Organisations, Works Council Elections, trade union participation, migrant activism at plant level

11:00-11:15 BREAK

8A   Reframing the Dynamics of Transformations in Diverse Spaces Within Uneven Migration Regimes [UG13]

Chair: Mary Rose Geraldine A. Sarausad, Asian Institute of Technology, Thailand

1103   Fathering and Social Integration among Japanese Migrant Men in Japanese-Filipino Families: An Ethnographic Inquiry

Jocelyn Celero

Japanese-Filipino families are historically one of the major outcomes of Filipino women's migration to Japan, or Japanese men's migration the Philippines since the 1970s. Intercultural encounters between Japanese and Filipinos have resulted in intimate unions, producing second and 1.5 generation Japanese-Filipinos who are born and socialized in and between Japanese and Filipino societies. Existing literature examining Japanese-Filipino transnational family formation predominantly has focused on the migratory experiences of Filipino women as entertainers and marriage migrants in Japan. Little research has focused on the role of Japanese men in intermarriages outside of Japan (e.g. Tokoro 2016).

Departing from previous studies that problematize their parental absence, the proposed ethnographic research looks into their migratory and family lives of Japanese men who moved to the Philippines over the last two decades. It focuses on the impact of the Philippines on gender norms, fathering practices, and familial relations. Building on the concept of positive masculinity (Kiselica et. al, 2016), this study seeks evidence of how the parenting approaches of Japanese fathers enable them to integrate to the socio-economic and cultural spaces of the Filipino society, negotiating the socio-economic, cultural and moral expectations of the receiving context.

1104   Creative Practices by Russian-speaking Migrant Artists in Japan: Negotiating Gender, Belonging, and Self-fulfillment

Ksenia Golovina

Migrant artists working on themes related and unrelated to the experience of migration have been reported to have a positive impact on the vitality of urban spaces and the attraction of local artists. Art has also proven to be an important tool for the consolidation of migrant communities and for diaspora activities in the political and cultural spheres. On a personal level, art plays a crucial role in building intimate relationships with the environment and thus has the potential to facilitate the integration of migrants. Art is also a means of self-fulfillment, both when a migrant is employed in the arts or elsewhere, but especially in a situation where employment in the local market has not been achieved. Based on fieldwork consisting of object-oriented interviews, home visits, participant observation and cyberethnography, this paper examines the situation of Russian-speaking migrant artists in Japan. For some of the informants, migration to Japan was associated with the loss of creative workspace, students, and artistic income. For others, however, migration meant rediscovering themselves as artists based on their past experiences or training. For most of the informants, themes emerged such as the need to organize one's space for making art in Japan and to adapt to changes in art forms and materials. Some of the artists stated that they had experienced a surge of creativity since migrating, attributing it not only to the novelty of the move but also to the beauty of the Japanese landscape. Art gave them a sense of self-fulfillment and opened up avenues for appropriating the environment through its intimate depiction. Others, reflecting on the negative aspect of art making, noted that it provided them with a form of escapism, allowing them to avoid contact with the locals and slowing down integration. In light of these findings, this paper aims to explore the gender aspect of these artists' journeys and to identify differences in the experiences of men and women. To this end, the paper examines the individual motivations for making art, the place that art practices occupy in these individuals' lives, the accessible opportunities for self-fulfillment and promotion of their work, the negotiations with family members around making and exhibiting art, and their visions of themselves as artists in the future. The study found that compared to men, migrant women use their art skills and products more proactively to connect with Japanese society and the migrant community in the role of community members rather than artists. In the case of mixed couples, men find more support from their Japanese wives to pursue art as a profession, while women's art activities are more often marginalized as hobbies by their Japanese spouses. The paper aims to shed light on how gender influences migrants' artistic lives and creations, and what strategies both genders use to navigate the host society as migrants and artists.

1106   Migration Management and Bordering Practices in Thailand and Vietnam

Mary Rose Geraldine A. Sarausad and Reinaruth D. Carlos

The socioeconomic and political landscape of many host countries are ever changing. Therefore, the systems that shape the migration process are also transformed which sometimes leave migrants with limited options. In Thailand and Vietnam, narratives of some Filipino teachers interviewed in the study revealed how borders have not only encouraged but also constrained them and other teachers from fully achieving their goals because of changing migration policies. Moreover, the experience of bordering practices plays an important role in the lives of migrants as these affect their ability to access employment and social welfare as well as in incorporating themselves in the host country. This paper applies a theoretical and methodological framework in exploring the concept of bordering practices and its relationship with migration management, and how this developed with the current migration policies in both countries. Within this framework, border spaces can also be understood through the various ways in which the Filipino teachers in the study are affected by their experiences as border crossers particularly when the COVID-19 pandemic disrupted mobility within and across borders.

1105   Social Integration of International Marriage Migrants: Comparative Analysis of Russian-Speaking Females' Experiences in Japan and South Korea

Viktoriya Kim and Natalya Yem

This paper aims to analyze difficulties that accompany integration processes of international marriage migrants in Japan and South Korea. Despite both countries positioning as homogenous societies and limiting influx of large number of international migrants, their stance is more positive toward (female) marriage migrants. However, migration policies and absence of such, as well as the local family structures still create obstacles for foreign female integration in the local society. This paper is based on the authors' qualitative data collected in the period of 2007 to 2014 with women from former Soviet Union countries, who were married to South Korean (54) and Japanese men (50). In this presentation, we introduce the concept of integration, review migration policies and attitudes toward marriage migration in both countries, as well as analyze women's individual experiences of multicultural programs. We argue that there is a need for comprehensive policies that will address (marriage) migrants' needs in the early stages of migration and empower them in the process of settlement in the receiving society.

8B   Theory and Methods in Migration Studies 4 [UG11]

Chair: H. Yaprak Civelek, Anadolu University, Turkey

193   The statistical immigrant: Immigration statistics in the Danish welfare state

Heidi Vad Jønsson

Immigration statistics has played a significant role in Danish and Scandinavian political debates for decaedes. While some policy makers have used immigration statistics to argue for a more restrictive immigration policy, others have questioned the legitimacy of "the immigrant" as a statistical category. Since the 1980s one of the key discussions in immigration debates has evolved around numbers and categorizations. Should immigration policies regulate entrance based on quotas?

Was the number of newcomers a problem or was the lack of integration measures the biggest issue to be solved by policies? In its essence, Danish immigration debates evolved around opposing problemdefinitions and diverging categorizations. In this process statistical knowledge became an important, powerful and highly contested tool of governance. Hence migration statistics received increased attention from the mid 1990s and in this process "the statistical immigrant" emerged as a category that could be used politically. This paper focuses on this important part of immigration policies and explores the historical development of "immigrants" as a statistical category in Denmark since the 1990s.

139   Comparative Geographical Analysis of Transnational Social Spaces: Georgian Diasporas in the USA and Latvia

Ia Iashvili and Tinatin Gvenetadze

Georgia, the post-Soviet country in the South Caucasus, has a population of slightly more than 3.7 million people. Georgian exodus is the phenomenon of the last three decades when the country started its transition to the market economy. Even though, during the Soviet era 96,4 % of all ethnic Georgians lived in the Georgian SSR (Gachechiladze, 1997) and the nation never was distinguished with active outmigration, moves of labour migration between the all union republics were not limited. However, after the dissolution of the Soviet empire amid political and economic crises, the international labour migration appeared the only way for many nationals to survive. After the 1990s the modest Georgian community that existed in former Soviet Latvia was filled with new arrivals, while in the USA Georgian's mass emigration resulted in the foundation of large diasporas and creation of transnational social spaces (Faist, 2013, 46). Transnationalism is a lifestyle and a "strategy of survival and betterment" by a migrant (a transmigrant) that spans international borders of more than one country, keeps homeland-host country ties and activities (Faist, 2013, 7). This paper aims to give the comparative analysis of Georgian Diasporas and transnational social spaces in two destination countries of Latvia and America. As our comparative study on Georgian outmigration flows from the Soviet era up today is being conducted for the first time, the presented issue is relevant. The selection of the target countries was motivated, on the one hand, by the research experience in the USA (2015-2021), where immigrants from independent Georgia form several community associations, and on the other hand, by the study of Soviet and post-Soviet Georgian immigration in Latvia, which we got the opportunity to do in 2022. The subject of the research is the Georgian diasporas in the USA and Latvia, while the target groups are members of these communities. The objectives of the research are to study the structure of the Georgian diasporas in the target countries (transformation in space and time) and transnational social spaces they create; at the same time to determine the degree of integration of the Georgian community through the involvement/less involvement of its members in the local societies and institutions of the host countries. Our key question is: what are the main differences in the level of integration of the Georgian diasporas in the USA and Latvia? In the research we refer to the theoretical concept of transnationalism by Nina Glick-Shiller (Glick-Shiller, et al., 1992) and the Diaspora theory by W. Suffran (1991). We practice qualitative research methods, particularly in-depth interviews with Georgian community members and field experts and discourse analysis. Due to well established connections since the Soviet period, the study confirmed our hypothesis about a higher degree of integration of the Georgians in Latvia than in the USA. Our research will contribute to the literature on diaspora studies and transnational social space.

140   Brazilian population abroad: the process of research and construction of a data virtual platform about Brazilian emigration

Camila Escudero

The goal of this text is to present the project "Brazilian population abroad – Data virtual platform about Brazilian emigration", the initial result of the academic-scientific research "Brazilian emigrants: Communication networks in the identification of the profile, living conditions, forms of organization and construction of identities", which began in Brazil, in 2022. It is an information base, with public and free access, about the subject of Brazilian emigration, with the objectives: 1) systematizing, organizing and giving visibility to data involving the presence of Brazilian population abroad; 2) serve as a point of support in the articulation of emigrants and community leaders, researchers, nonprofits organizations and government spheres involved with the theme.

The project was developed based on the follow three perceptions during previous work (IOM, 2021): 1) the fragility of concrete data and knowledge about the profile of the Brazilian emigrant population, even with a qualitative approach, estimated at 4.215.800 people (MRE, 2021) ; 2) the fact of Brazilian emigration process to be considered recent – it was only from the 1980s that Brazil, recognized throughout its history as a country of immigration, with the arrival of foreigners contributing to the formation of its national identity (Ribeiro, 1995), passed to be considered a country of emigration; 3) the interdisciplinarity of the theme, in general, studies on international migration processes are dispersed in several areas of knowledge, and occur in a trans and interdisciplinary way, in an "epistemological itinerary" (Sayad, 1998).

The idea is that "Brazilian population abroad – Data virtual platform about Brazilian emigration" will function as a kind of "observatory". In a virtual website format[1], released in February 2023, the platform was built based on concepts of architecture and information for the treatment of digital environments (Nielsen; Loranger, 2007), as well as composed with content resulting from bibliographic (Stumpf, 2011) and documentary (Moreira, 2011) researches. The material was systematized into categories, according to aspects of Thematic Analysis (Escudero, 2020): 1) Studies and research; 2) Legislation; 3) Demographic estimates; 4) Financial remittances[2].

It is intended, therefore, from the visualization and knowledge of the data, to stimulate the performance of theoretical and empirical interdisciplinary researches, from a transnational and intercultural perspectives, which explore the profile of the emigrant community abroad, its characteristics, demands, ways of social and economic organization and performance, networking, cultural practices, public policies, innovation and impact, as well as issues related to sustainable development.

References

Available in: www.brasileirosnoexterior.org.

We hope to improve new categories with future platform updates.

66   Embodied waste laborer: A study of identity, value, and social integration among Pakistanis in a Hong Kong's informal street economy

Terence Chun Tat Shum

While Hong Kong's economic affluence has given rise to mass consumption and mass-waste lifestyles among one sector of the population, the lower strata of society struggle to survive. Waste is often associated with dirt, uselessness, and redundancy; the people who work with it are therefore perceived as dirty, invaluable, and underprivileged. For more than a decade, a subset of the Pakistani population—a dominant South Asians in Hong Kong—has been appropriating this urban space during the late afternoons and evenings, creating a living from their marginalized social position as ethnic minorities who work with waste. This research examines their roles and activities in this "unregulated" part of the urban economy. Specifically, it explores the reasons behind their participation in the informal second-hand trade.

Drawing from in-depth interviews and participant observation with Pakistani informal waste laborers in the second-hand markets of Hong Kong, this research proposes the concept of "embodied waste laborer" to examine the embodied experience of waste work among Pakistani laborers in Hong Kong. It explores how the waste trade is carried out by the bodily efforts of Pakistani laborers and what the work is aiming to achieve. "Embodied waste laborer" refers to a site for skill production and value transformation that is actualized through the working body of Pakistanis positioned in relation to wasted consumer goods, people, the environment, and situations that confront them within an informal ethnic enclave. This site demonstrates how their informal work is performed, perceived, and challenged in the context of urban spatial ordering.

108   Complexity of parenthood in forced migration: Risk, commitment and moral concerns

Lejla Sunagic

The paper explores a complexity of the role of parents in forced migration and the moral considerations surrounding their migration choices. It is based on the reflections of Syrians who embarked on perilous sea migrations to Europe by focusing on their perceptions of their role as parents. The narratives often began with a justification of the risks taken, grounded in their commitment to securing a better future for their children. In that sense, the parents believed that sea migration was necessary to ensure their children's well-being, protect them from the traumas of war, and provide them with educational opportunities. Their reflection for the decision to migrate was intertwined with moral discourse centred around the protective nature of parenthood. However, parents who undertook the journey with their children faced a paradox inherent in the contradiction between their narrative positions: On one hand, they aimed to emphasize a social virtue by deciding to take risk with high stakes for the sake of their children's well-being; on the other hand, they acknowledged that they inadvertently had exposed their children to life-threatening danger. As a result of the paradox, their cognition oscillated between the functional attributes of migration embodied in achieved desired outcome and emotional attributes of the migration. The conclusion discusses the inevitability of placing moral considerations of parenthood in the framework of the migration policy governing forced migration. It suggests that moral dilemmas of individual risk takers in migration cannot be explores without raising issue of ethics of migration governance.

Key words: forced migration; risk; parenthood

8C   Education and Skilled Migration 3 [EG17]

Chair: Pascual Garcia, Universidad Técnica Particular de Loja, Ecuador

237   The Determinants of Migration Intention of the Healthcare Professionals in Morocco: An Econometric Analysis

Boutaina Idrissi and Sara Kawkaba

The health crisis that affected the world in 2020 revealed, among other things, the state of hospitals (lack of equipment, medicines, beds in intensive care units) and particularly highlighted the shortage of medical and nursing staff. It was also an opportunity to recall a little-known reality about the presence of health professionals with foreign degrees, particularly in Europe facilitated by a policy of attraction and migration chosen to attract more doctors and other health professionals to meet their needs in this sector.

In order to assess the intention of migration among professional healthcare and the push and pull factors that could encourage them to leave Morocco. A survey was conducted in 2022 that targeted 355 professional healthcare in the health public system in Morocco (doctors, nurses and paramedical staff (other than nurses) practicing particularly in the main hospital structures in Morocco including the University Hospital of Casablanca (hospital 20 August 1953) and the Regional Hospital of Health El Ghassani Hospital of Fez.

This paper aims to assess the key determinants of migration intention of healthcare professionals based on an econometric analysis by relying on several explanatory variables. Indeed, the migration intention can be formalized by a discrete choice structure where the health worker i intends to migrate $Y_i = 1$ if the health worker intends to migrate or $Y_i = 0$ If not. Since a variable is between the values 0 and 1, we need to use categorical variable econometrics.

The two most commonly used statistical distributions are the logistic distribution and the normal distribution, which then give the binary categorical models called Logit and Probit. In the case of this research, both models give equivalent econometric results. We have chosen to present the results of the Logit model since it offers an advantage in terms of parameter estimation technique and its mathematical basis is relatively simple.

490   Education and Mobility in the lifelong learning construct

Tanja Schroot and Roberta Ricucci

In 2016, the EU-Commission formulated and published the New Skills Agenda for Europe that calls local, regional and national policymakers and stakeholders for action to combat unemployment and to increase resilience on political and economic predicaments through competence formation.

The action plan strove to strengthen "human capital, employability and competitiveness" and increased labour market participation to overcome a situation where "skills gaps and mismatches are striking" (COM 2016). Missing, unrecognised or non-utilised qualifications elicits a situation that prevents from progress, innovation, economic growth and stability in the Union.

Recent data confirms that rather than skill production efficient skill utilisation represents one of the main challenges on the European labour market. Indeed, almost 40% of all non-European citizens and 30% of nationals of other European countries turn out to be over-qualified for the job they are performing (Eurostat 2023).

The European Commission reacts with the continuous promotion of the education-mobility nexus, that suggests high quality education as driver for spatial mobility and vice versa towards individual and economic growth. This has challenged provisions, thought and action patterns on individual, institutional and national level. Accordingly, this paper aims to embed the figure of the contemporary 'knowledgeable' mover into the thematic complex of a 21st century educational paradigm.

The discussion is thus set in an overall discourse on competencies as promoted by the European Commission and thus legal, socio-cultural and economic dispositions towards a European knowledge society, aspirations towards competence transfer, formulations of new skills wanted and concrete action lines pursued.

472   Discrimination Perception of International Students During their Internship and Graduate Schemes Applications in the UK

Musa Kandemir, Sabrina Colombo, Ibrahim Sirkeci

International students are skilled immigrants, and they bring a high level of human capital to the host countries. They contribute to society and organizations in a variety of ways, such as by broadening the environment and raising knowledge of various cultures in both the host and the home country. International students are educated immigrants who contribute highly skilled labour to their host countries.

This study addresses the experiences of international students in the context of internships and graduate schemes, which have become a necessity rather than an option for students to increase their competitive advantage in the labour market. The aim of this study is to reveal discrimination perceptions of the international students from Birmingham Business School and Aston Business School during their internship and graduate schemes searches.

This is a qualitative study and the researcher conducted 14 semi-structured interviews. The participants were recruited with convenience sampling and snowballing sampling techniques. After the qualitative content analysis, four themes emerged. These themes are nonending disadvantages, uncovered expectations, damaged confidence, and uncertainty. While most of the students claimed that they have not felt any discrimination, they claimed that they are in a disadvantageous position in the UK in several aspects which also can be seen by codes, categories, and themes.

8D   Migration, Law and Policy 8 [EG15/16]

Chair: *Ülkü Sezgi Sözen, Universität Hamburg, Germany*

1130   Fachkräfte-Einwanderungsgesetz von einer anwaltlichen Sicht

Martin Manzel

1131   Fachkräfte-Einwanderung aus der Recruiting-Praxis

Hayriye Yerlikaya-Manzel

1132   Zuwanderung nach Deutschland aus der Perspektive einer Fachkraft

Aysenur Kölgesiz

8E   Docentes Inmigrantes [BG3/4] VIRTUAL ACCESS

Chair: *Natalia Ferrada Quezada, Universidad de Santiago de Chile, Chile*

1109   Tendencias de la literatura sobre el profesorado inmigrante: ¿dónde está el foco?

Natalia Ferrada Quezada y Cherie Flores Fernández

Se exploran las características bibliométricas de la investigación sobre la inmigración de profesores. Los documentos indexados se recuperaron de la base de datos Scopus y se analizaron con el programa informático VOSviewer. Se estudiaron 700 artículos que representaban a 55 países y 160 revistas. Se oberva que la literatura en el área comienza a aumentar desde 2017, siendo Estados Unidos, Canadá y China los países con mayor producción en este campo. La mayoría de los artículos se publicaron en revistas de educación y estudios culturales. Las instituciones más activas en publicaciones fueron de Sudáfrica y Canadá. Si bien hay autores en el área que destacan por sobre otros, no se observaron grandes productores de investigación, además de que la colaboración entre investigadores es escasa. No se encontraron referencias a países Latinoamericanos a pesar del aumento de su población migrante en los últimos años en esta región. Estos resultados sugieren la la realización de estudios locales y en colaboración para profundizar el conocimiento sobre esta minoría y desarrollar políticas públicas adecuadas para poblaciones cada vez más diversas.

1110 ¿Qué nos dice la literatura acerca de las iniciativas para incorporar profesores inmigrantes al sistema escolar?

Natalia Ferrada Quezada y Cherie Flores Fernández

Se presentan los resultados de una Scoping Review que examina las iniciativas que permiten acceder y permanecer en la profesión docente a los profesores inmigrantes. Para responder a las preguntas: ¿Cúales son las iniciativas? y ¿Cuáles son sus características? se utiliza el protocolo del Instituto Johanna Briggs y el PRISMA-Scr. La búsqueda bibliográfica se efectuó en ocho bases de datos, seleccionándose 27 documentos publicados entre 2006 y 2021. Se observó una gran cantidad de estudios realizados entorno al profesorado inmigrante, sin embargo, solo unos pocos han estudiado las iniciativas de acceso y permanencia a la profesión en los países de acogida. También, la investigación en este campo está desequilibrada entre regiones o estados particulares, siendo las iniciativas más estudiadas las de recertificación. Se concluye como necesario ampliar la investigación relacionada con la retención del profesorado inmigrante.

1111 Los profesores inmigrantes en Chile desde sus experiencias profesionales

Natalia Ferrada Quezada y Cherie Flores Fernández

En Chile, los estudios sobre inmigración y escuela se han enfocado mayoritariamente en investigar a los estudiantes inmigrantes, pero no han puesto su foco en los educadores que logran reinsertarse en las escuelas. Datos recientes informan que en el período 2015-2020 aumentó en un 218,9 % la participación de los y las docentes inmigrantes en el sistema escolar. En este trabajo se presentan los resultados preliminares de un proyecto de investigación que busca analizar las experiencias profesionales de 8 profesores inmigrantes que se desempeñan en los niveles de educación primaria y secundaria en diversas dependencias escolares. Se utiliza un diseño fenomenológico con un alcance exploratorio y descriptivo. Para recoger la información se efectuaron dos focus group virtuales. Los resultados señalan que los profesores, en su mayoría, no contaron con redes de apoyo e información oportuna para reinsertarse al trabajo. Una vez trabajando, los profesores encuentran diversas complejidades para adaptarse a la cultura escolar relacionadas con la enseñanza, el uso del lenguaje y el manejo del aula. Comprender las experiencias de estos educadores es importante para implementar programas gubernamentales más efectivos tanto para la reinserción como para su desarrollo profesional, pero también para la transformación de las escuelas en comunidades interculturales, capaces de aprovechar la diversidad cultural.

END OF IN PERSON SESSIONS

VIRTUAL SESSIONS

Day Three 25 August 2023 Friday

Day Three 25 August 2023 - 11:15-12:45

9A   Migration, Law and Policy V1

Chair: Hanna Franz, Universität Hamburg, Germany

339   Workshops for Improving Digital Literacy Skills among Refugee Populations

Mythili Menon, Kaitlyn Hemberger, Mohd Sabra, Murtuza Jadliwala

Introduction

The availability of technology combined with access to smartphones and digital devices sets the landscape for social engineers to target people with poor digital and language skills, such as refugees. Phones and emails are often the first technology that newly arriving refugees interact with, and effective usage of technology is imperative to their successful integration in the U.S. society [1]. However, the usage of these technologies in a culturally new and linguistically diverse environment can be challenging to the resettled refugees, making them susceptible to fraudulent scams due to two main factors: a) the digital divide in the usage of this technology in non-U.S. countries and communities, where something considered as dubious in the U.S. may be completely normal in the communities from where the refugees are arriving from, thus making them easily vulnerable to such attacks, and b) language is a barrier to comprehension as majority of these community members lack the literacy in English and/or English language skills required to truly understand and parse a fraudulent scam in a language which is not their home language (mother tongue).

Digital Literacy Workshops and Methodology

Although digitization and the role of digital tools have increased post COVID-19, refugees systematically lag in their ability to use digital tools [2]. To address this gap, we recruit both refugees from DRC (N = 94) and Afghanistan (N = 94) to participate in digital literacy workshops at the local public library. The goals of these workshops are three-fold: a) to assess English proficiency of the participants, b) to assess digital skills of the participants, and c) to prime participants for phone and email usage. The language proficiency of each participant will be assessed using the LEAP-Q questionnaire [3]. Interpreters and translators of Swahili and Pashto will be hired to work with the focus groups. Communicative Technologies proficiency will be assessed using the Digital Skills Questionnaire from vINCI [4]. In addition, a demographic questionnaire will be administered.

Results

The study is currently ongoing, and we expect to have results by the start of the conference. We will present the results of the three questionnaires- the LEAP-Q questionnaire assessing language proficiency, the digital skills questionnaire assessing digital skills and communicative technologies, and the demographic questionnaire.

Conclusion

The results of the digital literacy workshops can inform government policymakers, educators, and humanitarian and resettlement agencies on the importance of providing additional educational resources to improve educational outcomes in the refugee community, and aid in improving and prioritizing more inclusive cybersecurity policies. In addition, digital literacy skills open a wide variety of opportunities to refugees, including allowing them to find employment online and thereby as a corollary making them more employable.

Reference

Alencar, A. (2018) Refugee integration and social media, Communication & Society, 21:11 [2] Kaurin, D. (2020). Space and Imagination, Rethinking refugees' digital access. UNHCR Research Briefs. [3] Language Experience and Proficiency Questionnaire (LEAP-Q). (2007). by Blumenfeld, & Kaushanskaya, Journal of Speech Language and Hearing Research [4] vINCI (n.d.) Retrieved on December 09, 2021 from https://vinci.ici.ro/

203   From the politics of closed ports to the politics of faraway ports: Piantedosi decree as a new frontier of populism

Veronica Romano

Since the new italian government headed by Giorgia Meloni took office, the practice of assigning safe but distant ports to humanitarian ships that rescue migrants in distress at sea has become established. On closer inspection, the policy of faraway ports is symptomatic of the government's desire to limit the presence of NGOs in the Mediterranean, and takes the form of a further punitive gesture, all the more so given the simultaneous allocation of landing ports in Sicily and Calabria to the vessels of the Coast Guard and the Financial One.

The policy of faraway ports therefore rides – along the lines of the Minniti, Salvini and Lamorgese decrees – the wave of punitive populism that, as argued by Luigi

Ferrajoli, «leverages on incitement to hatred and defamation of conducts that are not only lawful but virtuous and even heroic, such as saving human lives at sea»[1].

As a matter of fact, the origins of the criminalisation of search and rescue activities can be traced back to the codes of conduct of 2017 which subjected NGOs cooperation in Italian authorities' search and rescue activities to the respect of several rules, such as the prohibition to obstruct the Libyan Coast Guard's activities (a rule that aroused lively controversy, because of the refoulement operations carried out by Libyan authorities, with the italian financial support[2]).

Piantedosi decree[3], on the one hand, incorporates the rules already provided for in the codes of conduct, and, on the other hand, introduces new ones, such as the duty for the master of the ship to reach the assigned port "without delay".

Even though this provision was drawn up with the intention of prohibiting the so-called "multiple rescues", the obligation to save lives at sea is bound to prevail, given its international and constitutional rank. However, it cannot be denied that the heavy sanctioning apparatus, connected to the violation of insufficiently determined prescriptions (such as the duty for the master of the ship to transmit the "relevant data" of the persons on board) may discourage NGOs from saving lives. Based on this, the present paper aims to critically analyse this new discipline, also in the light of its concrete implementation in the near future.

References

L. Ferrajoli, Le politiche contro i migranti tra disumanità e illegalità, in M. Giovannetti – N. Zorzella (edited by), Ius migrandi. Trent'anni di politiche e legislazione sull'immigrazione in Italia, FrancoAngeli, 2020, p. 17 (available at the following link: https://series.francoangeli.it/index.php/oa/catalog/view/553/358/2674).

The reference is to the Memorandum of Understanding between Italy and Libya, whose incompatibility with human rights has been denounced by the Indipendent Expert on Human Rights and International Solidarity of the United Nations (URL: https://documents-dds-ny.un.org/doc/UNDOC/GEN/N19/221/01/PDF/N1922 101.pdf?OpenElement).

Law-Decree 2 January 2023, n.1.

329   The solidarity's principle in the government of migration between criminalization and sustainability

Filomena Pisconti

During the presentation of report "Punishing compassion: solidarity on trial in fortress Europe" (2020), Amnesty International asked European governments to stop the criminalization of human rights defenders in the UE and to introduce a system of safe and regular human mobility.

The vague dispositions of so-called "Facilitators Package" (Council Directive 2002/90/EC), born in European law to oppose to trafficking in human beings, has contributed to produce the effect of "criminalization of solidarity", for humanitarian conducts without profit purposes, which cannot be considered as example of migrants' smuggling. It takes a new reform of these dispositions, to forbid States from criminalizing humanitarian assistance activities at sea.

The "chilling effect" of the criminal sanction and, even before that, of the risk of criminal trials creates a preventive dimension which prevents incoming flows and, in general, humanitarian activities in the Mediterranean.

There are example cases of criminal trials for facilitation of irregular immigration: in Croatia, against the NGOs "Are you Syrious" and "Center for peace studies" and in Greece, for rescuers Sarah Mardini and Seán Binder.

In France, Cédric Herrou was arrested for "délit de solidarité" for helping migrants to cross the border between Italy and France; despite the Conseil constitutionnel pronounces, in 2018, for the constitutional value of the principle of "fraternité", someone says that the crime of solidarity has not completely disappeared from French law.

In Italy, the commanders of NGOs, repeatedly subjected to criminal investigations, are left at sea for a long time without a place of safety where to disembark migrants, due to ministerial prohibitions. Furthermore, rescue activities are usually regulated through rules of conduct (the so-called, in Italy, "Codici di condotta") to deter their permanence at sea, wrongly considered as a "pull factor" for the departures of migrants.

All the critical aspects of European law show the attempts of European States to manage the immigration problem as an emergency, with the risk that national dispositions about migration repeatedly threaten the protection of human rights, in which it is difficult to divide humanitarian action from criminal one.

The migration issue has always been seen as an emergency of landings and invasions, as a fight against the illegality of migrants, used to carry a sovereignist vision, full of xenophobic and racist contents.

This management of migration is very far from the principles of sustainable development and other fundamental values of European Union, which proposes an integrated approach between search and rescue programs and reception and integration national ones.

The emergency perspective of European dispositions must be suppressed in the place of an idea of an orderly, safe, regular migration, as stated in Goal 10, Target 7 of the UN 2030 Agenda and specified in the Global Compact for Migration, which consider migrants and refuges of growing wealth for national economy, to allow to EU to have a strategic role in promoting a debate on "sustainable" immigration, to not be restrained in contemporary nationalist and populist visions.

204   Syrian Refugeedom, Post-War Reconstruction and Safe Return

Sandra Cvikić

Based on the Croatian experience of refugeedom, post-war reconstruction and safe return into formerly occupied territory of Eastern Slavonia, Baranja and Western Sirmium in late 1990s this paper will provide on one hand, an insight into the process of peaceful reintegration led by the UNTAES and international community (Cvikić and Živić, 2010); while on the other hand, it will discuss the predicaments of Syrian refugees' safe return and post-war reintegration after their long-term refugeedom in Turkiye (Cvikić, 2016; Cvikić, 2021). The aim is to discuss the feasibility of a peaceful reintegration project on a bigger scale for 3.6 million Syrian refugees from Turkiye as a potential solution to their prolonged and precarious refugeedom.

Seemingly successful UN project implemented in the post-war Croatia, the peaceful reintegration process of Eastern Slavonia, Baranja and Western Sirmium had introduced a blueprint for forced migration solutions deemed beneficiary for both, the international community and the post-war nation (Schondorf, 2009; Tuković, 2015; Kasunić, 2017/2018). However, conflicting interpretations of such 'win-win' solutions by numerous experts and scholars have shed doubts about migration policy outcomes that are not always beneficiary for the refuged populations in the long run. Therefore, produced knowledge by international and Croatian scholars/experts in this respect will be critically examined and juxtaposed to collected knowledge about the Syrian refugeedom in Turkiye. Such comparative analysis will test the viability of a peaceful solution to Syrian refugees' prolonged precarity in Turkiye – an international project supporting return to their homes in Syria.

This qualitative sociological inquiry is premised on a critical examination of scholarly/expert knowledge production about contemporary refugeedom and related international policy solutions using sociology of knowledge approach to discourse (Keller, 2020). Preliminary findings have so far indicated a greater need for realistic and people-oriented solutions which deploy improved sense and respect for the most vulnerable population in the world today – the refugees.

9B Arts, Literature and Migration V1

Chair: Anwesha Das, Manipal Academy of Higher Education, Manipal, India

75 The Middle Passage and Migration in West African Literature

Anwesha Das

This paper will reimagine the Middle Passage through the literary works of Anglophone West African authors Amos Tutuola and Ben Okri, and personal narrative of the West African slave Olauda Equiano (Gustavua Vassa). The violence of European "modernisation" manifested in the production of a racialised knowledge will be critiqued with reference to the "writing culture" debate started by James Clifford. This paper will argue that personal slave accounts in "writing up" their experiences and culture, provide an alternate anthropological account of the horrifying history of migration that counters a Eurocentric perception of life. How have the personal slave accounts re-defined the Middle Passage? This paper will analyse literary works to argue that literature and micro-histories play important roles in questioning the archived history of the Middle Passage. It contributes to ongoing debates on postcolonial critique and de-colonial thought in Europe by examining the production of Eurocentric knowledge.

425 "There is No Place Like Home": Searching for a Home in Özdamar's Seltsame Sterne starren zur Erde

Irem Elbir

As migration, whether forced or voluntary, has been an issue in various geographical areas for so long, subject positions shift inexorably, resulting in a proliferation of studies on diaspora, migration, post-colonialism, nomadism and transnationalism. While scholars probe how these social events shape human subjectivity, the experiences of migrants have entered into the literature by expanding the boundaries of not only the literary studies but also the intercultural communication studies. Borders have become both loose and tight, forcing many people to migrate as a result of postcolonial experiences, wars, domestic crises in countries, colonial history, political reasons and unequal distribution of the world's resources. In various contexts, this mobility is viewed as a threat to or a promise for an economic and cultural growth in the host countries.

This study presents a modified understanding of "space" with a discussion on the creation of a "home" in the migrant's experience. Basing upon the growing mobility of the world currently, this study claims that Emine Sevgi Özdamar's Seltsame Sterne starren zur Erde: Wedding –Pankow 1976/7 (Strange Stars Stare toward Earth: Wedding – Pankow 1976/77) (2003) is a quest for a home and provides new comprehension of a border as both "opening" and "closing" (Müller-

Funk, 2021: 23). As a result, a sense of place and belonging are transformed in the Seltsame Sterne zur Erde.

The protagonist in Özdamar's work, being both a part of and separate from a certain group, alters the spaces they are in to give them personal significance. They reshape physical locations, making them unique and rich in meaning. The character also takes control of their own situation by moving across the East-West German border for her professional improvement and work and asserting herself in spaces traditionally occupied by men. Therefore, travelling back and forth between West and East Berlin and between İstanbul-Berlin becomes essential for the protagonist's understanding of a sense of place. In this novel, the dynamic process in the relation between home and migration can be considered as Al-Ali and Koser (2002) stated. Seltsame Sterne starren zur Erde leads up discussions on the possibility of a "multicultural home" and the positions of the self and the Other.

206   Memory of emigration and the perception of immigrants in Italy

Luana Franco-Rocha, Dorothy Louise Zinn, Daniela Salvucci

Italy is a country well-known by its mobility of people: the important emigration flows in the years 1880s and various subsequent waves, and the more recent immigration flows since the 1980s, with a new phase from 2015 onwards. Having such a background in mind, the aim of this paper is to study how the memory of Italian emigration affects the perception towards immigrants arriving in the country. As memory is a socio-historical construct, it is conceivable to build a mnemonic archive that is part of everyday social relations to preserve a certain image of the past (Halbwachs, 1987). Thus, evoking the Italian emigration path as similar from the one taken by immigrants may conceivably be helpful in building an empathetic perception of newcomers. Based on interviews carried out with Italian citizens with family members who emigrated, this paper tries to correlate the images they have of their relatives and the current immigrants who have settled in Italy.

The interviews show the change of the image of Italian emigration across the time. If those who left the country in the 1880s are perceived as people in a difficult socio-economic situation that must leave to find better living conditions, recent emigration is seen as more connected to a will of cultural exploration and better work opportunities. In that sense, when asked to correlate the current emigration of Italians with the recent immigration flow, the rejection of such a comparison was unanimous. The participants stated that it is not possible to confront such different experiences, since Italian citizens who emigrate nowadays usually have a high education level and decided freely to move abroad. Instead, they claim that immigrants who arrive nowadays in Italy are more comparable to the historical

Italian emigration, since both groups are moved by a strong necessity to find a better place to live, due to armed conflicts in their home countries or economic need. Moreover, in several interviews there was an explicit reference to the many disasters and difficult situations that occurred in boat trips in both past Italian emigration and current immigration. Despite the similarities in struggling for living, the interviews show a reluctance to create a closer bond between emigrants and immigrants, as a sort of necessity to be detached from the image they have of immigrants. For instance, such a disconnection can be perceived when they claim that Italians who emigrated "were not as in need as immigrants", even if they have also escaped from an Italy that had a high rate of poverty and unemployment at that time.

Therefore, although most of the participants were able to build some links between the Italian emigratory past and recent immigration, there is still little allusion to such correlations in the social debates on Italian migration (Glynn, 2008), which may hinder a positive pro-migrant perception. Finally, the study shows that it is necessary to construct a positive collective memory of immigrants, in such a way as to create a more tolerant place for both Italian and non-Italian citizens.

325   Migration and culture: relocation of representatives of creative industries to Kazakhstan during the war period

Saida Negizbayeva

Historically Kazakhstan has been a territory of frequent migration flows. Two main factors contributed to it – nomadic lifestyle of Kazakhs that was predominant till 1930s and its geographic position in the center of the Eurasian continent.

People change their place of residence for various reasons – migration can be voluntary and forced, i.e. caused by natural disasters and wars. Evacuation accounts as a form of forced migration as well. In this regard, the WWII was marked for Kazakhstan by evacuation of creative community to Almaty (ex-capital of Kazakhstan). Almost 80 years later, in 2022 flows of people came to Kazakhstan from Russia, including those with creative background.

'By the number of magnificent names, by the amount of talent and intellect that hit Almaty in the early 1940s could probably be compared only with Odessa or Yalta of the post-October years, whery the flows of Russian cultural intelligentsia hoped to escape the revolution'. This creative energy transformed the cultural landscape of Almaty and gave a powerful impetus to the further development of the artistic scene in Kazakhstan.

With the outbreak of war in Ukraine in February 2022, and seven months later, when Russian President V. Putin announced 'partial mobilization' in Russia in

September 2022, a large number of Russians came to Kazakhstan. The situation resembled the one in the 1940s: war, people forced to leave homes and relocate to a new place. According to statistics, around 200 thousand Russians entered Kazakhstan.

As newcomers arrived, there was a sharp increase in interest in work prospects and opportunities in art & media in Almaty. Online group dedicated to help the newcomers with the search of work and housing was created on Telegram, which now has almost 200 participants. However, it should be noted that migrants seeking employment in creative sphere faced the same difficulties experienced by the local creative community – unemployment, lack of opportunities for self-expression, modest level of cultural life. It is important to note as well, that back in times of the 1940s evacuation, when Russian creative community was a leading force in the industry of the entire USSR, creative industry of Kazakhstan benefited greatly from newcomers. However, this was not the case this time – since 1991 Kazakhstan has been involved in the process of globalization, including cultural one, separately from Russia. This led the country to produce the same level art professionals & creators, that have equal access to world practice and experience.

Art lives always and everywhere, both in peacetime and in wartime. Representatives of creative industries are also involved in migration. As people move, they bring their traditions, knowledge, and beliefs with them. In this regard, migration comes not only with difficulties, but new ideas and cultural enrichment, that can change and develop artistic and creative landscape of the host country.

9C   Economics, Work and Migration V1

Chair: Sahizer Samuk, University of Pisa, Italy

413   Local policies of diversity in (post-)industrial cities: unpacking multiculturalism in Italy and Japan

Magda Bolzoni and Silvia Crivello

The paper aims at discussing how migration and diversity in the urban space are differently understood, framed and elaborated upon by local urban policies. More specifically, it explores if and how policies and interventions aiming towards migrations' local governance and migrants' social inclusion interact with those interested in promoting urban economic growth. In so doing, the paper intends to strengthen the bridge between migration studies and urban studies and to bring forward the debate regarding the persistence of multiculturalism at the local level and the ways it locally unfolds.

Multiculturalism, after considerable initial popularity, has largely come into question in Western countries: particularly in Europe, the dissatisfaction towards multiculturalism principles and the idea that we have entered in a post-multicultural era are largely shared. Despite this, policies with a multicultural approach are still quite widespread, particularly at the local level. Also, in some context, the explicit reference to multiculturalism is present in national policies too, as it is in Japan, where a national guideline on "multicultural existence", was released in 2006 and recently renewed.

At the same time, diversity in urban spaces has emerged as a feature to bet on to promote post-industrial neighbourhoods and cities: central ethnic districts and multicultural neighbourhoods have been increasingly marketed to attract visitors and prospective residents and diversity has come to be considered an element characterizing the authentic urban experience. Similarly, the capability to attract international high-skilled migrants and transnational elites has become a mark of success for cities, a relevant asset in the competition to attract further resources.

To unpack these different dimensions and to address how their interconnections (if any) take form at the local level in the field of urban policies, the paper takes into account the two sister-cities of Turin (Italy) and Nagoya (Japan). Both cities are characterized by a presence of migrants above the national average and by a strong relevance of the automotive industry, and they are located in national contexts similarly dealing with issues of ageing and shrinking population and adopting a "jus sanguinis" approach to the matter of migration. However, relevant differences are present too, for example in terms of debates on multiculturalism, services for the foreign population, vision for the city's future and the role the foreign population may have.

The analysis relies upon a multi-site qualitative research developed between 2017 and 2023 through qualitative semi-structured interviews to local authorities, NGOs and civic associations, as well as policy documents and materials analysis. The paper therefore is interested in exploring how local policies for urban growth and local migration policies interact, frame and address the issue of migration and diversity, specifically exploring if and how three field of policies may interact: 1) policies towards the social inclusion of low skilled migrants and local governance of migration flows; 2) policies towards the attraction of highly skilled migrants and transnational elites; 3) policies of urban promotion and branding in which diversity and internationalization are considered an asset.

497　New 'crisis', old challenges and responses: Labour im(mobilities) of Albanian migrants in Greece's COVID - 19 'crisis'

Maria Panteleou

The recent COVID - 19 pandemic has highlighted the interdependence of the global and the local through the imposition of an almost universal human immobility in order to prevent disease from moving. Restrictions on international travel, closure of borders, and lockdowns within national territories are some of the measures that have abruptly halted the international and internal mobility of labour migrants (Triandafyllidou, 2022; Papademetriou & Hooper, 2020). This presentation examines, on the one hand, how Albanian migrants conceptualize the labour precarity during the pandemic 'crisis' in Greece through the lens of their past experiences of the 'crises' in Albania [collapse of the communist regime in the 1990s] and in Greece [economic 'crisis' throughout the 2010s], in which they faced similar labour challenges. On the other hand, it studies how new 'structural constraints' (Schewel, 2020, p. 331) on human mobility, which were imposed 'from above' to prevent the spread of Coronavirus in Greece (e.g. total lockdown policy in March and April 2020), interact with old challenges, such as the de-legalization, which Albanians faced as early as the 2010s in the country and are transformed the cultural strategies and practices that Albanians adopted to deal with labour precariousness in the new, pandemic 'crisis'. Specifically, drawing on data collected during fieldwork (2015-2017) through participant observation and semi-structured interviews with Albanian migrants who have lived and worked in the city of Corinth and two nearby villages since 1998 and from ongoing (from 2022) fieldwork with the same Albanian migrants and in the same areas, the presentation highlights how their labour mobility takes on a new form in the pandemic 'crisis'. In particular, although labour mobility was the main strategy that Albanians adopted to deal with the past 'crises' they experienced in Albania [international migration to Greece and labour mobility within Greece in the 1990s] (Panteleou, 2022, p. 67-71) and in Greece [labour mobility inside and outside the wider region of Corinth in the 2010s] (Panteleou, 2022, p. 71-76), they seem to be immobilized in the Corinthian context during the pandemic, because they do not have work permit, which would allow them to move legally in the area to their jobs. However, they move irregularly within the local Corinthian context, where they live, and work in informal agricultural, domestic and construction jobs, which are secured by their network of 'acquaintances' with Greek employers. This network, which Albanians have built since 1998, who first settled in Corinth, helped them find jobs both during the economic 'crisis' in Greece and during the pandemic 'crisis' in the country. The presentation concludes that the case study of Albanian migrants highlights how a new 'crisis', on the one hand, intensifies pre-existing social inequalities (Sirkeci & Cohen, 2020) and on the other hand is dealt with by people in old ways, which have a differentiated form.

360   Which temporalities for asylum seekers and refugees? The perspective of street-level workers in the Italian asylum system

Pamela Pasian

In the last twenty years, Italy has faced the phenomenon of the so-called 'forced' international migration. As a result of its geographic position in the Mediterranean, this country constitutes, in many cases, the first reaching country for persons who look for international protection. The increasing numbers of asylum seekers have forced the Italian State to implement and organize a reception system characterized by emergency and exceptionality, which led to the implementation of a public policy with many shadows and little light, with multiple negative consequences, especially for the asylum seekers and refugees involved (Avallone, 2021). Currently this system is characterized by policies of subsidiarity where different actors, public and private, are involved at various levels of government. Generally, public authorities subcontract third sector actors and NGOs to provide inclusion and integration services to international protection seekers and holders. Despite central efforts to achieve harmonization on the national level, this scenario entails considerably differences between territories, in particular according to the commitment and willingness to promote paths of integration and inclusion from the third sector actors involved. The role of these agents, and in particular the discretionary practices they apply in order to cope with the task of implementing a state mandate concerning also the management of the condition of immobility that affect the temporality of refugees and asylum seekers, is the focus of this article.

Drawing on ethnographic research realized in the realm of the project "SIforREF - Integrating Refugees in Society and Labour Market through Social Innovation" founded by the Interreg Central Europe Program, I will follow a street-level bureaucracy approach (Lipsky 2010), to analyze how the politics of time have been managed by third sector actors involved in the reception system in two medium-sized Italian cities located in the region of Emilia-Romagna, Bologna and Parma, which are acknowledged as 'virtuous' systems of urban asylum governance (Campomori, Ambrosini 2020). Despite the central role of a variety of street-level workers – such as social workers, case-workers, police officers- in the everyday management of asylum seekers and refugees have been already investigated (Borrelli 2021; Giacomelli 2021), less attention has been devoted to the issue of third sector workers discretionary power and agency in dealing with the management of the legal and social limbo which caught asylum seekers and refugees while waiting to receive a status – and, therefore, a residence permit – for international protection or while trying to activate paths of work and social inclusion (Della Puppa and Sanò 2021). I argue that street-level workers considered in this study are aware of their discretionary power and use it as a tactic (de Certeau, 1984) to contrast the inconsistency of the Italian integration immigration policies (Barberis and Boccagni, 2014). While the mechanisms of the reception system stuck asylum seekers and refugees, street-level workers try to use this suspended and dilatated time to implement practices which reflect their integration and inclusion visions and values.

219   Talking about the meaning of work: The case of highly skilled Italian migrants abroad

Sahizer Samuk and Sandra Burchi

What do young Italians who decide to go abroad after their studies think about work? What are the working conditions they encounter with their positive and negative sides? What significance is attached to work and the opportunity to work abroad? In this article, we focus on the results of a research study investigating the career trajectories of high-skilled young people educated in Italy who have chosen to go abroad. The empirical basis of the research consists of 50 semi-structured online interviews conducted in 2020-2021. The substantial scientific literature on this issue has well highlighted a 'generational sentiment' that underpins the phenomenon of mobility, recounting the most conflicting aspects. It has been said that it is not only the economic driver that drives research abroad, but a broader range of motivations that unite young people from southern Europe and that include a strong critical instinct and impatience with the overall dynamics of countries that do not offer sufficient opportunities to young people (Bartolini et al. 2017). It is no coincidence that a type of 'meritocratic emigration' has been spoken of (Dubucs et al. 2017), i.e. motivated by the desire to move beyond employment and social systems with blocked access or polluted by unfair and non-transparent forms of access. Having dismantled the representation that portrays skilled migration as a typically cyclical 'flight' phenomenon that returned to Italy after the onset of the economic crisis, the research conducted has shown that this form of mobility has been accompanying the downward parabola of our country's economic system (and, within it, of its university system) for at least two decades, and that it can now be qualified as a structural component of its development and of the way in which it faces the challenges of globalisation.

In this article, we would like to highlight the elements the way young people abroad talk about work, the meaning they attribute to the work they undertake, the aspects relating to income and remuneration, but also those that signal autonomy and independence, the perception of professional and personal growth, and the ambiguous perception of risk and security.

9D   History and Migration V1

Chair: Caner Tekin, Ruhr University, Bochum, Germany

51   Human migrations, history and law according to "The Nomos of the Earth"

Orazio Maria Gnerre

Carl Schmitt (1888-1985) was the author of the famous essay "The Nomos of the Earth" (1950), with which he tried to define the geopolitical history of our planet through a whole series of concepts and images. A problem that he posed in this essay is that relating to the taking possession of the territory following the human migration of certain peoples, thus linking the migratory phenomenon – of very long historical ancestry – with the birth of political orders and laws. With this speech we intend to explore his ideas and propose some reflections starting from them.

221   Migrating beyond the "wave": transformations of the migratory experience of Brazilian migrants in Portugal (1960-2020)

Patricia Posch, Rosa Cabecinhas, Isabel Macedo

When the theme is Brazilian immigration in Portugal, we find reference, in scientific literature, to the different "waves" of this migratory flow. In the first "wave", between the 1980s and 1990s, migration had an economic character and was associated with the countercurrent movement of Portuguese emigrants in Brazil, qualified Brazilian professionals and political exiles. The second one, between the 1990s and 2000s, marks the densification and feminization of the flow, with the migration of people less qualified to occupy positions in sectors such as construction, food services, tourism and domestic services. The third, which some authors understand as a fourth (Cf. Fernandes et al., 2021), begins in the mid-2010s, when it started to be observed the migration of Brazilians with a high social status, among which are pensioners, investors and students, but also people with a higher social status in general, motivated by a "middle class malaise" (Millar & Fanini, 2022, p. 319) in the face of a political and economic scenario in Brazil perceived as unstable (Azevedo et al., 2022). In our study, we approached these transformations from a diachronic and qualitative point of view, with the objective of identifying the social and cultural reflexes that they caused at the level of the experience of migrating and being and/or immigrant. To this end, a Thematic Analysis of biographical accounts of Brazilian migrants in Portugal was carried out, with a time frame from the 1960s to 2020. These accounts were collected using the Life Stories method, a variant of Narrative Interview (Jovchelovitch & Bauer, 2002). As a result, it was possible to overcome symbolic boundaries (Chouliaraki, 2017) imposed by the dominant discourses and promote a change of agency that is empowering and emancipatory (Abadia et al., 2018), in order to understand the collective phenomenon from a look at the individual processes, in which are often involved "itinerary[ies] of difficulties", "failure in the realization of dreams", and "strangeness" (Fausto, 1998, p. 21). This historic awareness exercise (Freire, 1979) allowed the analysis of how the experience of being an e/immigrant is impacted in relation to changes in social and contexts over time, resulting in social and cultural challenges at the individual and group levels. In this article, we present a discussion based on some of the themes that stood out in the research, namely the influence of cultural ties between both countries on the experience of migrating, the changes observed over these decades in social and cultural dynamics and their impacts on identity negotiation, the nuances and meanings of social discrimination, and language as a demarcation factor of cultural difference and social asymmetries.

248   Situational Migration and Hidden Histories: A Case Study

Rochelle Fernandes

Introduction:

Typically, migration is examined from the position of origin and destination or from the perspective of whether it is voluntary or involuntary. However, between willing and coercive migration, there is another variety that has yet to be investigated. This is "situational migration", where migrants may find themselves in vulnerable situations due to the conditions they experience before migrating, in transit or on arrival, in addition to the social and political structures prevalent in the host society. This could project an identity onto the migrant, thus shaping their experience in the host country. To further examine the concept of situational migration, this research engages with the case study of Marie, an African poskem who, as a child, was brought to Goa, India from Mozambique.

Objectives:

To investigate the effects of situational migration on the identity formation process of the migrant.

To determine the role of other stakeholders in the migrational process such as the state and policymaking structures.

Methods:

The research utilises an empirical-qualitative analysis of the migration and life of Marie. Histories of the poskem have been excised from official documentation. Therefore, an email interview was conducted with the respondent, whose aunt and uncle adopted Marie and brought her to Goa. Theories of power are utilised to understand how migration shaped Marie's identity in Goan society.

Results and Discussion: The term poskem is derived from the Konkani verb "possunk," which means "to raise" (Porobo 71) or "to feed" (Carvalho, 2017) and was often used in reference to cattle. Such children were informally adopted by elite Goan Catholic families. Catholics, in pre-Liberation Goa, were prohibited from legally adopting as per the general laws of the land (Gracias 1996; 80). Because there was no formal agreement binding the adopted child to the family, the child was often exploited and forced into domestic servitude. Marie was taken in as a child by a Goan couple living in Lourenco Marques, Africa, because her parents could not afford to look after her. She was then brought to Goa to be looked after by the respondent's grandmother and in turn, to look after the grandmother in her old age. Marie was denied rights to education, marriage and inheritance and received no wages for her service. However, the respondent notes that Marie was well-treated and accepted by the local Goan community although she was African. As Goa was a part of the slave trade, this statement raises racial concerns pertaining to the vestiges of slavery. The research probes into whether Marie, a victim of situational migration, was explicitly aware of the identity thrust upon her.

Conclusion:

Marie's movement is an example of situational migration, as she was neither coerced nor given an alternative. Her status in Goa is the consequence of her family's circumstances coupled with a lack of regulations. The paper concludes with an analysis of how situational migration affects identity and can "free or imprison" (Castro et al. 14) the migrant in the host community.

Keywords: Situational migration; Portuguese Goa; Adoption; Poskem; Power; Identity

9E   Youth, Children and Families V1

Chair: Gul Ince Beqo, University of Urbino, Italy

271   Network to Credit: Role of Kinship in Punjabi Migration

Atinder Pal Kaur

The influx of migration from Punjab is not new; it is as old as Indian migration. Due to strong network relationships, Punjabis have become visible in all parts of the world. Network relations play a vital role in migration and provide required information about the country of migration. Similarly, Punjabi migration always remains influenced by the migrated kin or those that boost the migrants for migration. With this given background, the study attempts to understand a) the role of networks facilitating migration from Punjab b) and the role of kins to credit to meet the cost of migration. Theoretically, the study is based on an ethnographic and narrative approach. The ethnographic approach includes the nature of migration, place of migration, network relations, years of migration, and occupation of the migrants. The narrative technique is used to understand and analyses channels of migration and return migration. The paper will highlight the role of social networks in discovering employment opportunities and various typologies of debt used to meet migration demand.

Keywords: Punjabi Migration; Kinship relations; Social Networks; Credits

531   Youth Forced Migration Experiences in Southeast Asia

Rashin Lamouchi

This qualitative study investigates forced migrant youths' sense of belonging. The study was part of the Youth Migration Project, an ongoing investigation of how young forced migrants construct their identities, sense of belonging, and future aspirations while perched on the edge of mainstream society – without a voice in decision-making about their futures. A snowball recruitment method was applied to gather narratives of 52 forced migrant youth aged 11 to 17. In this study, I focused on the experiences of eight forced migrant female participants living in prolonged displacement in Malaysia. My research question was: How do the processes and experiences of forced migration shape migrant youths' sense of belonging? Through a mixed-method approach, including a novel, arts-based peer-mediated storyboard narrative method, now known as Storyboard Peers, and follow-up interviews, youth shared their migration narratives, the challenges they faced while living in Malaysia, and their expectations and aspirations for their futures. The theme of safety figured prominently in the girls' accounts, and I constructed the themes of physical safety and social safety to represent the data the girls contributed. The girls' sense of belonging and feeling at home had a direct relationship with feeling safe, valued, and loved. I found that physical and social environments inform sense of belonging. Sense of belonging is neither a static nor a fixed concept; rather it is a flexible, everchanging, and reconstructed with ongoing, everyday experiences, reflections on the past, and anticipations of what the future could hold. The girls' accounts conveyed those feelings of "belongingness" and "at home" shifted from tangible places and familiar faces to abstract concepts such as love, peace, and family. Overall, feeling safe and "at home" were rooted in basic needs being met. The findings call for governments and nongovernmental organizations to significantly reduce the length of time that youth spend in transit, promote safety, combat discrimination, fulfill basic needs, and ensure access to education and healthcare.

343   Separated but still one? On the complexities of translocal households: Results from a case study in Sierra Leone

Johannes Lückenkötter

In political and academic discussions about migration in West Africa, internal migration is largely neglected. Greater attention is paid to cross-border movements within the region or international migration to other continents (Teye 2022: 3; Romankiewicz/Gilles 2019: 9). But in terms of sheer numbers, internal migration within one country is far more prevalent. For example, while in 2016 the total number of Sierra Leoneans who live in other countries was estimated to be 336,000 and in 2019 only 187,100, more than twice that number migrated internally to a different chiefdom within Sierra Leone (UN DESA). Typically, this means rural-urban migration, which among others has contributed to rapidly growing cities.

Straddling the rural-urban divide, however, are so called translocal households whose members live in different places but continue to define themselves as a joint household. By splitting themselves between e.g. a rural and an urban location and maintaining intense exchange relations, these households try to stabilize their income and minimize livelihood risks, e.g. from adverse climatic changes in rural areas. Greiner (2011: 610) therefore defines translocality "as the emergence of multidirectional and overlapping networks created by migration that facilitate the circulation of resources, practices, and ideas and thereby transform the particular localities they connect." In particular, translocality is often seen as a (partial) solution to precarious living conditions in rural areas.

But despite the recent proliferation of studies on translocal migration in Sub-Saharan Africa (e.g. Ayele, Degefa 2022, Djurfeldt 2022, Kuiper 2020, Nord, Byerley 2020, Vibert 2020, Steinbrink, Niederfuhr 2020), the concepts and empirical findings are still fuzzy and many open questions remain: How long and based on what do such spatially separated persons still consider themselves as one household? Are risks really minimised by such translocal arrangements or replaced by a new combination of risks? How do the perspectives of the urban and rural members of such households differ? Are translocal livelihood arrangements able to stabilize rural communities or do they contribute to their disintegration?

This paper aims to identify, empirically investigate and discuss these and other complexities of translocal households on the basis of a bi-local household survey that was conducted as part of a case study in urban and rural areas of Sierra Leone. The study is part of the international research project "Migration and Translocality in West Africa", which aims to better understand internal migration in the region and is embedded in the West African Science Service Centre for Climate and Adapted Land-use (WASCAL).

446   Transmitting family culture and changing marriage decision strategies in the migration context: cultural and structural dynamics

Gul Ince-Beqo and Eralba Cela

While migration entails empowerment for many women escaping from patriarchal societies, when it comes to partner choices of their children in the destination countries, for some communities, attachment to the country of origin becomes prominent, in particular in the case of daughters' marriage. Marriage patterns of the second-generation are gaining increasing attention among migration scholars and many studies have focused on transnational marriages and partner choices and their impact on gender inequalities, schools dropouts and labour market careers. Relying on qualitative biographical interviews collected among Turkish migrants living in Italy, this article explores (1) the transmission of family culture in the migration context, with a focus on the mother-daughter relationship (2) migration experience and changing family practices, focusing particularly on the marriage decision. Italy is a nontraditional destination country for migration flows from Turkey, which means that families are lacking the support of the extended family that once was very strong and important in the transmission of family culture. In such lack of support of the family networks in the transmission of cultural-religious codes, migrant mothers' concerns grow in relation of their daughters' age and future partner choices/decisions. Our findings suggest that while migration experiences consolidate certain gender roles in the transmission of the culture of being a woman, as mother and wife, on the other hand, Italian migration policies, especially those on family reunification, determine the choices of future partners, shifting the focus from the context of origin to diasporic transnational spaces. In particular, the long waiting time for family reunification authorisation, particularly in the case of the future husband's arrival from the country of origin, determine changing patterns of partner choice 'channels. This relation is gendered since waiting for reunification seems to be more frustrating for men, when women are the sponsors. Such dynamics, along with others, increase the focus on the European diasporic space for the research of future partners, being this space free of bureaucratic restrictions that hinder free movement between European borders.

9F   Göç Çalışmaları V1

Chair: Betül Dilara Şeker, Van Yuzuncuyil University, Turkey

328   2013-2022 Arasında Türkiye'den Almanya'ya Nitelikli Göç ve İnsani Güven(siz)lik

Burçe Orhan

Bu çalışma, Türkiye'de 2010 yılından itibaren hızlanan, 2013 yılı itibariyle dikkate değer bir şekilde artan ve gerek medya gerekse politikacılar tarafından "Türkiye'nin nitelikli genç kaybı" ya da "beyin göçü" olarak dile getirilmeye başlanan, uluslararası göç akışı içerisinde de 1990'lı yılların ortası 2000'ler başı itibariyle eğitim ve uzmanlığın uluslararasılaşması ile gittikçe büyüyen bir öneme sahip olmaya başlayan yüksek nitelikli göçü ve profesyonellerin hareketliliğinin, Türkiye'den Almanya'ya doğru olan ayağının -ve Türkiye'de "yeni bir göç" dalgasının başlangıcı olarak ele alınabilecek- göç etme kararlarına ilişkin 33 katılımcı ile yarı-yapılandırılmış sorular içeren görüşmeler ile gerçekleştirilen niteliksel bir araştırmadır. Son dönem literatüründe, özellikle Avrupa, Amerika ve Kanada'ya doğru yüksek eğitimli göç ve hareketliliği için; 'life-style migration', 'free mover' gibi gitme kararlarında oluşan değişikliğe vurgu yapan farklı adlandırmalar bulunmaktadır. Yine son yıllarda Türkiye'den ayrılan kişiler için de aynı şekilde, 'yaşam tarzı göçü' ya da 'seküler göç' gibi tanımlamalar yapılmaktadır. Bu çalışma sonucunda, göç etme kararları arkasında yatanların sadece bireysel sebepler ya da sadece yapısal sebepler olmadığı; 2013 yılı itibariyle Türkiye'nin içinde bulunduğu siyasi, ekonomik krizler ve bunların insanların günlük hayatlarına, iş yaşantılarına, eğitimlerine etki etmesi ile birlikte, göç etme kararı veren insanların ortak deneyimlerinin sonucu olarak ortak bir duyguya/hissiyata sahip oldukları söylenebilir: Hayatın her alanındaki güvensizlik ve belirsizlik kaygısından kaynaklanan bir huzursuzluk hissi. Bu duygu; yaşam tarzına müdahale, politik çatışmalar, hukuk ve adalete güvenin kalmaması, ekonomik krizin etkileri, eğitim sisteminin sürekli değişmesi ve giderek kötüleşmesi, eşitsizlik, işsizlik, iş yerlerinde fazla çalışma ve özel/sosyal hayatın kalmaması, toplumsal cinsiyet eşitsizliği ve temel güvenlik hissinin kalmaması gibi makro, mikro ve mezo düzeyde, birçok kesişimi barındıran Türkiye'ye özgü bir göç olarak karşımıza çıkmaktadır.

538   Sosyo-Ekonomik Gelişmişlik Düzeyi ile Göç Arasındaki İlişki: Van İli Üzerine Bir Araştırma: Sosyo-Ekonomik Gelişmişlik Düzeyi ile Göç Arasındaki İlişki: Van İli Üzerine Bir Araştırma

Ceren Pehlivan, Bahadır Yüzbaşı, Gökhan Tuncel

The evolution of socioeconomic indicators in Turkey is critical to the survival of regional differences. Migration between provinces is caused by differences in development between regions. The concentration of economic activities in specific regions, as well as social and political issues, are the primary reasons for the formation of migration between provinces. When studying the concept of migration, the social and economic structure should be taken into account. Because migration is the phenomenon in which we see the most reflections of changes in the economic and social structure, Migration affects the demographic structure of cities, resulting in social mobility in settlements. Migration also transports the cultural structure, social characteristics, and lifestyles of cities. As a result, migration has a complex structure with numerous factors and characteristics. Another effect of migration on cities is an imbalance in the distribution of populations, human capital, and economic unions. Furthermore, the problem of social, economic, and cultural adaptation to newly settled places may arise as a result of migration. In our study, we investigated the concept of migration, which has many effects and features, in the context of Van province. Because it is a border city, the province of Van has become a city that receives immigration, and the surrounding provinces have faced economic and environmental problems, particularly terrorism, throughout history. The migrations experienced did not only occur between cities, but also a large number of people arriving in Van from neighboring countries, particularly Iran. Immigration to Van had an impact on the city's social, economic, and physical structure. The coming together of different cultures has added diversity to Van's cultural structure. At the same time, the presence of incoming human capital has improved the economic structure. The physical structure of the city has also evolved in tandem with the city's growing population. The relationship between socioeconomic development level and migration was investigated in this study for the city of Van. The Geographically Weighted Regression and Ordinary Least Squarses Analysis were used in the research. The level of socioeconomic development explained 36% of the total variance (adjusted R2) in migration, according to the OLS model. The GWR model explained 53% of the total variance in migration by socioeconomic development level. This represents a 17% increase over the OLS model. The GWR model showed an increase in model fit while the AICc decreased when compared to the OLS model. Similarly, the fact that the sum of squares is less in the GWR model now proves its superiority.

540 Ekonomik Yetersizlik İle Göç Arasindaki İlişkinin Ampirik Analizi: Van İlinden Kanitlar

Ceren Pehlivan ve Bahadır Yüzbaşı

Negative economic developments and periodic problems play a significant role in shaping the country's policies. The effects on economic indicators influence individuals' decisions about the current situation and the future. Migration is one of the decisions that people will make as a result of poor economic conditions. Migration can occur within the borders of the same country or it can occur by moving to different countries. People's desire to work and live in better conditions, as well as wars, ethnic, political, and cultural factors, all exhibit a dynamic structure. People who migrate may encounter issues with adaptation, settlement, and culture in the regions from which they came. This phenomenon is most noticeable when people move from rural to urban areas. Given its geographical location and geopolitical structure, Turkey has been both a receiving and a sending country at various times. Turkey, with its many ethnic and cultural structures, has become a crossroads for various cultures over the years. Many migration studies have been conducted in Turkey as a result of these characteristics. The topic of migration was investigated in this study using the province of Van, which is an important border city. For years, the province of Van has had a migration-receiving structure due to its productive agricultural structure, geographical conditions, political problems, and, in particular, terrorism in neighboring cities. The relationship between economic inadequacy and migration was investigated in this study through empirical analyses in the province of Van. GWR (Geographically Weighted Regression) and OLS (Ordinary Least Squares) analyses were used in the study. The level of economic insufficiency explained 3% of the total variance (adjusted R^2) in migration, according to the OLS model. The GWR model's F-statistic and p-value demonstrated statistical significance. Economic insufficiency explained 34% of the total variance in migration, according to the GWR model. The GWR model showed an increase in model fit while the AICc decreased when compared to the OLS model. Similarly, the fact that the sum of squares is less in the GWR model now proves its superiority.

504 Göç Sürecinde Kesişimsellik: Sosyal Psikolojik Bakış Açısı

Betül Dilara Şeker

The intersectionality theory, which has its origins in studies in feminist theory and sociology, was developed to understand the social experiences of disadvantaged group members. The concept emphasizes the interrelationship of the disadvantages brought about by different group identities. Despite the increasing importance of the concept in various fields such as psychology, philosophy, economics, law, and history, the ambiguity of its definition continues. In addition, discussions about using the concept as a theoretical perspective, an analytical approach, and a political tool for social justice projects continue and increase interest in the concept. Intersectionality theory; is essential in understanding and evaluating the complexity of the disadvantages that systems of power and oppression, such as sexism and racism, cause in individuals' lives. The field of social psychology considers intersectionality as identifying a social position rather than an individual difference that influences social attitudes and behaviour. Intersectionality; is regarded as a critical approach to exploring whether and/or how the combination of social justice, equality, and disadvantaged group memberships have social and personal meanings. According to the social identity theory, the process of acquiring identity is constructed due to the individual's group memberships and the process of comparing themselves with others. One's identity is associated with multiple social categories. The social psychological perspective focuses on multiple identities, how they are organized, how they interact, how they lead to forms of discrimination, and the individual meanings of belonging to multiply disadvantaged groups. During and after migration, the person moves from one identity hierarchy to another. The individual repositions himself in the new cultural structure with his multiple identities. For example, being a refugee can be grounds for discrimination, while identifying as a refugee woman can result in multiple disadvantages. In this sense, one's experiences and perceived discrimination cannot be explained by being a refugee or a woman. Multiple and permeable identities and combining these categories cause inequalities and disadvantages for the individual compared to a single identity.

Today, people move for different reasons. The disadvantaged and heterogeneous nature of the members of immigrant groups, especially in the migration process, makes the concept of intersectionality a concept that needs to be studied to understand the disadvantages and to produce effective solutions in creating and implementing social justice and migration policies. However, the history of the intersection concept in migration studies is relatively new. An intersectional perspective should be added to migration studies to understand immigrants' experiences in detail. The study aims to evaluate the concepts of intersectionality and intersectional awareness in migration studies as social psychological concepts and to reveal their contributions to the field. In the context of the concept of intersectionality, it is thought that determining the profiles of immigrant groups in Turkey, indicating how their identities affect their experiences, and raising awareness about the multiple disadvantages experienced will contribute positively to both immigrant groups and the host group in daily life and the process of policy making and implementation.

Keywords: Intersectionality; immigrant groups; social identity theory; intersectional awareness

9G   Las Migraciones V1

Chair: Pascual Garcia, Universidad Técnica Particular de Loja, Ecuador

355   Jóvenes españoles descendientes de familias inmigrantes en las migraciones intra-europeas: ¿la triple ausencia?

Alberto Capote-Lama y Mónica Belén Fernández-Suarez

The area of free mobility was implemented in the European Union in the mid-nineties. But it was not until the following decade that intra-European migrations took on a certain extent, first with the flows of young people from Eastern countries after successive enlargements, and then from southern Europe in the context of the 2008 economic crisis. In the case of this new Spanish emigration bound for Europe, some profiles have been more visible than others. In general, both in the media field and even in research, the youth with university studies who looks for opportunities to grow professionally or increase their cultural capital in countries like Germany, France and the United Kingdom has predominated. Within these young people we can find a subgroup: that of descendants of immigrant families. In other words, these are young people who were born in Spain to families of foreign origin or who arrived through family reunification. Their motivations may be similar to those of other Spanish youth. But in them it is possible to ask other types of questions such as the influence of the family migratory history, the relations they maintain with three countries (the origin of the parents, Spain and their destination in Europe) and how they perceive their identity within the European framework. And, in short, remembering the sociologist Abdelmalek Sayad and his work "The double absence", how it is lived to belong to three countries. The study is based on a series of semi-structured interviews with young people who have these characteristics and who have emigrated from Spain to the United Kingdom, France and Germany.

494   Discurso de odio en contra de la inmigración: desplazamientos del homo sacer moderno

Laura Natalia y Rodríguez Ariano

Los discursos de odio son elementos que se utilizan con frecuencia en contra de los grupos o colectivos vulnerables. En este caso, las y los inmigrantes irregulares son el centro de estos discursos que van en contra de los principios valores, derechos y dignidad que son básicos e indispensables en los seres humanos.Uno de los principales obstáculos para la incorporación de la población inmigrante al lugar de destino son los sentimientos arraigados que existen en su contra, lo cual incrementa las políticas de discriminación y exacerba discursos de odio que son reforzados por normativas de contención de los flujos migratorios, lo que provoca la criminalización de las y los migrantes irregulares.Los diferentes discursos de odio se encuentran latentes en la política del siglo XXI, en particular en los países donde la nueva derecha de carácter populista utiliza este discurso para dividir, violentar y vulnerar. Una de las principales características de la ultraderecha es el discurso antiinmigrante; donde la otredad aparece como el mal que amenaza el bienestar social y la identidad nacional. Esta postura política representa un grupo que mantiene como característica de identidad un discurso antiinmigrante, en donde su aceptación incrementa junto con su posicionamiento en la política internacional y se refleja en las contiendas electorales.Los discursos de odio en contra de la migración parten de la aceptación y normalización por parte de la sociedad, son considerados como aporófobos racistas y xenófobos. donde predomina la deshumanización, criminalización, violencia e infravaloración del migrante. Ante esta postura, el discurso antiinmigrante propicia la cultura de odio en sociedades democráticas que constituye un pilar importante en la necropolítica del Estado para la gestión del fenómeno migratorio.Otro punto relevante, son los crímenes de odio que poseen una relación estrecha con este tipo de discursos, esto se debe al impacto que tienen los mensajes de intolerancia que diferencian a los otros como una amenaza para el bienestar nacional, también se enaltece el rechazo y la posibilidad de comentar delitos de odio en contra de los inmigrantes irregulares que para el Estado receptor, los irregulares representan las vidas que no importan, vidas que son desechables, sin valor y reemplazables.Finalmente, nos encontramos con la ausencia de una agenda pública incluyente basada en los derechos humanos de las y los migrantes. El discurso de odio en contra de las migraciones es una práctica que se ha normalizado y se fortalece mediante acepciones de carácter racista, de xenofobia, exclusión, criminalización y marginación contra de la migraciónindocumentada. Axel Honneth señala que "el reconocimiento de la dignidad de personas o grupos constituye el elemento esencial de nuestro concepto de justicia".

184 The revitalization of rural areas in Spain through the chain migration

Paula Alonso, Leticia Santaballa, Laura Oso

This contribution analyses the processes of rural revitalisation from the perspective of chain mobilities. It attempts to go beyond the vision focused on the depopulation approach. The chain migration perspective is a dynamic means, as it considers the articulation between internal/international, historical/recent migrations and shrinking/revitalisation processes. Spatial mobility is also analysed in relation to the articulation of the local and immigrant population's intertergenerational social mobility processes. The research is based on intensive fieldwork (109 semi-structured interviews) conducted in several shrinking regions in Spain (Galicia, Andalusia and Castilla-La Mancha).

Our research reveals how the internal and international exodus of the second half of the 20th century in Spain, driven by the "Developmentalist" economic model, implemented by Franco's regime, is at the basis of the territorial imbalances and the configuration of rural shrinking areas in this country. It also shows how de-agrarianisation and the lack of intergenerational replacement explains the arrival of immigrant populations in rural areas from the turn of the century, in order to meet the needs of labour markets segmented by ethnic origin and gender. Along with newcomers, the shrinking areas are also benefiting from the arrival of returnees and root migrants (from both external and internal migration), who decide to go back to their roots, drawn by emotional ties. These groups of migrants (newcomers, returnees and root migrants) are different, yet complementary, in terms of sustaining life in rural areas. The impact of migration on the revitalisation of rural areas is visible in demographic, economic and social terms.

462 E Percepción negativa respecto a la inmigración venezolana por la mendicidad

Jessica Ordóñez

Este documento parte de una metodología cualitativa que tiene como instrumento grupos focales, se realizó en el año 2022 en la ciudad de Loja, sur de Ecuador, participaron: servidores públicos, empleados privados, estudiantes de secundaria y superior. El objetivo fue conocer la percepción respecto a la presencia de personas venezolanas en la ciudad. Los resultados muestran que existe una percepción negativa entre las personas que participaron debido a que, desde que se incrementó la inmigración particularmente de personas venezolanas en la ciudad, la imagen urbana ha cambiado notablemente, principalmente por la mendicidad en la cual participan adultos acompañados de niños menores de 5 años. Cabe mencionar que esta situación no se había observado con la presencia de personas inmigrantes de Perú o Colombia, al menos no en la misma magnitud.

12:45-13:45 BREAK

10A   Migration, Law and Policy V2

Chair: Jara Al-Ali, Universität Hamburg, Germany

436   Management of Massive Asylum Seeker Influx in Kenya and Turkey Through Policy and Law-Making

Abdülaziz Ahmet Yasar

The aim of this research is to analyse how Turkey and Kenya, two countries hosting millions of people under international protection, have responded to the mass influx of asylum seekers. In particular, the research paper examines the legal framework, policies and strategies used by governments in dealing with these crises.

The main research question is: How have the two main host countries of people under international protection, namely Kenya and Turkey, responded legally and politically to the mass influx of asylum seekers?

The hypothesis of the paper is that there are currently no optimal solutions for dealing with forced mass mobility, especially as temporary measures prevail in various asylum-affected countries. A comparative analysis combining the positive aspects of each approach will lead to conclusions that are more in line with international human rights.

The two main host countries of refugees and people under international protection have responded, inter alia, with policy decisions and the implementation and reform of domestic law to address major humanitarian disasters.

In 2014, Turkey introduced the Temporary Protection Regulation for asylum seekers and stateless persons from Syria to provide them with protection and basic services based on international human rights and refugee law, a year after it established its Presidency for Migration Management. The Kenyan governments of the 1990s responded to the mass influx of asylum seekers by no longer directly caring for the refugees, but leaving this task to the UNHCR through opening temporary refugee camps. The 2006 Refugee Act, which sets out the status, rights and restrictions a refugee has or is subject to, was passed after a decade. In addition, Kenya's Refugee Act created national institutions responsible for managing the country's asylum and refugee affairs.

The methods used are functional comparativism, comparative policy analysis, actor-network theory and content analysis, which provide a comprehensive and nuanced understanding of the role of laws and policies and the mutual impact on these areas of research.

253   Frontex's responsibility in third countries: Ensuring accountability in the Western Balkans

Adnan Smajic

Frontex, the European Border and Coast Guard Agency, has been increasingly cooperating with non-EU authorities, including those in the Western Balkans, to manage migration and enhance border control in the region. These collaborations are carried out through various arrangements, such as working arrangements and status agreements, which include deploying Frontex officers to the borders to control migratory flows to tackle cross-border crime, including migrant smuggling, trafficking in human beings, and terrorism. In light of this, there are concerns regarding Frontex's legal responsibility and potential complicity in human rights abuses by non-EU authorities, particularly in the context of pushbacks and violence against migrants and refugees. Moreover, the issue of standing corps' immunity raises questions about the accountability of Frontex personnel for their actions in third countries.

This research analyses the legal and policy frameworks governing Frontex's cooperation with non-EU authorities in the Western Balkans and evaluates their adequacy in ensuring compliance with human rights standards. It examines the specific cases where Frontex has been involved in border management activities, and explores the role of Frontex personnel in such activities. To address the issue of accountability, the research looks at the applicability of national and international human rights standards, such as the European Convention on Human Rights and the UN Guiding Principles on Business and Human Rights, to Frontex's operations in the region. Additionally, it analyses the potential for judicial and non-judicial remedies for human rights violations, including the shared responsibility of holding Frontex accountable for its cooperation with non-EU authorities in third countries.

The research provides policy recommendations to improve Frontex's legal compliance and human rights protection in its cooperation with non-EU authorities in the Western Balkans. The recommendations include analysing the adequacy of and strengthening the mechanisms for monitoring and reporting human rights abuses in the context of Frontex's operations in the Western Balkans; establishing clear accountability mechanisms for Frontex personnel in third countries, including measures to address instances of human rights violations; and enhancing transparency and public access to information regarding Frontex's cooperation with non-EU authorities in the Western Balkans, including the use of standing corps' immunity.

460   Addressing the root causes of migration and improving community resilience by accelerating climate action

Konstantinos Pappas

Introduction

The United States has prioritized supporting climate change adaptation and mitigation in Central America, outlining effective strategies to build resilience to address climate change and disaster risk impacts such as food insecurity, and to support sustainable development in the region. Its objective aims to increase the resilience of agricultural production, resource management, and infrastructure, as well as to enhance economic opportunities and increase the security, prosperity, and governance of the disaster-prone region via partnerships with the private sector and civil society (Vice President Kamala Harris on July 29, 2021).

Climate change impacts exacerbate poverty, inequality, and food insecurity, and research increasingly suggests that climate change and disaster risk are major contributing factors to migration. From 2014 to 2020, an average of 311,000 people migrated from the Northern Triangle (El Salvador, Honduras, Guatemala) to the United States annually, with many fleeing extreme weather events. Projections estimate that in the next 30 years, 3.9 million climate refugees will flee Central America due to the climate crisis.

Comprehensive approaches to climate adaptation and mitigation efforts, including through energy transition, resilient infrastructure, and a better-integrated development of economic sectors could offer an opportunity for sustainable development, strengthening resilience and addressing the root causes of migration.

Objectives

The main scope of this research project is to: 1) identify key systemic inter-dependencies of the energy-food-migration nexus in the Northern Triangle, in the context of climate and disaster risks, 2) propose a framework for quantifying these interlinkages in support of informed decision-making by climate-threatened small and medium businesses and local communities and 3) identify anticipatory action areas and interventions for disaster risk reduction and improving community resilience.

Methodology

We will develop convergence research through example case studies, bringing together multiple disciplines including the following activities:

Review the literature to identify key interconnection between migration, food, and energy under climate-related risks and disasters.

Review existing global best practices for disaster risk reduction and improving community resilience relevant to the energy-food-migration nexus in the Northern Triangle

Develop a framework for energy-food-migration interconnections, with a list of potential interventions that can be made across the interconnected sectors

Co-identify the social, economic, and environmental indicators to evaluate the impacts of the different interventions

Focusing on the agricultural sector and using El Salvador as a case study, experiences of climate-threatened small and medium agricultural businesses and farms as well as local communities will be identified, and decision-making frameworks will be co-created that will support evidence-based decisions while fostering an environment of multi-national cooperation toward climate action and disaster resilience.

Results

Share information and build capacity related to the systemic interdependencies of food, energy, and migration with implications for climate action and disaster risk reduction interventions in El Salvador.

Co-identification and ranking of different identified interventions, as well as the social, economic, and environmental indicators critical to assess these interventions according to stakeholders.

Analysis of systemic interactions and evaluation of the developed framework, policy, and barriers for resilient pathways.

381   The Human Rights of Refugees: Status Transition from Illegal Migrants to Asylum Seekers regarding the Supression of Migrant Smuggling as a Transnational Crime

Blerta Ahmedi, Bekim Nuhija, Stefani Stojchevska, Betim Jahja

When considering the protection of refugees, it is important to consider that seeking asylum represents their guaranteed human right. Given the situation when an asylum seeker is a person who has left his or her motherland with the intention to seek protection from serious human rights violations and from persecution in another country, he or she has not yet obtained the status of a refugee in a legal manner until the reception of the decision on their asylum claim. Appropriately, the right to seek asylum – as an established human right – is protected by both national instruments of the Republic of North Macedonia and international instruments, such as the 1948 Universal Declaration of Human Rights, the United Nations 1951 Convention Relating to the Status of Refugees and the 1967 Protocol

Relating to the Status of Refugees guiding national legislation concerning political asylum. This research paper consists of two parts, where the first part of the paper aims to analyze the human rights of refugees, with a particular focus placed upon the right of obtaining asylum, while the second part of the paper aims to analyze the criminal offense of Migrant Smuggling, incriminated within the national Criminal Code of the Republic of North Macedonia, defined as a crime against humanity and international law. In addition, statistical data for the time period 2006 – 2022 originating from the Republic of North Macedonia will be scrutinized in detail, concerning the numeral aspects of such phenomenon. The research paper is further enriched with two practical case-studies, where the first case-study regards migrant smuggling (a national case) and the second case-study is taken from the international court of human rights, whose objective regards is the right to obtain asylum by a migrant in the Republic of Slovenia (an international case).

Keywords: Migrant Smuggling; Asylum; Refugees; Human Rights; Transnational Crime

10B   Economics, Work and Migration V2

Chair: Sadaf Mahmood, Women University Multan, Pakistan

257   Understanding the network of diaspora donors, collection, distribution, and utilization of resources by diaspora-funded organizations and institutions; Diaspora philanthropy in Kerala, India

Afsal K. and Reshmi R. S.

Migration has had a significant role in the socioeconomic and demographic features of Kerala in South India, particularly the Gulf migration after the 'oil boom' of the 1970s (Prakash, 1998). With the help of Gulf migrant workers in Kerala, numerous charitable organizations and institutions operate in the areas of education, health, social welfare, rehabilitation, and community development.

This paper aims to comprehend diaspora donor networks as well as how diaspora-funded organizations and institutions distribute and employ resources for philanthropy. For the study purpose, 26 in-depth interviews with executives of different diaspora-funded and -supported charitable organizations and institutions operating in the areas of health, education, social welfare, rehabilitation, and community development were undertaken. A categorical content analysis approach was applied using NVivo 12 for the analysis.

The research highlights that organizations and institutions establish locality, destination, and philanthropic project-based diaspora donor networks in order to utilize diaspora resources for various types of charitable activities in Kerala. These organizations used different methods for resource collection from diaspora communities such as membership campaigns, monthly collections, special collections, sponsorship, and challenge programs. The distribution of philanthropic funds is categorized: as locality-based distribution, distribution to specific groups, and distribution based on an immediate issue or response. Finally, a large portion of the resources collected by philanthropic organizations is spent on four areas: health education, social welfare, and rehabilitation projects. This study proposes the idea of implementing a new framework for the optimum utilization of philanthropic resources from the diaspora.

476   Socio-economic Determinants of Labor Movement From Georgia to the Eastern Black Sea Coastal Cities

Kerim Taşkın

For more than 30 years, there has been an intensive, unilateral, cyclical, sensitive to economic and political developments, regular and irregular labor migration from Georgia to the cities of the Eastern Black Sea region, with tens of thousands of migrants each year, although the actual number is never known. The literature on labor migration from Georgia to the Eastern Black Sea region is mostly concerned with seasonal agricultural workers coming to rural areas. Although most of these studies are related to rural areas, it is observed that they cover the entire region in terms of their results. However, some of these migrants participate in the labor force only in rural or urban areas while others participate in the labor force in both rural and urban areas. This paper focuses on the effects of cyclical labor movement particularly in the coastal cities of the Eastern Black Sea. The research aims to reveal the labor movement of Georgians with different influences in the cities and their interactions in socio-economic life.

9 cities of different scales (Ordu (Altınordu, Fatsa, Ünye), Central Giresun, Trabzon (Ortahisar, Akçaabat), Central Rize, Artvin (Hopa, Kemalpaşa)) located in the coastal provinces from the western end of the Eastern Black Sea to the Georgian border were selected as the research field. The data were obtained from the field through the interview technique. Interviews were conducted with 40 people who have relations and knowledge about Georgians (employees of migrant associations, administrative unit managers, intermediaries who carry out migration, neighbors, etc.). Phenomenology method, which is a qualitative method, was used in this research in order to determine the effects of Georgians in Eastern Black Sea cities on socio-economic life.

Observations in field studies and data obtained from expert interviews revealed fundamental differences such as the fact that Georgians work in different sectors in cities, (entertainment, trade, health, care services, tourism sector, etc.) that the mobility pattern in cities is different from seasonal agricultural labor in rural areas and that labor movement is longer lasting and under the influence of different dynamics compared to rural areas. With the findings obtained, the differences and details of labor movement in the Eastern Black Sea cities can be determined.

434   Urban-Rural Migration and Its Impact on New Business Models

Ferah Ozgoren Sen, Ebru Bilgen Kocaturk, Nevin Karabıyık Yerden

Considering the extraordinary events that have emerged in recent years, it would be appropriate to talk about the concept of migration. The first of these is the first Corona case in our country in 2020. The second is the February 2023 earthquake, which we started to normalize after the pandemic. In parallel with the change in lifestyle due to Corona, people who moved away from the city centers had to migrate again to our country due to the earthquake. In this sense, the way of life in places where places to go are limited should be much different than in big cities. This study is aimed at investigating the sources of motivation and the impact of the rapid migration after the earthquake on business models. It covers new business models and their implications for marketing and examines the change in the housing sector. The case study method is used in this study to examine how migration from cities to rural areas affects the housing sector. It has been shown that social events such as pandemics and earthquakes in Turkey have caused reverse migration, which has led to the emergence of new houses that provide a transition to simpler lifestyles.

1120   Human Capital Accumulation and Career Development of Pakistani Labour Migrants in Germany. What Determines their Success?

Sadaf Mahmood, Beatrice Knerr, Izhar Ahmad Khan

In the early 21st century, international migration for the sake of better job opportunities is increasing day by day and human capital becomes an essential ingredient for the career development and labour market adjustment of immigrants in the host countries. Pakistani immigrants' communities in several developed countries are the core example of this. 7.6 million Pakistanis studying, residing, and working abroad. They are engaged in several occupations including students, employed, and self-employed, and utilizing their accumulated human capital stock by participating in labour market as well as enhancing it for their career development. Our study is based on the human capital theory by Schultz and Becker as they stated that the schooling and capabilities of an individual are called human capital that maximizes their lifetime earnings (Schultz, 1971; Wossmann, 2001). Younger people are more interested to invest in migration and education as in our case, Pakistani young people invested in both than other groups in the interest of better return on this decision (Becker, 1975; Sjaastad, 1962). The study by Mahmood *et al.,* (2015;2017,2022) strengthens these theories. The focal point of this research is to explore the human capital stock of Pakistani immigrants in Germany and its effects on their career development while the comparison of gender was also done in this perspective. A face-to-face field survey was conducted in different German cities with a significant number of Pakistanis and the results were analyzed via descriptive and inferential statistics. In total, 264 respondents were interviewed with different occupational statuses in Germany. The results illustrate that commonly, Pakistani male respondents were involved in self-employed and paid-employed activities while students and women were not actively participating the in-labor market. Among the students' group, males were dominant in number whereas females were also significant in this category. It was also found that human capital accumulation has a strong relationship with occupational status. Another indicator of human capital in addition to education, previous work experience has also played a significant role. It is concluded that the accumulated human capital is significantly contributing to their career development at their destination. Individuals with advanced human capital are better to grow in the job market as well as integrate into the host society and play their role effectively in the development of the country. Globally, the "race of talents" is a competition for the sake of human capital accumulation and attracting talent which is increasing day by day.

References

Becker, G. (1975). Human Capital: A theoretical and empirical analysis, with special reference to education, second edition, NBER. 0-226-04109-3, p. 13-44

Mahmood, S., & Knerr, B. (2015). Asian Students in Germany: Contexts of their Studies, Living Conditions and Future Plans 2. (Chapter 7: Students from Pakistan Social relations and human capital formation of Pakistani students in Germany), Volume: 11, pp. 156-175, *Kassel University Press GmbH.*

Mahmood, S. (2017). Human capital, occupational status, and social integration of Pakistani immigrants in Germany: Gender Perspectives, (Vol. 20). Pp. *Kassel University press GmbH.*

Mahmood, S., Knerr, B., Khan, I. A., Shabbir, M., & Mahmood, R. (2022). A Gender-Sensitive Analysis of Social Integration Challenges. Evidence from the Pakistani Diaspora in Germany. *Migration Letters, 19*(4), 437-448.

Sjaastad, L. A. (1962). The Costs and Returns of Human Migration, Journal of Political Economy, 70(1), 80-93

Wossmann L (2001). "Specifying human capital: A review and some extensions", KielInstitute of World Economics, [August 2001].

10C Education and Skilled Migration V1

Chair: Dr Pınar Yazgan, Sakarya University, Turkey

227 The "Not Migrant" Narrative and its Causes: Self-Categorization of the Highly-skilled Migrants in Budapest

Pınar Dilan Sönmez Gioftsios

Who are those highly-skilled individuals moving in high circularity and temporariness? How do they self-identify, and why? Debates around migrants' sense of belonging point out that how migrants self-identify and how they represent their identity constitute complex processes (Bielewska 2021). The self is considered a social actor, a motivated agent, and an autobiographical author, and cares deeply about social acceptance as well as social status to consolidate its autonomy. In this sense, the self-identification of highly-skilled migrants who are portrayed as a privileged, wanted group of cosmopolitans (Weinar et al.; Bielewska 2021; Smith and Favell 2006) suggests an interesting case for understanding and explaining how the narrative identity interacts with the external categorizations throughout the mobility experience. Through the analysis of the interviews conducted with 30 highly-skilled migrants in Budapest in 2022, this article explores the ways how highly-skilled migrants make sense of categories and self-identify. Combining the literature on self-categorization theory with the critical discourse analysis approach, this study seeks to answer the question of why 'migrant' has turned into an undesired category and become a "heavy word" that migrants refused to be categorized as migrants. It is argued that using "non-migrant" categories such as foreigner, foreign worker, and expatriate, these individuals try to free themselves from the category of migrant to feel more secure, and more capable of avoiding discrimination in their social, psychological, economic, and political interactions. They either refuse any kind of label or recategorize themselves as a foreigner which is a general category that does not directly indicate racial, ethnic, and cultural connotations which may trigger social biases. This research also argued that reconceptualization of categories in migration studies within a crisis frame, the negative and pejorative connotations the words 'migrant' 'immigrant', and 'refugee' have attained play a significant role in the emergence of today's understanding of the migrant. The discursive tendency to use these terms as interchangeable categories made them more contested, confusing, negotiated, and resisted in praxis.

373 Barriers and challenges in emigration of semiskilled and unskilled workers of Indian Villages

Md Musharuddin Sk

India is the highest number of migrants sending country in the world. Migrant labourers and their households face various obstacles in of migration process. Migrant workers encountered barriers in decision-making to arranging migration costs. The migrant workers experienced challenges in the destination countries also.

The highest sex ratio criteria was fit for the study. The selected two villages in Murshidabad district reported the highest sex ratio (1204 and 1190) and had more than 200 households in the latest census of India, 2011. They are located in West Bengal in the eastern part of India. An interview schedule was developed to survey 214 Households covering 260 migrant workers between October 2020 and October 2021. Face to face In-depth interviews were also conducted with 12 stayed-back wives who are heads of households, 12 elderly persons, one agent, and 15 migrant workers abroad over the telephone to understand the dynamics of labour migration.

About 43 per cent (91 out of 214) households and emigrants took money from moneylenders (37 per cent), sale or mortgage of land/ gold or property (16.5 per cent) to meet their first migration cost. As the number of emigrants gradually increased, remittances accelerated migration.

One-third of emigrant labourers suffered a loss in earnings in the workplace for diverse reasons. However, recently (after 2015), emigrated labourers reported less wage loss than their predecessors. Of 88 emigrant labourers, more than half reported a full loss in destination earnings because of no work or proper work and then returned to India. One-third of them reported a partial loss in earnings for having no adequate job. These semiskilled or unskilled migrant workers had lower educational levels and could not report or manage the challenges in the proper channel in the destination countries.

41   Innovation and flexibility: Nigerian women in Durban's informal economy

Sunday Israel Oyebamiji

The primary aim of this paper is to examine the livelihood strategies of Nigerian female migrants in Durban, South Africa in the informal economy where the majority engaged in informal trading. Nigerian women are known for their diligence in trading and setting up their own informal businesses to be financially independent. Thus, it is interesting to understand the experiences of Nigerian women in the informal sector. This paper relies largely on a qualitative methodology drawing on in-depth interviews with Nigerian women. It reveals that the proceeds of informal trading may sometimes appear insignificant considering the constraints and hurdles, as most of the women talked about their struggles in making ends meet and their challenges as they adjust to a new environment that is now polarised by the crises of Covid-19. At the same time, the majority of the women described aspects of their lives that have changed positively through adjustment and adaptation since they arrived in South Africa and the advantages that some have been able to identify. The study concludes that the experiences of Nigerian migrant women demonstrate the need for a new approach to the informal sector since this will be beneficial to all other groups irrespective of citizenship status.

10D L'émigration V1

Chair: Erhan Kurtarir, Yildiz Technical University, Turkey

348   La Place des ONG dans le cadre normatif de protection internationale des réfugiés

Samira Bikarden

The multifaceted presence of non-governmental organizations (NGOs) on the international scene and their increasingly important involvement in complex and globalized issues such as that of refugees is at the heart of cooperation and the global governance of international refugee's protection. Therefore, understanding the place and the role granted to this new actor of international relations in the regulation of this global issue is a major challenge.

This contribution is part of a larger research endeavor on the actions and limits of NGOs involved in the international protection of refugees. It seeks to understand the role and place assigned to NGOs in the normative arsenal governing international refugee law. It is based on an in-depth analysis of international refugee law (IRL) but also international human rights law. It aims to identify the positioning of NGOs vis-à-vis State and inter-State actors and to explore the room for maneuver available to them, allowing them to contribute to the strengthening of the international "protection" of refugees or, on the contrary, weakening their intervention at this level.

113   L'émigration des ingénieurs marocains à l'étranger : une analyse empirique

Djamila Chekrouni, Zaynab Benabdallah

Partout dans le monde, le métier d'informaticien (ingénieur ou technicien) est très recherché, bien rémunéré et offre de nombreuses opportunités. Avec l'internationalisation des marchés du travail, l'accélération des flux d'informations et de compétences, les informaticiens se trouvent dans l'obligation de rester constamment à la pointe et de s'adapter à un contexte numérique en perpétuel changement (Big data, intelligence artificielle, etc.).

Le phénomène de la fuite des ingénieurs et des techniciens marocains en informatique vers l'étranger constitue un sujet d'inquiétude pour les entreprises et les autorités dans le pays. Ce phénomène universel découle d'une mobilité générale des compétences entre les continents, en quête de conditions de travail et de recherches scientifiques plus appropriées.

Au Maroc, Selon l'ex-ministre de l'Education nationale, de la Formation professionnelle, de l'Enseignement supérieur et de la Recherche scientifique, 600 ingénieurs partent chaque année.

De même, l'Association des Ingénieurs de l'École Nationale Supérieure d'Informatique et d'Analyse des Systèmes (ENSIAS) a affirmé que, sur les récentes promotions, jusqu'à 80% des lauréats ont été embauchés par des entreprises européennes.

Pour le secteur IT, la Fédération Marocaine des Technologies de l'Information, des Télécommunications et de l'Offshoring (APEBI) a annoncé que le secteur IT au Maroc perd chaque mois 50 ingénieurs et que trois entreprises étrangères viennent tous les 15 jours pour recruter une dizaine d'ingénieurs.

Bien que le Maroc a augmenté de 87% ses effectifs de lauréats ingénieurs entre 2011 et 2016 pour répondre aux besoins engendrés par ses plans de développement notamment son plan d'accélération industrielle, les entreprises qui recrutent continuent de déplorer une carence de profils d'ingénieur sur le marché de l'emploi marocain particulièrement dans le domaine informatique. Le schéma explicatif de ce phénomène est assez complexe. En effet, certains pays développés comme : la France, le Canada, la Chine, l'Inde, l'Allemagne, l'Autriche, la Belgique, le Denmarck, les pays bas, le suède et le Royaume unis ont besoin des travailleurs hautement qualifiés pour des activités économiques à haute intensité de connaissance. À cause de leurs pénuries, ces pays créent indirectement une chasse aux talents en offrant aux jeunes ingénieurs marocains une meilleure qualité de vie, une évolution de carrière plus intéressante et des conditions de travail et de recherches scientifiques plus appropriées.

Par ailleurs, selon les motivations théoriques et empiriques il existe 3 types de déterminants de l'intention d'émigrer chez les ingénieurs en informatique : les déterminants personnels, les déterminants environnementaux externes ou contextuels, et les déterminants environnementaux internes ou organisationnels.

L'objet de cette étude est d'étudier les caractéristiques et les motivations d'expatriations des informaticiens marocains installés à l'étranger (plus particulièrement dans : l'Allemagne, la Belgique, le canada, la France et l'Emirats) afin d'essayer d'expliquer plus précisément les motivations de cette émigration.

Cette intervention analyse les différents aspects de cette migration, en mettant l'accent sur les axes suivants:

Une analyse descriptive de la situation de la fuite des ingénieurs au Maroc;

Une étude empirique à l'aide d'un échantillon. Les résultats des estimations souligneront les variables explicatives de l'émigration des ingénieurs à l'étranger.

510 Réinventer la migration dans la vallée du fleuve Sénégal

Mohamadou Sall

Depuis la période coloniale, la vallée du fleuve Sénégal est une zone de départ pour les migrants internes et internationaux. En fonction de l'évolution politique et économique des zones de destination, cette migration a toujours su s'adapter, trouvant au niveau des zones de départ, de transit et de destination, des ressorts à perpétuer.

Depuis la période coloniale, la vallée du fleuve Sénégal est une zone de départ pour les migrants internes et internationaux. En fonction de l'évolution politique et économique des zones de destination, cette migration a toujours su s'adapter, trouvant au niveau des zones de départ, de transit et de destination, des ressorts à perpétuer.

Le but de cette communication est d'examiner les nouveaux ressorts mobilisés aujourd'hui pour donner un nouveau souffle aux migrations internationales et d'étudier l'articulation entre les anciens ressorts et les nouveaux ressorts, les légitimités qui construisent ces articulations et comment, ces articulations relient les espaces locaux, les zones de transit et les espaces de destination.

Le but de cette communication est d'examiner les nouveaux ressorts mobilisés aujourd'hui pour donner un nouveau souffle aux migrations internationales et d'étudier l'articulation entre les anciens ressorts et les nouveaux ressorts, les légitimités qui construisent ces articulations et comment, ces articulations relient les espaces locaux, les zones de transit et les espaces de destination.

10E   Las Migraciones V2

Chair: Pascual Garcia, Universidad Técnica Particular de Loja, Ecuador

354 La llegada a la jubilación de los antiguos inmigrantes: la experiencia francesa a través de los marroquíes

Alberto Capote-Lama

The objective of this proposal is part of an interest in studying a group that is often invisible: the population that emigrated for work reasons and reaches retirement age in the country of destination. This new phase in their life cycle makes us ask ourselves questions such as their position upon return, living conditions in retirement, their state of health, if their situation differs from that of autochthonous retirees, the migratory capital acquired and what balance they make of their life trajectory since they emigrated. The French case, because it is a country with a long tradition as a country of immigration, may be representative of a sociodemographic reality that is also beginning to be perceived in Spain and will grow in the medium term. Therefore, we analyze the French experience regarding people of Moroccan origin, who are also the first foreign national in Spain. The analysis is based both on a series of interviews with Moroccan retirees in the Parisian region who have shown their testimony, as well as a balance of the studies carried out. The results show problems they face (living old age between two countries), loneliness problems, but also meeting points and initiatives to promote active ageing.

122   El Derecho a la Salud de la Población Migrante Venezolana en Colombia

Juan Pablo Serrano Frattali

El derecho a la salud en Colombia representa para miles de personas un viacrucis; de hecho, únicamente hasta el año 2015 el derecho a la salud en Colombia fue consagrado como derecho fundamental. Este sistema con graves falencias ha llevado a que las víctimas de este sistema de salud deban acudir inexorablemente al Juez, para tratar de resolver sus problemas de salud. Este panorama nacional es aún peor para la mayoría de los dos millones de migrantes venezolanos que se encuentran en Colombia los cuales deben enfrentar también las desigualdades sociales. El propósito de esta presentación es describir el sistema de salud colombiano y cómo funciona este sistema para la población migrante venezolana en Colombia.

115   Court-To-Court Dialogue: Challenges For The Protection Of Children In Migration Processes

Laila Roxina y Moliterno Abi Cheble

This paper aims to explore the role of supranational courts in guaranteeing the rights of children in processes of human mobility. Thus, it is important to take into account the context in which children live and "differentiate in order to protect", as law as a social science cannot remain oblivious. The number of children in processes of human mobility is growing significantly and therefore modifying the debates surrounding migration previously understood in terms of adults and men. The issue becomes relevant as thousands of children are crossing international borders both in Europe and the Americas, such as the war situation in Ukraine and

Syria, as well as the mobility processes in the Central American region. During these movements, which entail risks and opportunities, situations arise that place them in a situation of increased vulnerability, as some are separated from their families or migrate alone. This calls for an adequate study and an enriched or reinforced protection by understanding the various key actors (families, children and States themselves through public policies). This study highlights the value of soft law instruments and the role of supranational courts in guaranteeing children's rights. To this end, international law instruments (treaties) that contain references to the terms "children" or "children" are taken up, specifically the Convention on the Rights of the Child, additional protocols drawn up by the Committee on the Rights of the Child, the International Convention on the Protection of the Rights of All Migrant Workers and Members of Their Families, etc. In addition, soft law documents (which allow for the constant evolution of the law) such as the New York Declaration, the 2030 Agenda for Sustainable Development, the Global Compact for Safe, Orderly and Regular Migration are analysed. These instruments are used as a framework for the study of cases in the Inter-American Court of Human Rights (IACHR) and the European Court of Human Rights (ECHR), the highest guarantors of law in the respective regions. Based on the cases, points of coincidence and divergence between the understandings developed and the interpretation of the courts are pointed out. While recognising the sovereignty of states over the control of their borders, the importance of international cooperation in border management is highlighted. It is concluded that the term vulnerability(ies) is a point of convergence between the two Courts, as well as references to the best interests of the child, the need for context analysis, detention as a measure of last resort. However, divergences are noted (for this purpose, the standards indicated by the IACHR and the ECHR are demarcated) and the lack of a fluid dialogue between the courts. Finally, dialogues for the construction of a new legal framework for the protection of human rights are pointed out as a valuable tool.

404   Reflexiones teórico-metodológicas para el estudio de los vínculos familiares transnacionales en México y en Estados Unidos: apuntes de trabajo de campo

María José Grisel Enríquez-Cabral y Ismael García Castro

La familia transnacional representa un ejemplo heurístico de la perspectiva transnacionalista, este tipo de familia se encuentra bajo el lente académico de quienes están interesados en vencer al nacionalismo metodológico (Pries, 2017). Se apuesta a que, en la distancia, son los "vínculos transnacionales" los que permiten la continuidad de la unidad familiar. Diversos aportes teóricos afirman que dichos vínculos se reproducen a través prácticas como el envío de remesas económicas y emocionales, contacto "virtual" facilitado por el uso de las tics. En alunas reflexiones que van más un poco allá, se argumenta que no son las tics, sino el deseo de mantener la familia lo que les da vida (Faist, 2005; Nyberg, 2016; Castañeda y Román, 2021). Gonzálvez (2016) también abona a la necesidad de comprender a la familia transnacional y sus vínculos desde otros cuestionamientos y se interroga, ¿Qué novedad aporta "lo transnacional" con respecto a los significados de familia? ¿Aporta algo más que enfatizar la gestión de los vínculos desde la distancia? (Gonzálves, 2016: 3). En esta ponencia, como producto de un trabajo de campo realizado con familias transnacionales sinaloenses con vínculos en Estados Unidos, se sostiene que el deseo y/o la densidad de las practicas (envió de remesas emocionales o económicas, co-presencia virtual) no son un sustento que permita dar cuenta de la complejidad de los vínculos. Aunado a ello, es necesario incluir en la teoría y metodología del análisis de los vínculos transnacionales el sentido o intención que imprimen los actores a dichos intercambios, en deseo carente de voluntad es letra muerta. Es preciso cuestionarlos sobre el sentido que le dan a enviar dinero, a las llamadas por teléfono etc, porque desde el lente del investigador suele atribuírsele que es con el afán de dar continuidad a los lazos familiares, caemos en el error de operacionalizar los vínculos transnaconales sin incluir las causas, motivos, fines subjetivos individuales de los mismos.

10F   Migration and Social Integration V1

Chair: Carla De Tona, University of Bologna, Italy

336   Forging Refugee Identity: On Liminal Spaces, The Arts, and Transcultural Exchange

Sarah Koellner and Kerrigan von Carlowitz

Forced migration suspends almost all qualifiers of a stable life—security, home, employment, health, kin connections. Further, in resettlement, refugees encounter the systemic discrimination of welfare systems and neoliberal economies, amidst the emotional tumult of displacement, linguistic isolation, and the loss of spatial identity (cf. Gowayed, Refuge). Under this imposition of liminality, demonstrating Victor Turner's anthropological theory of communitas, refugees find agency, voice, and community through artistic expression. In recent years, scholars associated with the Critical Refugee Studies Collective have turned to artistic expression to analyze "the livability of refugees," and the ways in which artistic creation enables them "to speak back to the law to insist on their humanity" (Espiritu, Departures, 52).

Contrary to the imposed "language of fear," which is demanded of refugees to "gain entry" into host countries and permeate the legal structures of the asylum process (57), artistic production, as we will argue, creates a language of belonging. Employing a comparative ethnographic approach, combined with an aesthetic analysis of artistic production, our paper offers a transdisciplinary approach—mirroring the hybridity of the refugee experience. Such an approach will illustrate how translingual language production and the cultural exchange between refugee and host country populations expedites identity reconfiguration, fostering a cultural paradigm shift regarding a refugee's otherness. (cf. Alastair, 2010). Our analysis catalogs the commonalities in two transcultural innovations: the songs of diasporic Hmong rap artist Louicha in France and the German-English poetry from Sam Zamrik, a Queer Syrian refugee living in exile in Germany.

Evoking key feelings of nostalgia for Hmong culture and resistance against the color-blind French majority, Hmong rappers forcibly displaced from Laos cultivate an artistic identity because of their liminality, not in ignorance of it (cf. Shi, "Between Return and Resistance"). Illustratively, the lyrics of the song Npawg "connect [Louchia's] in-betweenness with the Hmong diaspora" and "connect their future with the idealized past" (238). Rap's intrinsic amplification of minority voices collaborates with refugees' specific yearning for self-definition in this adaptive work of creativity. Channeling the same concomitant nostalgia and frustration of Hmong rap songs in France, Syrian refugee Sam Zamrik confronts their legal and social marginality through German and English-language poetry. While their poem "Bureaucracy" can be interpreted as an artistic attack on the law that foregoes questions of refugee livability, other poems such as "Patchwork" invite the reader to reflect upon identity, belonging, and the creation of community through translingual writing.

Both artists, as we will conclude in our presentation, demonstrate the liberty in escaping identity loss either through assimilation or chronic "refugeeness" which assigns individuals the same, tragic refugee story (Espiritu, 112.). Their artworks counter such narratives by giving voice to their unique experience of displacement, and to the creative potential of poetic and musical language production to foster transcultural exchange. Ultimately, both artists make a strong case for the pivotal role of refugees in shaping their own sense of belonging, and the cultural fabric of their host countries; refugees, as creative agents, forge a new canon of transcultural identity.

1123 Which co-participation is possible with migrants? A critical reflection on the organization and co-design of the Usability Tests and of the Public Pilot Implementation during the H2020 MICADO project in Bologna, Italy

Carla De Tona

Among the key objectives of the MICADO project was that of designing a digital tool to facilitate the exchange and communication between migrants, public administrations and civil society organizations engaged in promoting integration, on common and clearly defined fronts (housing, education, health care and work) but often with distinct and non-integrated tools and fields of operation. The key approach of the project was that of co-participation and co-design with all relevant stakeholders, including migrants themselves. This paper presents a critical reflection on how co-participation has been organised in testing the validity of the digital tool's prototype (through Usability Tests and Public Piloting Implementation). It also reflects on what the main achievements have been (inclusion of gender, linguistic and ethnic minorities) and on what challenges it faced (particularly the failure to reach migrants with limited digital and linguistic skills and with short-term or precarious legal status).

541   Investigation of Migration due to Social Environmental Pressure by Geographical Regression: The Example of Van Province

Çetin Görür and Bahadır Yüzbaşı

Migration; In the historical process, it has an important place for people and societies because of the reasons and results it took place. Regardless of the duration of the migration and the place of migration, the reasons leading to the displacement of the population are largely similar. Individuals who decide to change their living space basically have problems arising from the area they live in. These problems are generally defined with the concept of push factors and they are poverty, ethnic-ideological-religious and political pressures, unemployment, war etc. problems are counted among these factors. From past to present, migration in Turkey is generally from rural areas to urban areas, especially from underdeveloped eastern and inner regions to developed western regions. While economic reasons were among the most important reasons for internal migration in the beginning, the security problem started to come to the forefront since the 1980s. Migration occurs due to the fact that life is more difficult in regions where social pressure is intense. Analyzes of migration flows and their influence factors are usually conducted at the aggregate country level, thus ignoring the existence of large regional disparities. Because regions are so diverse, the main drivers of migration are likely to vary in space and act with varying intensity, creating different regional patterns. In this study, the factors affecting migration under social environmental pressure were examined using Ordinary Least Squares and Geographical Weighted Regression methods. The Ordinary Least Squares method is a statistical method used to analyze the relationship between the dependent variable and the explanatory variables. In parameter estimation, the appropriate value is assumed to be the same for all observations or regression points. However, if the observations are recorded in a regional or regional data known as spatial data, it becomes difficult to obtain reliable results. The Geographical Weighted Regression method gives healthier results by including spatial changes in the model by using the weighting matrix depending on the proximity between the observation location. In this study, it was aimed to determine the relationship between migration under social environmental pressure and independent variables, to examine which of the models used for analysis gave stronger results, and to examine the effects and significance of the variables on maps. In this study, face-to-face surveys were conducted with 440 individuals who immigrated from the provinces with first and second degree borders to Van, and it was observed that the Geographical Weighted Regression method gave stronger results than AICc and R^2 values in the analysis results.

177   Chinese women in transnational marriage migration in two British cities, UK

Lan Lo

This paper presents a joint research study involving ten couples in two British cities: Nottingham and London in UK that were interviewed to explore their transnational relationships, families, and experiences of marriage migration. This paper explores the following research questions in the context of Chinese women's transnational relationship and marriage migration to the UK:

What are the culturally situated understandings and experiences of intimate citizenship between Chinese women and their partners?

How do Chinese women negotiate perceived cultural, national, and ethnic differences within their relationships?

How does transnational migration shape their experiences of intimacy, and vice versa?

In terms of methodology the paper uses a qualitative interview-based approach. Thus, ten couples in two British cities were interviewed pre-pandemic who met the following criteria: 1) currently or previously in a committed relationship; 2) the Chinese woman was born in the mainland China; 3) the western partner was born in the UK. The interviews lasted approximately 90 minutes and took place at a time and place of the participant's choice. The participation was entirely confidential, and their responses were anonymised, as per the British Sociological Association's code of ethical research.

The paper will set out the main findings from the data in areas of such as cultural differences, maintaining spousal relationships, transnational family ties, and employment issues. We will also define the future direction of travel of the research which will explore the extent to which these findings remain constant or have changed in the post-pandemic world. To this end, the original participants will be reinterviewed using the same methods as during the pre-pandemic phase. Our working assumptions are that the main difference will be in the area of employment issues and possibility in terms of maintaining spousal relationships. We predict at this stage that there will be fewer changes in relation to transnational family ties and cultural differences. This paper is original in three main ways: firstly, its focus on Chinese migrant women; secondly, its methodology and thirdly, its pre and post-pandemic comparative focus.

15:15-15:30 BREAK

11A   Migration, Law and Policy V3

Chair: Andrea Romano, University of Barcelona, Spain

45   The use of the transformative intercultural mediation model for immigrants

Amel Ketani

Mediation is a form of intervention in which a third party – the mediator – assists the parties to a dispute to negotiate over the issues which divide them. The mediator has no stake in the dispute and is not identified with any of the competing interests involved. In every mediation, the interests and needs of the parties will be the focus of the mediator and the participants.

This paper will focus on intercultural mediation for immigrants. An intercultural mediator is a mediator who facilitates communication between immigrants and the host society in trying to promote the integration of immigrants. But how can intercultural mediators achieve this? Which mediation model can they use to assist them achieve this objective?

There are several mediation models such as: structured, narrative and ecosystemic mediation models. However, this paper will focus on the transformative mediation model and will argue that if this model is used in an immigration context and is successful, this will help transform the parties' attitude towards the dispute. This paper will argue that, through the use of the transformative intercultural mediation model, mediation has the capacity to engender transformative effects that benefit the parties and that for mediation to give rise to such transformative effects, the mediator's approach and philosophy must seek to achieve recognition and empowerment. It is arguable that recognition arises when, as a result of acknowledging each other's views and feelings, the parties become more sensitive to each other's needs. In other words, empowerment promotes the freedom of the parties to consider the case carefully and to then determine their course.

This paper is based on research that solicited the views of practising mediators. Therefore, this paper is based on empirical research with data analysed from questionnaires and interviews. Once the questionnaires were collected, interviews were organised with fifteen mediators who gave their opinion on the transformative mediation model. Their identities are kept confidential so numbers will be assigned to each mediator.   The collected data was analysed using thematic analysis. Thematic analysis is a method for identifying, analysing and reporting patterns (themes) within data. Thematic analysis was used in this research, with the aid of the NVivo 11 software, to analyse quantitative and qualitative information and to systematically gain knowledge and understanding of the transformative mediation model. Thematic analysis was used as a way to gain an accurate and deep understanding from the data gathered.

1108   Retrieving the Solidarity Pillar: Reframing the future of the EU's free movement of persons from empowering historical legacies

Cristina Blanco Sío-López

This paper critically analyses the relevant role of the European Parliament (EP)'s debates in the consolidation of solidarity approaches to a key policy at the core of fundamental rights decision-making: The EU's free movement of persons. More particularly, this contributions looks at the role, actions and discourses of fundamental players at the European Parliament (EP) articulating differential resilient responses to evolving crises of human mobility rights since the inception of the Schengen Area in 1985. These contributions constitute, indeed, inspiring new points of departure to reframe the essential role of the solidarity principle when articulating migration policies around the respect to fundamental rights and freedoms. Furthermore, this paper aims to recover empowering historical critiques towards the socalled 'Schengen Laboratory' which could be relevant today to find inclusive ways of responding to the asylum and migration external dimension challenges currently being posed with regards to the EU's free movement of persons. This enquiry on EP sources is based on archival research at the Historical Archives of the EU in Florence, at the Historical Archives of the EP in Luxembourg and at the EP Research Services. These sources also include a large set of Oral History interviews conducted with key decision-makers at the European institutions comprising discursive utterances on ways of influencing the dynamics resulting from introducing a 'solidarity' and a fundamental rights element within the EU's 'free movement of persons' policy-making.

410   Private International Law and Migration: Insights from a Brazilian approach

Laís Silva Lopes Tavares, Marilda Rosado de Sá Ribeiro, Luís Renato Vedovato

Private International Law shows an important potential to contribute to global migration governance, considering its methodologies and techniques. Furthermore, there is an evident connection between both fields, considering that international migration entails private international law issues, such as recognition of foreign documents, legal status of individuals, among others. International cooperation, particularly, reveals important relevance in this regard, when taking into account a multilateral global framework in which countries of origin and destination would assume responsibilities, consult and cooperate on a regular basis.

An administrative cooperation between Central Authorities, for example, could upgrade the migration governance to a more efficient level.

In order to accomplish an important background for future ways out of the migration crisis of the contemporary Era, this article aims to survey the recent developments of the Brazilian approach in regard to migration. Most specifically, a specific case is scrutinised: the "Welcome Operation" project (Operação Acolhida). The initiative, initially conceived as an answer to the substantial number of refugees and migrants coming from Venezuela, is a coalition between the military force, governmental bodies, international organisations, NGOs, private parties and the civil society. With the analysis of its contradictions and positive aspects, it is aimed to analyse and illustrate what can be expected from the possible cooperation between Central Authorities in regard to migration.

363   Enviromental Refugees and the 1951 refugee convention

AlBaraa Quradi

This paper argues that the 1951 convention should protect environmental refugees. This paper incorporates evidence from the literature and case laws on "environmental refugees" to discuss the recognition of environmental refugees under the 1951 refugee convention using a desk literature review method. It argues that Environmental refugees fulfill the criteria of the 1951 refugee convention of who falls under its protection. Furthermore, this notion is supported by the 1951 refugee convention concept of non-refoulment and the related case laws testifying for this argument.

11B   Education and Skilled Migration V2

Chair: Lan Lo, University of Nottingham, UK

350   Testimonios as decolonizing tools in EFL teacher education programs to promote reflection and action

Irasema Mora Pablo

Testimonio as a research methodology has been described as a "verbal journey of a witness who speaks to reveal the racial, classed, gendered, and nativist injustices they have suffered as a means of healing, empowerment, and advocacy for a more humane present and future" (Pérez Huber, 2009, p. 644). This presentation offers perspectives to help applied linguistics researchers and teacher trainers think through the intersections of different domains of analysis when it comes to the study of experiences, emotions, power, and conflict that return migrants and transnationals experience as they face relocation in Mexico or as they move across borders between   Mexico and the United States. Based on narrative data from central Mexico, the data show evidence on how the learning experiences, values, and linguistic capital of these youths become the subject of mockery, discrimination, and rupture inside learning spaces.

Using a decolonizing lens, I strive to create awareness to rethink learning spaces for understanding and learning from diverse methods of cooperating and interacting in the educational space. The aim is to challenge the notion of education as a process of knowledge transmission; to give way to new forms of knowledge construction anchored in multiculturalism and the interplay of knowledge derived from emotional engagement and action (Ghosh & Galczynski, 2014; Hargreaves, 2003). Participants in this study shared their experiences on returning to Mexico, moving between both countries and engaging in language learning and teaching. Their bilingualism does not meet the social requirements of the educational communities on either side of the border. As these returnees and transnationals engage in English as a Foreign Language Teaching Education Programs (EFLTEPs) and become student-teachers, they are in a relevant position to reflect and consider new ways to approach students who have similar traits. While EFLTEPs have been around for years, not all have opened to critical conversations regarding the consideration of thinking, feeling, and acting characteristics. In looking at these experiences through the lens of testimonios we can help at validating and re-signifying the knowledge(s) and linguistic practices of returnees and transnationals in the context of their professional training.

References

Ghosh, R. & Galczynski, M. (2014). Redefining multicultural education: inclusion and the right to be different. Canadian Scholars' Press.

Hargreaves, A. (2003). Teaching in the knowledge society: education in the age of insecurity. Teachers College Press.

Pérez Huber, L. (2009). Disrupting apartheid of knowledge: Testimonio as methodology in

Latina/o critical race research in education. International Journal of Qualitative Studies in Education, 22(6), 639-654.

334   Creating a Bilingual Digital Game-Based Learning Platform for Teaching Refugee Children Middle-School Science

Mythili Menon and JaeHwan Byun

Introduction

A truly inclusive and accessible educational system caters to a wide variety of learners. Considering the large influx of refugee students, the U.S. educational system, which is traditionally a "one-size-fits-all" model, needs to adapt to the changing needs of new learners and provide support for their differences. Refugee children often experience disruptions in schooling and overcome limitations and barriers to adjust to the new educational system in their new yet foreign home. With the goal of providing equitable educational access to all, we launched a project called 'Project Education for All' by creating the 'Center for Educational Technologies to Assist Refugee Learners' in October 2020. After collecting information through a needs-assessment survey, we built an innovative, digital game-based learning platform called 'Gorilla Bay' for refugee middle school children. This platform, built in Unreal Game Engine has both a desktop version as well as apps for both Apple and Android platforms. The game is built to supplement middle school science curriculum and the modules are created using the state's Science Standards and the Next Generation Science Standards, as well as the State Department of Education's English Language Arts and Literacy Common Core Standards. The game is currently being beta-tested in Kiswahili for refugee children from Africa in the public school system.

Gorilla Bay- Digital Game-Based Learning Platform

Gorilla Bay is a role-playing game designed for students to learn the science content embedded in the game by navigating the game area and interacting with Non-Playing Characters (NPCs). The main objective of the game is to take pictures of various objects corresponding to the module (such as planets in space, organs in the human body, etc.) while exploring game environments after receiving requests from Dr. Kayembe, the primary NPC who guides them through the game.

Methodology

The beta testing and focus group interviews are currently ongoing and is expected to be complete before the start of the conference. All student participants tested are in the Newcomer Program. The Newcomer program is a specially designed initiative for newly arrived immigrants, refugees, and English second language learners to help them transition to a new country, new school, and new language. In total, 60 students in the Newcomer Program (30 Kiswahili-speaking refugee students and 30 other language-speaking refugee students, immigrants, and English learners) will participate in focus group interviews and beta testing. In addition, 30 parent participants in total will beta test the platform and participate in focus group interviews (In Kiswahili or English). Four teachers in total will be participate in the beta testing and the focus group interviews in person at the school. All interviews will be recorded.

Conclusion

The results of beta-testing the digital game-based platform as well as the focus group interviews can inform government policymakers, educators, and humanitarian and resettlement agencies on the importance of providing additional educational resources to improve educational outcomes in the refugee community, and aid in improving and prioritizing refugee childrens' educational needs.

515   The Importance of Intercultural Competence of Educators: Non-EU Lecturers in Baltic States

Vaiva Chockevičiūtė and Karin Kuimet

The migration context in Baltic states changed significantly during the last few years. In a relation to hybrid attack from Belarus, 2021, and War in Ukraine, 2022, non-European migrants' numbers rose. Therefore, a discussion of intercultural competence in Higher Education settings takes on a new level of relevance.

Due to resent migrant crisis on the Border with Belarus, the Law on the Legal Status of Foreigners was amended to make it easier for non-European students and researchers to look for work in Lithuania (EMN, Country Factsheet, 2022). In 2021 after COVID-19 restrictions were removed, the number of international students from third countries increased 102% in Estonia (EMN Annual Report, 2021).

Studies show correlation between ability to adapt to diverse cultural contexts directly affecting both performance and satisfaction (Henderson, Stackman and Lindekilde, 2018). Such an ability should be developed and maintained at all levels of Educational Settings. A study of Immigrant parents in Lithuania shows several challenges towards inclusive education, such as: the lack of preparedness of teachers to work with culturally diverse groups; ethnocentric approach in teaching; lack of culturally diverse teaching content (Simoniukštytė and Chockevičiūtė, 2021). From the perspective of inclusive education, a teacher dealing with cultural differences needs to maintain a balance between respect for students' cultural identity and equal opportunities for every student (Simoniukštytė and Chockevičiūtė, 2022).

The research aims to supplement the data collected for the research the importance of intercultural communication competence of educators in multicultural classroom. One of the research's limitations was the lack of intercontinental and racial diversity between focus group participants. Assuming the experience might differ between EU and Non-EU lecturers, the decision was made to collect additional data with the help of qualitative in-depth interviews.

The data of 4 in-depth interviews allowed to supplement the data of Focus group research with the insights from non-EU lecturers' perspective, revealing issues faced by lecturers and students arriving in the Baltic states. The findings supported the need of integrational assistance for the international personnel, while additional efforts towards non-EU lecturers' and students' integration should be made, considering possible cultural shock and other individual challenges. Culturally aware environment and consistency in intercultural competence development creates better international career opportunities and local integration prospects for students and lecturers.

References

European Migration Network (2022). EMN Country Factsheet. Lithuania 2021. Available at: EMN_factsheet2021_LT.pdf .

European Migration Network (2021). EMN Annual Report on Migration and Asylum 2021. National Report Estonia. Available at: arm2021_estonia.pdf (europa.eu).

Henderson, L.S., Stackman, E.W., Lindekilde, R. (2018). Why cultural intelligence matters on global project teams. International Journal of Project Management 36. P. 954– 967.

Simoniukštytė, A., Chockevičiūtė, V. (2021). Inclusive Education from The Perspective of Immigrant Parents: The Lithuanian Case. The Migration Conference 2021. Transnational Press London. P. 84-85.

Simoniukštytė, A., Chockevičiūtė, V. (2022). Competences Needed for an Inclusive Teacher. The perspective of Roma and Refugee Parents Living in Lithuania. Reimagining Parenthood in Diverse Contexts. University of Malta. P. 99-125.

11C   Remittances and Development V1

Chair: Deniz Yetkin Aker, Tekirdağ Namık Kemal University, Turkey

236   Remittances, Healthcare and Education in Morocco: A Micro Econometric Analysis

Boutaina Idrissi, Sara Kawkaba, Ezzrari Abdeljaouad

Morocco's current population is about 37 million with an estimated of 5.4 million Moroccan nationals living abroad[1] 80% of which are settled in Europe mainly in France, Spain, Italy, Netherlands, Belgium and Germany. More recently, a growing number of Moroccan migrants have settled in Canada and the U.S. Among migrants from Maghreb countries, Moroccans living abroad are those who transfer the most of their revenues to the country of origin[2]. Remittances are an important source of revenue for Moroccan economy and play a key role in adjusting Morocco's balance of payments. During the last decade, remittances represented up to 7% of Morocco's GDP, amounting US$7 billion per year.   During 2022, remittances registered a new peak, attaining US$9 billion[3].

This paper aims to address the following question: Do remittances from Moroccan migrants allow households remaining in the country of origin to meet their social needs?

A heightened interest in understanding the remitting practices of migrants and their impact on a variety of socioeconomic aspects such as healthcare and education has emerged as remittances flows to developing countries have risen substantially over the last decades.

From Migrants perspectives, there are various reasons for remitting, ranging from consumption smoothing and target saving to altruism and insurance purposes (Amuedo-Dorantes et al. 2005). Similarly, there are a number of uses for remittances among which are daily living expenses, paying back loans, investing in education, paying for health expenses, funding a new business or building residential and nonresidential structures.

Compared to empirical work, Hanson, G. H., & Woodruff, C. (2003), proves that remittances may have both positive and negative effects on the education attainment of school age children, there may be differential effects by gender of the children.

Another interesting finding can be highlighted through the work of Mawuena, K., Okey, M. K. N., Pelenguei, E., & Kafando, B. (2022). The authors present in their article the results of a study on the impact of remittances from migrants on the health expenditure of recipient in Togo by using the propensity score-matching model and data from the 2015 Unified Questionnaire of Core Indicators of Well-being survey. The results show that remittances have a positive impact on the use of public health services.

This paper uses an econometric model to assess the impact of remittances on consumption in Morocco, based on the National Survey on Household Consumption and Expenditure (ENCDM) of 2013-2014 or the most updated one (2018-2019) conducted by The High Commissioner for Planning if it is available.

In this paper, the propensity score matching method (Rosenbaum and Rubin, 1983) was used as a key instrument. It consists of associating each household that received remittances from a Moroccan living abroad with a household that did not receive remittances but that has similar demographic and socio-economic characteristics. This second sample serves as a comparison group. Matching is based on the estimation of propensity scores, using a Probit model (default). The variable to be explained is binary: if the household receives remittances and otherwise (control group household).

142   Social remittances from Gulf: Impact on different dimensions of autonomy of the non-migrant wives in Kerala

Mohd Imran Khan

The inflow of financial remittances has continuously been assessed as a significant channel through which migration contributes to alleviating poverty, aiding job creation and improving overall socio-economic conditions in the origin countries. However, the financial aspect of remittances has dominated migration research. The study of the non-economic dimension of remittances remains relatively limited. Migrants send financial remittances and act as a transfer channel for social remittances such as social norms, health practices, educational systems and political structure from the host country to the country of origin. Social remittances are "ideas, behaviour, identities and social capital that flow from receiving to sending countries". Social remittances are broadly categorized into norms, practices, identities and social capital (Levit, 1998; 2001). Apart from these, there are other references to non-economic remittances, such as the transfer of technology by return migrants, often in the form of tacit knowledge and political remittances, including the transfer of political identities and ideologies from the host to the migrant-sending country.

In the Kerala context, few studies have examined the impact of social remittances. Studies have found that Emigration can strengthen religious identities (Osella and Osella, 2007) and have an effect on religious practices (Oommen, 2016); Emigration affects public provisioning (Bhavnani & Peters, 2015) and the education and Autonomy of non-migrant women (Osella and Osella 2000). Also, it creates morbidity differentials between emigrants and non-emigrant wives (Ali et al., 2017).

This study examines the impact of migration and remittances on women empowerment taking the case of women whose husbands have migrated to the Gulf. As the previous literature suggested, women's Autonomy is higher in emigrant households than the non-emigrant households. Autonomy can be pure because of the absence of the husband or a household head and not the changes in gender norms. We will distinguish the existence of social remittances by categorizing the women whose husbands are currently abroad to those whose husbands have returned to their households. Another significant departure from the current literature is that instead of taking the remittance amount or remittance as binary variables, which is a usual norm for examining the impact of remittances, we are focusing on the patterned remittances, i.e., the frequency of remittances, which seems to have a significant effect on the receiving households as evidenced by the recent literature in left-behind women's Autonomy in taking health-related decisions (Green, Sharon H., et al. 2019). We use the gender module of the Kerala Migration Survey conducted at the Centre for Development Studies, Trivandrum, for 2016 and 2018 for our analysis. We take a sample of married women living in nuclear families and compare across three categories – whose husbands are emigrants, husbands are return emigrants, and husbands have never migrated. We consider six types of Autonomy to analyze multiple dimensions of women's empowerment: economic participation, financial Autonomy, Participation in household decision-making, Autonomy in mobility, Autonomy in health decisions, and Reproductive Autonomy.

23   A Quantitative Analysis on the Effect of Remittances on the Socio-Economic Development of Return Migrants

Sarbani Thakur, Kailash Chandra Das, Tushar Dakua

This research is based on the Middle Ganga Plain (MGP region) which encompasses 37 districts of Bihar and 27 districts of Eastern Uttar Pradesh and covers an area of 144409 square kilometres. Migrants send remittances in form of cash or kind to their households. The objective of this study is to analyse the impact of these remittances on the socio-economic development of the household of return migrants as perceived by them. The data reveals that more than 57 percent of the households from the MGP region have at least one member who had migrated for economic purposes and 7% of these households have return migrants. We take up a quantitative approach, by initially checking the internal validity of the Perceptive statements using Cronbach's Alpha and then develop an 'Impact Score' based on these perceptions of the Return Migrants regarding their social and economic development. We then employ, Ordinal Logistic regression and infer that remittance utilization in which field have a significant association with the Impact Score. We see that, nearly 30 percent of return migrants feel that they may migrate again and two-thirds would encourage their children to migrate. This study would help us to know the level of satisfaction and degree of upliftment in the lifestyle and socioeconomic characteristics, based on various determinants, among the return migrants in the MGP region of India.

Keywords: Remittances, Return migrants, Socio-economic development, Middle Ganga Plain, Quantitative Analysis

11D Youth, Children and Families V2

Chair: Almudena Macías León, University of Malaga, Spain

1   Culture of migration and aspiration of youth in Kerala

Sulaiman KM

Context: Kerala, one of the prominent spots of international emigration, depicts historical migration trends and the development of a stable migration stream towards Persian Gulf countries and other developed countries. The widespread diffusion of this migration also affects those without any direct links to migrants and the community. The study intends to go beyond the conventional emphasis on the economic benefits of migration and remittances and investigate the effects of migration and social remittances on status relations at home and the youth who live in a culture where migration is a crucial part, how their future decisions are shaped by the cultural consensus related to migration.

Objectives: The collective aim of this study was to understand if there is a culture of migration in the Kerala community. Further, how the young Keralites perceive, represent and interact with the significant factors of the culture of migration influenced the migration from Kerala to Gulf for over three decades. In the end, there is a need to derive a definition for the concept of culture of migration that can be applied in the context of Kerala.

Data and Methodology: The study used the anthropological demographic method. Anthropological demography is an empirical research approach that includes a mix of quantitative and qualitative methodologies. The study used the primary data collected during 2019-20 from Calicut, Kerala. In a quantitative survey, students from six colleges in the study area, three from each professional and non-professional course, were selected, and 491 respondents were interviewed. For the qualitative study, urban and rural areas were selected from the same district; from this chosen small study area, 43 open-ended interviews were conducted among potential migrants, migrants and non-migrants using respondent-driven sampling. Key informant interviews were also conducted with different community leaders and travel agents. The qualitative data is used narratively to understand the presence of the culture of migration. Relevant bivariate and multivariate techniques were applied to analyse quantitative data in the context of the study's objectives.

Findings and Conclusion: The summary of this study will be that Kerala has a culture of migration; more than four decades of migration from Kerala to the Gulf induced changes to the local culture in a way that motivates and facilitates further migration. Even though many youths find migration a potential life choice, they are more aware of the pros and cons of migrating. Youth have a sense of hope that if they find a suitable job in their native land, they can build their life in Kerala. The study explained that in Kerala, migration is considered a potential life choice that can help the person to have meaningful employment, Support children's education and live a middle-class lifestyle. The culture of migration in Kerala can be described as "the migration was widespread based on the history of movements, this migration history and previous migratory experiences influenced the cultural perception and values, which buttress the celebration of migration and migrants. Migration decision-making became an everyday experience for individuals, and migration became a dignified life choice for households and individuals to attain economic and social well-being." The culture of migration in Kerala is a product of historical migration patterns and experiences, which developed a cultural scenario where migration is treated as a day-to-day activity. Migration became a socially accepted and economically feasible way for people who want to meet household and community expectations.

503   Adolescents' decision to migrate following parental labour migration. Questions of agency, opportunities, and constraints

Georgiana Udrea and Gabriela Guiu

In recent years, the migration of temporary labour, whether skilled or unskilled, has led to one of the most dramatic population shifts in Eastern Europe. Countries such as Romania, Ukraine and Poland have some of the largest migrant populations in the region (McAuliffe & Triandafyllidou, 2021) and the current Russian-Ukrainian conflict seems to further deepen existing migration trends and flows. Our paper focuses on the Romanian diaspora, which exploded when the borders of the Romanian labour force were opened (Beciu, Ciocea, Mădroane & Cârlan, 2018) and explores the consequences of parental migration on adolescents left at home.One of the major consequences of the massive out-migration of Romanians is that a significant percentage of children have grown up without the irreplaceable support of their parents (Iancu, 2013; Onu, Pop, Chiriacescu, Preda & Roman, 2019). According to official statistics, the total number of children whose parents work abroad is estimated at between tens of thousands (National Authority for the Protection of the Rights of the Child and Adoption, 2021) and hundreds of thousands (Save the Children Romania, 2020; Toth, Toth, Voicu & Ştefănescu, 2007). Most of these children live in regions with high unemployment rates, especially in the north-east and south-west of the country and most come from rural areas (Bălţeanu, Moldoveanu, Ichim, & Dobrescu). Based on these realities and hypothesising that work migration inevitably leads to multiple changes that affect families' lifestyle, life quality, communication, relationships, etc., our study discusses some of the main transformations generated by parental migration from the adolescents' own standpoint. This perspective is less common in the Romanian academic literature, which tends to devote more attention to migrant narratives than to the perceptions and experiences of the children left behind. Our focus is on the teenagers' capacity to self-educate and organise themselves to perform well at school and in everyday activities following parental migration – young people's agency, which is less studied in Romania. We also investigate on their future career plans and their intentions to migrate.To understand adolescents' perceptions of both the benefits and risks of belonging to a transnational family, we conducted in-depth interviews with 21 adolescents aged 16–18 years from rural Oltenia, a region in south-western Romania that ranks second in statistics on the places of origin of left-behind children. Results show that the parental out-migration can trigger positive outcomes for our participants, who tend to show a high level of learning agency and a mature and responsible attitude towards school. Taking their studies seriously means both a better career path and a chance to re-pay the sacrifices their parents made. Asked about their future plans, with very few exceptions, respondents said that they want to live, study and work in Romania and dream of the moment when their families will be reunited. Thus, in addition to making the reality of these adolescents better known, our approach provides information that can be turned into policy solutions aimed at improving their life quality.

445   Approach to the situation of Unaccompanied Migrant Children in Spain

Almudena Macías León

Spain is one of the countries with the most significant influx of immigrants and, specifically, of Unaccompanied migrant children (hereafter, UAMC). The UAMC numbers have increased considerably in recent years. The arrival of these children is constant, especially in the Canary Islands and Andalusia, as well as the Autonomous Cities of Ceuta and Melilla, having experienced a sharp increase in recent years. This group has become one of the priority groups for intervention within the child protection system in Spain.

Most are male, come from Morocco, and are accommodated in regionally-managed state reception centers across the country in Andalusia, Melilla, Catalonia, the Basque Country, and Madrid. However, there are increasing reports of children who are not in shelters and find themselves destitute on the streets or in informal accommodations.

Despite the low volume they represent within our country's total number of entries, minors constitute a particularly vulnerable group. The insufficiency of protection services or the shortage of training itineraries and voluntary abandonment of protection services would be the leading causes of vulnerability of this group. This voluntary abandonment of services means that in many of these cases, the whereabouts of these minors are unknown.

In this work, we will approach the situation of this population in Spain. First, we will approach the volume and sociodemographic profile of this population. Secondly, we will analyze the legal resources and procedures of the child protection system to deal with these minors. Finally, we will analyze the vulnerable factors of this population.

205   From Left-behind Children to Low-skilled Youth Labor Migrants: chain migration within the kinship networks in Do Thanh Commune (Yen Thanh District of Nghe An Province of Vietnam)

Thi Van Cao and Thuy Linh Nguyen

Since the 1990s, and even before that, the low-skilled Vietnamese in Do Thanh Commune (Yen Thanh District, Nghe An Province of Vietnam), which was once a poor commune, has now become "a billionaire village" in the eyes of Vietnamese people, have found ways to work abroad and they have now formed several large family lineages in the overseas countries. The continually growing number of Vietnamese migrant workers raises important concerns about the living environment of the left-behind children. Existing literature (Hoang et. al. 2012, 2014, 2015; Yeoh et.al. 2012; Lam et.al. 2013) are mainly concerned with how to ensure the lives of these people, not being shed light on their attitudes and reactions to the labor migration in their hometown. Drawing on about 200 surveys and 20 in-depth interviews with Vietnamese return migrants and their family members in Do Thanh Commune, this paper first examines the kinship networks, particularly the various ways the networks are expected to assist Vietnamese left-behind children during their transnational migration processes. Vietnamese youths migrate at a young age by taking the different advantages of their kinship networks to facilitate their chain migratory endeavors. They regard these networks as not just the source of information and practical support but also the guarantees for their migration and work in labor-receiving countries. The "chain migration" has enhanced the likelihood of successful migration and settlement in the destination countries, left a belief that the labor migration is inevitable for a better life. The paper also provides deep insights into the way migration choices are often made by Vietnamese youths in a village of Central Vietnam and, at the same time, underscores the effects of their migration choice.

11E   Insecurities and Migration V1

Chair: Afzalur Rahman, University of Chittagong, Bangladesh

239   Migrants, the State and Human Trafficking in Trinidad and Tobago

Andel Andrew and Lue Anda Francis-Blackman

The United States Department of State's 2022 Trafficking in Persons report on human trafficking in Trinidad and Tobago (T&T) triggered a surge of media reports from local media houses on human trafficking in T&T. The opportunity has not been missed by political parties and public figures alleging the existence of human trafficking and pointing fingers at each other about secrecy, lies, cover ups, non-disclosure, and involvement. The common denominator in all of this has been migrants at the centre of human trafficking in T&T with claims of Venezuela and Dominican Republic female migrants being exploited and forced into prostitution. Such a context provides the impetus for this study as human trafficking is evolving in T&T and further it calls into question state capacity.   State capacity speaks to state efficiency and state capabilities. It speaks to the ability of the state institutions to operate effectively. While in T&T the anti-trafficking legislation exists and there also exist public bodies such as the Ministry of National Security and the Counter-Trafficking Unit, the question which guides this research remains: How does state capacity affect the ability of the state to address human trafficking in T&T? To answer this question, this study examines the bureaucratic quality of the Counter-Trafficking Unit at addressing Human Trafficking. The study also assesses the Anti-Trafficking legislation of T&T at being equipped to address the current wave of human trafficking in T&T. As such, in exploring the issue of state capacity and human trafficking. This study will take the form of a qualitative research design through the use of semi-structured interviews. Given the nature and sensitivity of this study the snowballing technique would be utilized.

192   The Old Route is New Again: Female Migrant Journeys from The Gambia to the Canary Islands

Catherine Conrad

Although the Gambia is the smallest country on the African continent, per capita, it ranks among the highest contributors of irregular migrants. This paper presents the results of ethnographic field work undertaken in the Gambia, West Africa during the period 2018 through 2022. Narratives from the Atlantic migration route between West Africa and the Canary Islands are discussed in an effort to better understand the return to this dangerous route. Female migrant journeys have been largely neglected in the literature of the Gambia, and yet women are increasingly attempting irregular migration routes in the context of local understandings of chances of success in seeking asylum. Particular attention will be placed on the impacts of climate change as a contributing factor to migration decisions. Bettering the understanding of the connections between desire, motives, actions and deprivations will allow us to consider more meaningful ways to support West African mobility.

461   New Trend, Illegal Migration from Turkey to the USA

Emrah Cengiz

United States' southern border has been witnessing a record increase in illegal entrance of Turkish citizens. According to the border patrol agents, during the 2022 fiscal year, 15.445 Turkish citizens entered the country illegally through the US-Mexican border, particularly through the border crossing at El Paso. Although it has not gotten much attention in media and academic studies mainly because there are other nationalities constituting higher numbers of migrants entering US illegally such as Mexicans, Venezuelans, Nicaraguans and several others, the rate of increase in the number of Turkish citizens entering the United States illegally is alarming. While the main reasons of the high numbers of people migrating from Erdogan's Turkey seem to be the general insatiateness regarding economic and political problems, substandard working conditions, underdeveloped fundamental human rights protection system and other deficiencies in the country, United States' prestigious image in the world, decent working conditions, strong economy and promising future can be counted among the main reasons that migrants prefer it as destination country. The surprising rise of Turkish citizens choosing Mexico as a transit country to enter the States is allegedly attributed to the transnational criminal organizations' connections to Turkey. The dire circumstances Turkish people experience and their endeavor to somehow "get out of Turkey" plays into the hands of cartels. This study aims to point out this multilateral phenomenon and to elaborate the reasons behind migrants' choosing United States as destination country.

346   Syrian Refugees in Turkey: Mental Health Challenges and Risk Factors

Selen Subaşı and Klára Tarkó

The Syrian conflict has resulted in a major humanitarian crisis, with millions of people seeking refuge in neighboring countries. Among these countries, Turkey has the largest number of Syrian refugees, with more than 3.6 million individuals residing in the country. However, many refugees struggle with psychological consequences related to their displacement.In an effort to understand the mental state of Syrian refugees in Turkey, identify potential symptoms of mental health disorders, and assess demographic and psychosocial factors associated with increased risk, a survey was conducted among 250 participants using the Mental State Questionnaire. The results revealed that 71% of the participants were either "vulnerable" (39.5%) or "endangered" (30.8%), while 28% were classified as "mentally healthy." The analysis found no significant differences in mental health status based on age. However, females were found to be more likely to be classified as mentally vulnerable. Marital status did not show any strong association with mental health status. On the other hand, higher education levels were linked to a lower risk of being classified as mentally vulnerable or endangered.These findings highlight the need for interventions and support programs targeting refugees who are classified as mentally vulnerable or endangered, especially females who appear to be at a higher risk. Addressing mental health concerns could have a significant impact on the overall well-being, productivity, and quality of life of refugees and society as a whole. Future research should explore the relationship between gender and mental health to identify potential contributing factors.

11F   Migration Governance V1

Chair: Ana Vila-Freyer, Universidad Latina de México, Mexico

228   Managing Mobility Dangers and Irregular Migration from Africa to Europe: The Role of Migration Governance

Adedeji Oso

The continent of Africa is facing a multitude of political and socioeconomic challenges such as poor leadership, poverty, bad governance, lack of job opportunities, and insecurity. As a result, many Africans are leaving their homeland for Europe in search of better opportunities. While some adhere to legal migration regulations, others migrate irregularly due to bad advice, defiance, inducement, frustration, desperation, or personal decision. Meanwhile, the irregular migration of many African migrants to Europe has resulted in predatory and security-threatening conditions, including death, drowning, rape, abduction, and forced labour. Ironically, while much attention is being given to the security dynamics of the irregular journey, only a little attention has been given to the institutions involved in the accountability of migration in Africa, found in national, regional, and continental spaces; to realize the efforts they have deployed to deter or reduce these crises, including the successes and failures therein. This paper aims to fill this gap in the literature and develop strategies, policies, or approaches for addressing irregular migration through an effective migration governance model. In the end, the study relies on relevant theoretical and conceptual frameworks to bridge the gap and promote migration safety and accountability regarding migration from Africa to Europe.

Keywords: Mobility Dangers; Irregular Migration; Migration Governance

106   Tunisian 'Escapees'- Sub-Saharan 'Invaders': Tunisian Media Discourse(s) on Crimmigration

Amal Hlioui

Tunisia has long been conceptualized as a sending country for immigrant workers/ illegalized harraga . Yet, after the 2011 political upheaval, a new variable was thrust onto the Tunisian migratory equation with the entry of thousands of sub-Saharans to Tunisia. Subsequently, migration occupied an important space in mediated debates after the so-called 'Revolution' and the media discourse swayed between myopia and problematization. Indeed, media attention shifted towards 'irregular' sub-Saharans with a rhetoric of fight against deviation. This manufactured 'illegality' and their construction as "potential criminals" blurred the lines between migration/ criminal laws, leading to crimmigration.

This study hinges on three gaps in existing literature: (i) absence of research on crimmigration in the Tunisian context, (ii) scarcity of systematic investigations of Tunisian media discourse on immigrants and (iii) the almost exclusively economic and ethnographic perspectives of sub-Saharan migration in Tunisia. Research failed to ruminate on sub-Saharans' reception and representation in their host society. Indeed, this article proposes to examine Tunisian media discourse(s) on crimmigration by scrutinizing the representations of Tunisian emigrants and sub-Saharan immigrants in Tunisian news and contrasting the discursive strategies used to crimmigrate them. Finally, it aims to understand whether the media discourse(s) around these two groups are convergent or divergent and if they reflect the overall social perception of Tunisian emigrants as 'escapees' and sub-Saharan immigrants as 'invaders'.

The corpus consists of news pieces published between 2019 and 2020. Data collection was done through systematic media monitoring of Tunisian media outlets, using key words pertaining to migration. The finished syndicated corpus is categorized, translated, then coded according to crimmigration thematic headings and the relevant discursive strategies. Building on crimmigration theory as advanced by Stumpf (2006) and adapted by Kmak (2018), the study adopts a Discourse-Historical Approach. The analysis follows a mixed-method and two-level design, cross-referencing the discourse topics with discursive strategies used for each group.

The quantitative/ qualitative findings yielded unforeseen answers to the research questions. Against odds, most news reporting addresses crimmigration as a fallacy and criticizes it rather than adopts it. The media's crimmigration rhetoric revolves around "harga", rather than illicit immigration. This shatters assumptions that

Tunisian media are fixating on sub-Saharan 'infiltrations' to Tunisia. Indeed, most news pieces tackling "harga" involving Tunisians and Sub-Saharans treat both groups similarly and use the same legitimation, nomination, argumentation discursive strategies. The indistinguishable use of "illegal" and "irregular" in the same pieces is indicative of the absence of ideological drive and a terminological confusion on the part of journalists. For instance, a news briefing dated December 16, 2020, titled "Ministry of Defense: 51 Africans caught while Surreptitiously crossing the borders", in the Arabic version of Business News uses both terms throughout the article, interchangeably. This lexical confusion is also displayed in the paradoxical headlines which use incongruous terms, crimmigrating and legitimating migrants at the same time. It is worth noting that words like "interception" or "arrestations" often occur in the same headline as "rescue" or "victims".

466   Old wine in New Bottle? Old Wine in new bottle? Migrants, Discipline and Surveillance in the New Workplaces: A Global South Perspective

Sumeetha Mokkil Maruthur

The world of work is changing at a pace we could never imagine before. Historically, technology has of course altered the organisation and structure of work. Today we are in the midst of a new wave of Industry 4.0 often termed as the Fourth Industrial Revolution that is eroding many jobs and creating new ones demanding re-skilling and training of the workforce. The work-life line is now too fluid that to transcend it and to encounter it every day is a challenge. Global South migration can be seen as two different streams of migration- South -South Migration and South North migration. More than 40 per cent of all international migrants worldwide in 2019 (112 million) were born in Asia, primarily originating from India (the largest country of origin), China, and South Asian countries such as Bangladesh, Pakistan and Afghanistan (IOM, 2019:26). When the new work structure requires a revamping of the shop floor dynamics changes in technology and surveillance becomes pivotal. Structures to discipline migrants and control them are devised in new workplaces too.Workers in many workplaces are monitored by using wearables-like wristbands that monitor their stress levels and time of work. In the context of industry 4.0 it would be important to explore how new surveillance mechanisms are actually implemented. When AI dominated technology is used, it can result in polarisation of jobs, with highly skilled and low skilled jobs dominating and middle skills almos disappearing, the position of migrant workers and the precarity it will add to their work life has to be observed. While international mobility of capital is often desired, nation states shy away from discussing international mobility of labour. In the growth of industry 4.0, this work proposes to analyse the new technological revolution, surveillance and unabated flow of international migration. The entire discourse of labour process analysis throws up interesting questions as to the organisation of work and the incorporation of new groups of workers into the workshop. Worker resistance or class- consciousness have challenged the structural constraints in all workplaces. The formal subordination of labour coupled with the real subordination of labour (Marx, 1976), with the dominance of technology, result in capital's control to be elusive in the workplace. Resistance to capital structures and responses of the workers reiterate workers' agency in the workplace.In this paper I would like to take forward the new developments in segmentation theories, take it as a base for analyzing the changes in the shop floor dynamics when technological disruption is the norm. Technology promotes highly skilled workers and may even wipe out jobs that require manual labour. The argument put forward is that despite use of sophisticated technology, when it comes to controlling migrant workers- diverse forms of surveillance and discipling mechanisms are adopted. Thus control still remains as an inveitable tool to define power relations in the workplace.

210   For every action, and equal reaction? The two paths guiding the (re)making of the North American Migratory System

Ana Vila-Freyer

In the 1990s, Mexico first recognized itself as a transit country, along with its traditional expelling migrants' tradition. Thirty years later, the country is emerging as a country of settlement (Giorguli, García, & Masferrer, 2016; Cruz Piñeiro & Hernandez Lopez, 2021). The Mexican approach of migration management cannot be understood outside the path (North, 1990) adopted by the United States since 1993, when the Clinton administration launched Operation Blockade and began the construction of the border wall. By the 2020s, the presence of Central American migrants trying to reach the US had surpassed that of Mexicans, giving rise to a process of reshaping of a centennial migratory system, until then centered on Mexico and the United States (París-Pombo, 2016; Durand, 2016). Mexico has adopted a pragmatic strategy to adapt to the pressures exerted by the United States and by grassroots migrant protection organizations (Vila-Freyer & Estrada Lozano, 2021). Both strategies frame migrant agency to challenge states and transborder migration management in a context of criminalization and illegalization.

11G   Migration and Social Integration V2

Chair: Apostolos G. Papadopoulos, Harokopio University, Greece

475   Problematising the migration-wellbeing nexus in rural Greece in unequal times

Apostolos G. Papadopoulos and Loukia-Maria Fratsea

In the last thirty years, Greece has changed from a country of emigration to one of immigration. During this period, international migration flows contributed to new socio-economic realities in the country, both in rural and urban areas. The economic recession starting in 2008 and the related austerity measures affected both the size, net migration and labour market integration of migrants in Greece, while in 2015 the economic crisis in the country coincided with the recent migration/refugee crisis. This paper draws on empirical research conducted as part of the IMAJINE H2020 project to examine the multiple mobilities and their links with actual and perceived social and spatial inequalities found in both urban (Attica region) and rural areas of Greece (Western Greece region). In Western Greece, we conducted 59 qualitative semi-structured interviews between 2017 and 2020 with different (non)migrant groups such as Romanian migrants, Syrian refugees, internal migrants in Western Greece, and the local population, while we conducted a follow-up in 2022. Interviews were combined with ethnographic observation in both research areas, and interviews with stakeholders and key informants (i.e., policy makers, NGO representatives, farmers, and local authorities) at the national and local levels were used to triangulate the information obtained from the interviews. The aim of our study is to discuss the changing conditions and challenges posed by newly arriving migrants and refugees in rural areas of Greece, as well as the views of local people on the impact of new arrivals in their rural areas. The empirical analysis problematizes the changing linkages that emerge between migrants and refugees and the economy, society, and culture in rural host areas. In this context, we reflect on the conceptualizations of rurality and well-being among different populations and contrast the challenges associated with well-being with the different mobilities that exist in rural and urban areas in Greece.

1124   Repopulating small towns by international migration: a mutual interest relationship?

Michela C. Pellicani

The picture of Italy, in particular in the last ten years, is a demographic black hole. The micro-towns (less than 500 inhabitants), more than others, are losing on average 11.6% of their population; the towns with 500-1,000 inhabitants 9.0% and the towns with 1,000-3,000 inhabitants 7.0% 1 (ISTAT, 2022). Following the ISTAT projections, this trend will even intensify in the next years compromising the cultural identity and the sustainability of fundamental social services like education, health, etc. Southern Italy is particularly affected by this phenomenon induced by a consistent drop of births combined with a resurge of important levels of young adults' emigration. In such a scenario, our questions are: "Could this trend be reversed?"; "By which strategies?"; "Considering the population ageing and the depopulation of small-medium towns on one hand and the numerous problems related to the integration process of the migrants on the other hand, could it be possible to trigger a positive trade off of mutual interest?" The entrepreneurial dimension of the small towns, as a matter of fact, is more oriented to the local know how and the prevalence of the crafts and agricultural activities is positively correlated to the territorial peripherality. At the same time, a large number of immigrants are characterised by an important know how for crafts and agriculture activities associated with high entrepreneurial skills. Basing on these attitudes and competences, a possible path to explore is, therefore, to promote immigrant' active integration policies to repopulate and revitalise small and medium towns through the development of new enterprises in the crafts and agriculture sectors.

References

ISTAT (2022), La geografia delle aree interne nel 2020: vasti territori tra potenzialità e debolezze.

22   International Migration, Nigerian Diaspora and Gender-Based Violence in the Global North: International Migration, Nigerian Diaspora and Gender-Based Violence in the Global North

Oláyínká Àkànle and Timileyin Asala

The Nigerian diaspora is best understood within the context of intersectionalities of migration and development. This is largely so because the formation of Nigerian diaspora, particularly in the global North, is heavily belied by the realities of international migration for livelihood and socioeconomic survival abroad against the backdrop of excruciating poverty and underdevelopment at origin. This is why Nigerian diaspora is one of the most bourgeoning diasporas globally. The socioeconomic and underdevelopment quagmires of Nigeria continue to propel Nigerians' migration up North. Common destinations in the global North among Nigerian migrants are; United Kingdom (UK), Canada, The United States of America [U.S.A], Australia and the European Union (EU) for survival and existential reasons. Of particular interest in the persistently increasing up North migrations among Nigerians is the booming spousal/family migration strategy where women sometimes go as advance team to destinations ahead of the men (or together with their men). Hitherto, migrations were gender selective with men been mostly migratory while women are left behind. Due to more debilitating harsh economic realities in Nigeria and more inclusive socioeconomic opportunities in Northern countries, there are usually role reversals, at destination, where women often become breadwinners (or equal-breadwinners), have better life-chances and have more gender/rights protection. These increasingly lead to role conflicts as well as power imbalances among spouses/couples/family members coming from patriarchal sociocultural systems like those of Nigeria and Africa. These reversals/inversions of roles, life-chances, rights and power dynamics become drivers of gender-based violence among Nigerians in the global north as gender-based violence becomes prevalent among Nigerian migrants in the diaspora. This calls for more studies/papers such as this. This paper, based on qualitative empirical research conducted in 2022 among Nigerians in the diaspora, therefore, contributes to intellectual conversations on the intersectionalities of migration and development and interpersonal/intraspousal gender-based violence in context of international migration in the global North. The research design used in the research that informed this paper was exploratory. Data were from primary insights, autoethnography, primary data and secondary data. This paper offers original empirical and theoretical findings and experiences through migration and development and gender-based violence experiences of Nigerian diaspora in the global North.

281   Intergenerational transmission of domestic violence in refugee families in Durban, South Africa

Kassa Maksudi and Shanaaz Hoosain

"The World Health Organization (2021) recently reported that 1 in 3 women worldwide are affected by gender-based violence (GBV). South Africa has gained notoriety for its high rates of GBV, particularly against women and children, including domestic violence (DV) (Gouws, 2021). Despite this, less than 20 peer-reviewed articles have been written about the experiences of refugee women in South Africa who suffer from DV. Given their refugee status this marginalized and vulnerable population is disproportionately at risk of violence (PASSOP, 2022). Consequently, I became curious about the experiences of African refugee women from war-affected countries, who are often unseen victims of violence, and the role that women play in DV. Specifically, I focused on how DV is transmitted intergenerationally within refugee families between mothers and their adult daughters from Burundi and the Democratic Republic of Congo in Durban, South Africa. To answer this research question, I conducted a qualitative embedded single case study inquiry with 30 pairs of mother and adult daughters, consisting of four focus group discussions with 20 women and 40 semi-structured individual interviews. The study revealed that refugee women and their adult daughters face(d) varying degrees of violence within the home, which are attributed to a range of risk factors, including their refugee status, economic challenges/dependency, religious misconceptions, poor parent/guardian-child relationships, and adherence to strict gender norms. The study's aim is to change the way we perceive and address DV in refugee communities by examining and comprehending DV in refugee families in relation to intergenerational transmission as well as by acknowledging the role of women in violence.

17:00 END OF DAY THREE SESSIONS

Day Four 26 August 2023 - 09:30-11:00

12A   Theory and Methods in Migration Studies V1

Chair: Ruchi Singh, Tata Institute, India

432   A Collaborative Open-Source Migration Research Platform

Jimmy Krozel, Mark Peters, Athina Bikaki, Shaili Dave, Luke Lorentzatos, Ioannis Kakadiaris

To understand global migration patterns, study scenarios, design effective policies, address researcher needs, and identify how these needs change over time, accurate, reliable, and timely migration data are needed [1]. However, migration data are often inadequately quantified, classified, have spatial or temporal gaps, or are nonexistent. In this paper, a collaborative, open-source research platform is introduced to facilitate the gathering of data, studying and analyzing of migration trends, problems, and concerns. The platform allows for easy access to structured and unstructured datasets, mathematical and graphical functions for cleansing and transforming data, computational models, and additional research artifacts.

157   Quality of data on migrants in the Indian Census

Reshmi R S, Ram Bhagat, Shalini Sen

Census provides valuable socio-economic and demographic data which is useful for the public welfare. Policies based on demographic estimation heavily depend upon the accuracy of the data and the use of statistical methods employed. Tests of accuracy on data related to age, headcount and/or vital events help to identify the underlying deficiencies in the datasets used. There have been studies focused on accuracy and adequacy of census data. However, there are only a few studies which evaluate the data of migration including its characteristics. The present paper, based on data on migrants collected from census of India, focuses on the quality of data on age and duration of residence of migrants. The study uses the migration data from Census of India during the years 1991, 2001 2011. The analysis will focus on the quality of age reporting and duration of stay and how the quality of data has changed over the last three decades and also how it varies among sex and place of residence. Further, detailed analysis will be carried out state-wise to show the pattern of digit preference in age and duration of stay.

15   Highland-Lowland Interaction in Mountain Regions: A Study of Changing Patterns among Bhotiya Tribes of Garhwal Himalaya

Saurav Kumar

Highland-lowland interaction amongst the Bhotiya tribes is a centuries-old tradition and practice. They have two dwellings – highland and lowland. During the winter when the highland areas are covered with huge snow, the Bhotiya migrate to their valley dwellings and during the summer, they migrate to the highlands with their animals for grazing. Recently, the trend of highland-lowland interaction is changing, mainly declining. This study examines the changing highland-lowland interaction amongst the Bhotiya tribes. A case study of eight villages was conducted and a total of 292 households in all villages were surveyed. We have noticed that the practice of highland-lowland interaction has decreased by 55% during the last two decades. A village has been abandoned. There were a total of 662 households living in the highland villages in 2001, which has reduced to 292 households in 2021. The occupational structure of the people has transformed. Earlier, their main occupation was practicing agriculture and rearing livestock mainly, goats and sheep. Now, only a few households are practicing them and most of the Bhotiyas are working in tertiary activities. This study suggests that the traditional practices of agriculture and livestock rearing can be revived by increasing infrastructural facilities – transportation, education, markets, and employment. The role of the state government and local people is noteworthy to conserve the traditional practices of highland-lowland interaction.

1114 Impact of Machine Learning based Data Imputation on the Prediction and Classification Performance of Refugee Modeling Dataset

Kazi Tanvir Islam, Esther Mead, Nitin Agarwal

As part of the continuous effort to improve our global refugee prediction and classification models, this work explores the effectiveness of various data imputation techniques. Our refugee dataset contains 233 countries and territories with 27 predictive features/columns. Global peace index (gpi), corruption perception index (cpi), discrimination and violence against minorities (dvam), and freedom of religion (fr) are some essential features of the dataset. However, the dataset contains a significant number of missing values. The feature column with the lowest missing values has 18%, while the highest has 60% missing values. This study was inspired by our existing research [1].

Data imputation is a common way to deal with the missing value problem where the missing values get substituted through statistical or machine learning techniques [2]. The simplest way to handle this problem is to ignore the missing values. However, this technique is ineffective when the amount of missing value is significant [3]. Jerez et al. [2010] stated that machine learning imputation techniques are usually much more flexible than the standard statistical models and can capture higher-order interactions between the data, which results in better predictions [4]. Khosla el. Al [5] utilized mean, median, and linear regression on a Cardiovascular Health Study dataset. Among the imputation methods, Linear Regression gave the smallest RMSD (Root Mean Square Deviation) and MAD (Mean Absolute Deviation) values, which suggested that it achieved the highest imputation accuracy [5].

In this research, we have utilized four machine learning (stochastic regression, deterministic regression, KNN, and missForest) and three traditional data imputation techniques (mean, median & mode). To begin with, we generated seven separate datasets using the mentioned imputation techniques. Later, we performed feature importance analysis using Pearson's correlation technique to determine the imputation techniques' impact on the imputed dataset and validated the result using multicollinearity analysis. The in-depth analysis of feature importance & multicollinearity is out of the scope of this article. Therefore, we will include that in our final full paper. In the concluding step, we determined the prediction and classification performance of the imputed datasets and compared the result with the original dataset (with all the missing values removed). Figure 1 and Figure 2 exhibit the comparison of regression and classification performance correspondingly.

The regression and classification performance confirms the effectiveness of data imputation. Stochastic regression, the best-performing imputation method, achieves 88% adjusted R-squared value in linear regression, while the original dataset achieves only 55%. In classification, the best performing KNN imputation achieves 90% accuracy, while the original dataset yields 80% accuracy. Consequently, in both cases, the rest of the imputation datasets have performed significantly better than the original dataset.

Any machine learning model's performance greatly depends on the dataset's quality. A dataset with huge potential descends into a useless dataset due to the missing value problem. Our study confirms that machine learning-based data imputation can significantly improve a dataset's quality, yielding better prediction and classification performance.

Acknowledgment

This research is funded in part by the U.S. National Science Foundation (OIA-1946391, OIA-1920920, IIS-1636933, ACI-1429160, and IIS-1110868), U.S. Office of Naval Research (N00014-10-1-0091, N00014-14-1-0489, N00014-15-P-1187, N00014-16-1-2016, N00014-16-1-2412, N00014-17-1-2675, N00014-17-1-2605, N68335-19-C-0359, N00014-19-1-2336, N68335-20-C-0540, N00014-21-1-2121, N00014-21-1-2765, N00014-22-1-2318), U.S. Air Force Research (FA9550-

22-1-0332), U.S. Army Research Office (W911NF-20-1-0262, W911NF-16-1-0189), U.S. Defense Advanced Research Projects Agency (W31P4Q-17-C-0059), Arkansas Research Alliance, the Jerry L. Maulden/Entergy Endowment at the University of Arkansas at Little Rock, and the Australian Department of Defense Strategic Policy Grants Program (SPGP) (award number: 2020-106-094). Any opinions, findings, conclusions, or recommendations expressed in this material are those of the authors and do not necessarily reflect the views of the funding organizations. The researchers gratefully acknowledge the support.

References

Mead, E., Islam, K. T., & Agarwal, N. (2022, December). EXPERIMENTATION WITH DATA IMPUTATION METHODS TO IMPROVE REFUGEE REGRESSION AND CLASSIFICATION PREDICTION MODELS. In The Migration Conference 2022 Selected Papers (Vol. 23, p. 111). Transnational Press London.

Abidin, N. Z., Ismail, A. R., & Emran, N. A., (2018), PERFORMANCE ANALYSIS OF MACHINE LEARNING ALGORITHMS FOR MISSING VALUE IMPUTATION. International Journal of Advanced Computer Science and Applications, 9(6).

Aljuaid, T., Sasi, S., (2016), PROPER IMPUTATION TECHNIQUES FOR MISSING VALUES IN DATA SETS. 2016 International Conference on Data Science and Engineering (ICDSE), pp. 1-5, doi: 10.1109/ICDSE.2016.7823957.

Jerez, J. M., Molina, I., García-Laencina, P. J., Alba, E., Ribelles, N., Martín, M., & Franco, L., (2010), MISSING DATA IMPUTATION USING STATISTICAL AND MACHINE LEARNING METHODS IN A REAL BREAST CANCER PROBLEM. Artificial intelligence in medicine, 50(2), 105-115.

Khosla, A., Cao, Y., Lin, C. C. Y., Chiu, H. K., Hu, J., & Lee, H., (2010), AN INTEGRATED MACHINE LEARNING APPROACH TO STROKE PREDICTION. Proceedings of the 16th ACM SIGKDD international conference on Knowledge discovery and data mining (pp. 183-192).

12B   Insecurities and Migration V2

Chair: Afzalur Rahman, University of Chittagong, Bangladesh

168   Exploring Two Categories of Ukrainian War Refugees Abroad, and Their Common Way to the Sure Victory of Ukraine

Oksana Koshulko

The abstract presents the preliminary results of the last 9 years of research on refugeeism and asylum-seeking of Ukrainian war refugees abroad, in Turkey, Poland, Germany, the Czech Republic, Austria, and Ireland during 2014-2023.

First war refugees from Crimea have been meeting by the author in Istanbul, Turkey, in 2014, after starting the occupation of Crimea by the Russian invaders

(Aslund, 2018), when they have not been recognized in host countries as refugees yet. Logically that this research continues today, in 2023, after Russia attempts a full-scale invasion of Ukraine in 2022.

The methodology of the research during these years was qualitative methods of research, among the methods were case studies; qualitative interviews, such as semi-structured and in-depth; as well as, fieldwork in the mentioned countries.

The research is extremely important because it united the Ukrainian and the Crimean Tatar populations, including refugees, into one common nation of the state of Ukraine (Okean Elzy, 2014). Besides, the research explored two different ways for the Ukrainian and the Crimean Tatar populations to flee the mainland part of the country during the attempts of the full-scale invasion in 2022, and the occupied peninsula during 2014-2023.

In addition, the research showed the efforts of the Ukrainian war refugees in different host countries in their fight and resistance against Russia, the 'state sponsoring terrorism and using terrorist means,' recognized by the European Parliament in 2022 (Goleanu, 2022).

Therefore, this study is extremely important and timely for understanding new approaches to studying two categories of Ukrainian war refugees abroad, the Ukrainian and the Crimean Tatar, and their common way to the sure victory of Ukraine.

References

Aslund, A. (2018). Kremlin Aggression in Ukraine: The Price Tag. The Report: The Atlantic Council of the United States, Second edition, 20 p. Retrieved from http://surl.li/efwdc

Goleanu, L. (2022). EP recognizes Russia as a state sponsoring terrorism and using terrorist means. The Renew Europe Group. Retrieved from http://surl.li/etsub

Okean Elzy. (2014). Coldly (In Ukrainian). ATR. Retrieved from http://surl.li/efzrq

371   The hero across borders: the contemporary myth of the migrant-hero

Patricia Posch

The empirical enterprise of collecting biographical accounts of migrants over the last few years have led to an unexpected likeness regarding the arrangement of happenings and the meaning that migrating and being an e/immigrant has to migrants themselves and the collectives. Despite the richness in detail and the singularity of each account, the tone underlying the narratives is very similar: they are stories of courage, strangeness, negotiation, resilience and perseverance. But what is this thread that sews the diversity of contemporary migration experiences as a part of a broader common sense? This fundamental question guided the development of the study presented in this essay. Having the case of Brazilian migration to Portugal in recent years as a starting point, it stresses the existence, in contemporary times, of a myth of the "migrant-hero" that shapes migration narratives to its structure and meanings. The theoretical ground of this proposition includes a review of archetypes theory as in Jung (1959), with a special attention to the archetype of the Hero, followed by an elucidation of the concept and mechanisms of operation of the myth as seen in Barthes (1957/1993). The idea is further developed in a re-reading of the cosmogonic cycle of the hero's adventure, detailed by Campbell (1949/2004), which corresponds to the main phenomenological events in each of the phases of the said journey. Each of these stages is accompanied by the corresponding situations and contexts in the migratory process and in the experience of the migrant person in the light of the literature available in this disciplinary field, in order to draw parallels and similarities. The intersection of this theoretical repertoire with the empirical studies of migrations allowed us to understand the broad applicability of the myth in the case of international migrations, besides providing evidence of how this intertwining can take place. Based on this study, some generic conclusions could be traced. First, despite the space-time and causal specificity of each migratory experience, it is observed the validity of the hypothesis of the existence, in contemporary times, of a myth of the migrant-hero. Second, the myth transcends cultural boundaries, and consequently, individually and collectively shapes the perceptions about migrants and their experiences of migration at different junctures. Finally, by not operating at a conscious level, but rather silently and (sometimes) unintentionally, it can be recognizable through all sorts of manifestations of subjectivity, such as verbal or visual narratives. Although it is impossible to limit all the diversity contained in migratory experiences to the myth of the migrant-hero, its identification and the understanding of its mechanisms of influence on individual experiences and socially shared discourses are of immeasurable value to bring to light the invisible subjectivities and structures that influence representations of the experience of migrating. Moreover, by bringing to light a force that signifies, it allows a more comprehensive look at the narratives of/about migrants, leading to a gain of consciousness that contributes to sociocultural individual and collective empowerment.

181   A Risk Taken to Serve the Decision: Challenges of the journey of the Irregular Sub-Saharan African Migrants

Siham Soulaimi

Unpleasant experiences can make people consider changes in their lives to find more pleasant ones. Sub-Saharan African migrants had compelling reasons to flee their home countries and embark on perilous journeys. In order to get to their destination, most of them arranged with smugglers and used irregular and unauthorized routes. Europe has become a difficult destination due to strict migration policies and border controls, making Morocco an immigration country. Sub-Saharan irregular migration is full of challenges that might cause a delay for the migrants, announcing a death sentence for many others. Our research study is dedicated to uncovering the driving forces that push Sub-Saharan African migrants to choose dangerous, off-the-beaten-path routes, as well as how these routes are fraught with dangers.

379   Rohingya Refugees' perilous journey from Myanmar to Southeast Asia and South Asia: An assessment through criminalization approach

Afzalur Rahman

This study explores the approach of host countries towards irregular migrants leveling them as a criminal. Furthermore, the adoption of such an approach to deal with the movers exacerbates the insecurity of the migrants. Thus, it fails to represent the actual scenario of the movers. For the present paper, the case of Rohingyas' movement from Myanmar to Southeast Asia and South Asia due to persecution has been assessed by using mixed research methods with taking field data. In particular, the lives and living of Rohingyas who are living in Bangladesh have been evaluated as a case study to know the perception of the host and their experience. Rohingya is one of the most persecuted ethnic minorities in the world. They are living in various South Asian and Southeast Asian countries for a better life. However, host countries like Bangladesh frame them as a criminal who is responsible for creating social unrest. As a result, the root causes of the movement of Rohingyas can't be understood always. Additionally, the host community considers the movement of the Rohingyas in Bangladesh, India, Malaysia, and Indonesia as a security threat to their society. In a nutshell, the discourse of seeing through a criminalization and insecurity lens would be a new perspective to know the real scenario.

12D   Göç Çalışmaları V2

Chair: Betül Dilara Şeker, Van Yuzuncuyil University, Turkey

408   Kahramanmaraş-Türkiye Depremleri Sonrası Yaşanan Deprem Göçü Üzerine Sosyolojik Bir Çalışma

Senem Gürkan ve Erkan Perşembe

Migration is a phenomenon that is experienced in many geographies and for various reasons and has some sociological consequences. Migration, which has increased especially as a result of globalization, may take place due to many reasons such as wars, natural disasters, marriage, health, and may sometimes be compulsory and/or on demand. This study aims to present a sociological research on the earthquake migration experienced by the individuals who experienced the 2023 Kahramanmaraş-Türkiye earthquakes. In this context, within the scope of the qualitative research, in-depth interviews will be conducted with 40 individuals who migrated to Samsun and sociological inferences will be made by applying content analysis on the data set. The results of the study will be presented during the conference presentation.

453   Türkiye'de Deprem ve Göç İlişkisi: Deprem Özelinde Göç

Sibel Terzioğlu

Asırlardır tarihin çeşitli dönemlerinde gerek zorunlu gerek gönüllü olarak Türkiye coğrafyası birçok göçü bünyesinde barındırmıştır. Bu durumun kilit noktası stratejik konumu nedeniyle Türkiye'nin bir tampon bölge olması ve göç rotalarının geçişinde olması ile açıklanabilir. Göç olgusu yıllarda teknoloji ve değişen dünya dinamikleriyle küreselleşme kavramını da kapsayarak yeni bir boyut kazanmıştır. Dolayısıyla beşeri ve sosyal faktörlerin akabinde farklı dünya dinamikleri ve sorunların da eklenmesiyle Türkiye'de ve dünyada dönüşen şartlar neticesinde göç politikaları yeniden gözden geçirilmelidir. Tarihte birçok dezavantajlı kesim vardır fakat trajik ve olumsuz sonuç doğuran en önemli konulardan biri de zorunlu göçler ile beraber yer değiştiren göçmenler olmuştur. Zorunlu göç her ne kadar devlet politikaları ile iyi yönetilmeye çalışılsa da beraberinde birçok sorun getirmektedir. Bu durumlar yaşanırken ülkelerin dünyada aynı zamanda beşeri faktörler ve mücbir sebeplerden dolayı; siyasi endişe ve korkular, hane halkı yoksulluğu, gün geçtikçe artan kıtlık, sel ve deprem afet durumları söz konusudur. Dolayısıyla bu çalışma doğal afet gibi yıkıcı etkileri olan; maddi manevi büyük kayıplara neden olan deprem gerçeği sonrası ortaya çıkan deprem göç olgusu özelinde ele alınmıştır.

Yapılan çalışmanın amacı 2023 Şubat ayında maddi manevi büyük yıkımlara neden olan tüm dünya basınında günlerce yer alan 7.7 ve 7.6 büyüklüğünde Türkiye'nin 10 ilinde ciddi kayıplara neden olan deprem sonrası değerlendirmeler göz önünde bulundurmak olmuştur.M'Asrın felaketi' olarak nitelendirilen deprem olgusu sonrası maddi ,manevi, sosyoekonomik etkileri ortaya konmaya çalışılmıştır. Akabinde göçün yaratmış olduğu etkiler ve doğal afet durumlarında kriz yönetiminin psikolojik ve sosyal boyutu, süreçte yapılması gerekenler, sürecin etkin yönetilmesinde dezavantajlı gruplardan biri olan göçmen kesime yönelik tespitlerde bulunmaya çalışmak hedeflenmiştir. Ortaya koyduğumuz çalışma yerel nitelikte bir araştırma olmakla beraber deprem gibi büyük yıkımlara neden olan durumlarda uluslararası çalışmaları da ilgilendirmesi bağlamında büyük önem arz etmektedir. Özellikle deprem kuşağında yer alan Türkiye ve diğer ülkelerin deprem akabindegerçekleşecek olan iç ve dış göçlerin yaşanmasıyla nüfus hareketliliğine hazır olması,yaşanabilecek krizlerin sağlıklı yönetilebilmesi, göç politikalarının nitelikli geliştirilmesi bağlamında literatüre katkı sağlanacağı hedeflenmiştir.

Anahtar Kelimeler: Göç; Deprem; İç göç

Kaynakça

AFAD (2023). https://www.afad.gov.tr/, Erişim tarihi:14.03.2023.

İÇDUYGU, A., SİRKECİ, İ. (1999). "Cumhuriyet Dönemi Türkiye'sinde Göç Hareketleri", 75 Yılda Köylerden Şehirlere, Editör Oya Baydar, İstanbul: Tarih Vakfı Yayınları, s.249-268.

YENER, S. (1977). "1965-70 Döneminde İllerarası Göçler ve Göç Edenlerin Nitelikleri", Ankara: Devlet Planlama Teşkilatı

WILLIAMS, A., PATTERSON G. (1998). "An Empire Lost but a Province Gained: A Cohort Analysis of British International Retirement in Algarve", International Journal of Population Geography, 4, 135-155.

505   Understanding the Attitudes towards Refugees among the Residents of Izmir, Turkey

Betül Dilara Şeker and Ibrahim Sirkeci

Different groups live together in society. Today, human movements continue to increase for various reasons. Cultural contacts and changes experienced after migration are essential for newcomers and host people/groups. Refugees face different challenges in the host country. The increasing number of people fleeing war, conflict or other forms of danger requires more knowledge and effort to understand the social integration of these groups and the cultural conditions they face. Individuals have identities to guide themselves and their actions in daily life. Social identity theory makes it easier to understand the factors that affect individuals' behaviour in groups and classifies them as "they" and "us" through social categorization. Refugees differ from host group members because of their cultural backgrounds and traumatic experiences.

Individuals emphasize similarities with ingroup members and focus on differences with outgroup members. In social categorization, the host group may feel negative emotions (prejudice) and hostility towards outgroup members, such as anxiety and uncertainty. They may tend to act accordingly (discrimination). Intergroup relations are shaped depending on the perceived balance between the welfare of the refugees and their own welfare by the host group members. From the perspective of host groups, immigrants/refugees are agents of change and uncertainty. Refugees are seen as either passive, needy, and victims or unstable and dangerous, although host groups often have guaranteed rights related to refugee groups. However, it is known that these perspectives are not static and are shaped according to the context. In social categorization, perceived realistic and symbolic threats to refugees can lead to prejudices. Different studies show that symbolic and realistic threats about outgroup refugees create a basis for prejudices. For this reason, the study was designed to reveal the attitudes of host group members toward refugees.

The study aims to examine the attitudes of host group members living in İzmir towards refugees. There are quantitative studies that reveal the attitudes of host groups towards refugees in general and towards Syrian refugees in particular. However, it has been observed that qualitative studies on this subject are limited. The study aims to reveal the participants' attitudes towards the refugee groups that come to mind first, without specifying any refugee group. Twenty-seven people living in Izmir, a host group member, participated in the study. Twelve of the participants were women, and fifteen were men. Participants are between the ages of 19-61. Semi-structured interviews were conducted with the participants. The data were evaluated in the research with thematic analysis, which can summarize the basic features and allow flexible and rich descriptions. As a result of the study, the prejudices of the host participants in the context of perceived symbolic and realistic threats were revealed. The study evaluates which groups the host participants perceive in the refugee concept and their positive and negative attitudes towards those groups. In addition, it is thought that describing the prejudices against refugees will contribute positively to the host and refugee groups' mutual adaptation processes and policies in the long run.

255   Beklenen İstanbul Depremi Özelinde Teknoloji: Görüntü İşleme ve Yapay Zekâ Algoritmaları Adaptasyonu

   Enis Çetin

We find it very difficult to understand and describe the Kahramanmaraş earthquake disaster that shook the society deeply. On the second day of the earthquake, we, as the Esenyurt Youth movement, participated in the aid campaign and formed a team with our friends to distribute them to the earthquake zone. What happened there wasn't a disaster, it was total apocalypse. The earthquake is not a new thing, but when we consider the destructiveness of the earthquake, which is recorded in history as the Kahramanmaraş earthquake, as well as the number of people affected and the breadth of geography (Eda Esma EYÜBAGİL1, 2023), and the human error factor that causes it, we face terrible facts. What's going on here with technology could be overcome.

12E   Migration and Integration V1

Chair: Venera Tomaselli, University of Catania, Italy

384   Extra-European Immigration by Media in EU Public Opinion

Venera Tomaselli and Rossana Sampugnaro

Media affect public opinion on crucial current issues.

Which media mainly distress the public attitudes towards no-European immigration?

In different research fields, the scientific findings of many studies do not agree on the role performed by different media.

To address the research question of the present study, legacy (TV, press, and radio) and new media (website and online social networks) are considered in order to evaluate their relationship with the EU citizens' attitudes towards immigration. The legacy media, indeed, have characterized the communication until the advent of the digital platform, while the new media have changed the equilibrium of the media ecosystem. So, the use of legacy and new media could differently affect EU citizens' attitudes towards immigrants from outside EU.

By the data analysis of latest 3 Eurobarometer waves from 2019 to 2021, EU citizens' opinion on no-European immigration is investigated by estimating multilevel statistical models with the aim of explaining whether new and legacy media differently affect EU public opinion on immigration issues.

The estimation of the parameters of the models reveals significant implications for media communication skills affecting the European citizens' opinion about non-European immigration.

The main findings point out that the use of legacy media rather than new media shows a similar impact on the European public opinion especially when the migration crisis becomes very serious. When the level of immigration is low, the use of legacy media implies not so negative opinions on no-European immigrants.

The new media use, on the other hand, performs a rather negative opinion, especially when the number of immigrants increases.

30   Refugees Integration in Greece and Italy (2010 -2020): A Comparison Study

Dimitrios Georgiadis

Europe is facing the largest population movement since World War II. This is expected to continue in the future as people escape from armed conflicts, extreme poverty, lack of human rights and climate changes. The aim of the presentation is to present a comparative overview of recent policy developments in the reception and integration of refugees in Greece and Italy, two transit countries which have recently had to face unexpected and unprecedented arrivals of asylum seekers and migrants at their borders.

These countries strongly differ from main destination countries, due to their more difficult economic and labor market conditions, and weaker institutional capacities for labor market integration. The focus of the analysis is on the policy reactions between 2010 and 2020, progress achieved and main challenges with a view to integration of refugees including changes in perceptions of key stakeholders, political actors and society.

Our research is based on a review of the literature and a survey of refugees who have been living in Greece and Italy for the last ten years. In the context of this work, we examine the difficulties of integration into Greek and Italian society.

310   Migration and Radicalization with Violence

Merve Önenli Güven

Migration is a sociological phenomenon in which its central subject is identity. With the action of migration, the prior identity of an individual turns into an immigrant. Migration is a process, which starts with the reasons that push the individual to migrate and composes of the migration conditions and the post-migration experiences. When the migration is because of mandatory reasons, the main concern of the immigrant is security. With the arrival of the immigrant to the host country, perception towards immigrants is shaped by security concerns, as well. Perceived threats of the immigrants and towards immigrants lead to extremism on both sides.

Especially, the conditions of the migrants in the host country can lead to radicalism processes starting with the ideology that turns into the motivation to use violence in order to represent the radical ideology. This radicalization process with violence, especially the conditions of the refugee camps, which are thought to be temporary for the immigrants prepares the structure for the radicalization with violence. The conditions of the refugee camps for the immigrants such as lack of free movement, inability to access educational opportunities, economic deficiencies, and lack of basic physical necessities with the feelings of the loss of identity, alienation, inferiority complex, and loneliness result with desperation, anger, and frustration in individual level. This situation also prepares a fertile ground for terrorist groups to benefit from these situations for the recruitment and dissemination of their ideologies.

This study aims to reveal the reasons behind the result with a relation between migration and radicalization with violence by analyzing the conditions of the refugee camps. Under this purpose, conditions of the refugee camps will be researched based on common and diverse aspects of these camps in the world. This research aims to reveal through what conditions lead to vulnerabilities, then marginalization to extremism, and end with radical violence. This scale from vulnerability to radical violence will be studied by searching for the parameters of the refugee camps' physical, security, social and economic conditions, which will be searched at the open source.

539   Examining the Factors Affecting Cultural Similarity in the Post-Migration Adaptation Process by Geographical Weighted Regression Method: The Case of Van Province

Çetin Görür, Bahadır Yüzbaşı, Gökhan Tuncel

Migration can be expressed as the relocation of people from the region where they live their lives to another region. In this context, while migration can go back to the history of humanity, it still continues today. The spatial migration of people does not mean that they will adapt to that region. Since people have different regional characteristics and backgrounds in many respects such as religion, language, culture, customs and traditions, migrations should be handled in socio-cultural terms and regionally. Migration has been in a continuous circulation in the world from the first ages to this time. People from different cultures interact within this framework. However, at this point, the fact that immigrants suddenly start living in a completely different culture together with the cultures they have been familiar with for years, affects them both psychologically and socio-culturally. Therefore, the cultural similarity of immigrants with the society they migrated accelerates the adaptation process. In this study, the factors affecting cultural similarity in post-migration adaptation processes were examined using Ordinary Least Squares and Geographically Weighted Regression methods. If the variations in populations are located in the spatial domain, the Ordinary Least Squares method may yield unrealistic results because the Ordinary Least Squares method assumes that all relationships are constant. Geographically Weighted Regression, on the other hand, handles behaviors differently according to regions or individuals and gives results according to these differences. Unlike Ordinary Least Squares method, Geographical Weighted Regression analysis looks for geographic differences and looks for spatial variations in the relationship between the dependent variable and independent variables. Therefore, in this study, it was aimed to determine the relationship between the benefit of cultural similarity and independent variables in the post-migration adaptation process and to examine which of the models used for analysis gave stronger results. At the same time, the effects and significance of regional variables were analyzed on maps. In this study, face-to-face surveys were conducted with 440 individuals who immigrated from the provinces with first and second degree borders to Van, and it was observed that the Geographical Weighted Regression method gave stronger results than AICc and R2 values in the analysis results.

12F   Wellbeing and Migration V2

Chair: Sadaf Mahmood, Women University Multan, Pakistan

314   Children in the Trauma Trail: From Being Human to Well Being

Surbhi Kumar, Shubhra Seth

The last few decades, have witnessed a quantum increase in the volume of forced migrations across international borders and internal displacements of people within the state as a result of civil conflicts and most recently the COVID-19 pandemic, which have caused immense trauma and a considerable need for mental health and psychosocial support for those affected. Refugees are highly susceptible to experiencing traumatic events that can be categorised into three phases: before, during, and after migration (Chen, Hall, Ling, & Renzaho, 2017). Trauma exposure, in this sense, tends to be cumulative.

In this paper, we trace the experiences of particularly children who have experienced migration. Forced migration due to conflict or persecution can expose children to violence, trauma, and loss of family and community, leading to mental health problems such as anxiety, depression, and post-traumatic stress disorder (PTSD). The experience of migration itself, including the journey and resettlement, can also be stressful and challenging for children, particularly if they face language and cultural barriers and have to adapt to new environments and social norms. Moreover, migration can disrupt children's education, social connections, and access to healthcare, which can have long-term consequences for their development and future opportunities. Children who migrate may also face discrimination, stigma, and xenophobia, which can further exacerbate their stress and trauma.

The paper further traces the role of social support in mitigating the impact of trauma and the challenges of providing effective support in the Global South. The paper also delineates strategies for providing culturally competent, trauma-informed care for children in particular. Using the systemic and interactionist perspectives, the paper provides a useful model synthesizing two key areas in migration-induced trauma - children and support.

Reference

Chen, W., Hall, B. J., Ling, L., & Renzaho, A. M. (2017). Pre-migration and post-migration factors associated with mental health in humanitarian migrants in Australia and the moderation effect of post-migration stressors: findings from the first wave data of the BNLA cohort study. The Lancet Psychiatry, 4(3), 218-229.

400   Overcoming Adversity: An Investigation of Psychological Well-Being among Syrian Refugees in Turkey

Selen Subaşı

The Syrian conflict has given rise to an immense humanitarian catastrophe, compelling millions of people to flee their homes and seek asylum in nearby nations. Out of these countries, Turkey has become the primary host to a vast number of Syrian refugees, exceeding 3.6 million people. Nevertheless, despite finding a new home, the psychological toll of displacement and trauma remains a significant issue for many refugees. This research paper examines the levels of psychological well-being (PWB) among 253 Syrian refugees in Turkey, ranging in age from 16 to 62 years (M=32, SD=9.33). The concept of psychological well-being (PWB) is a positive approach to psychology and emphasizes the promotion of positive human functioning. It encompasses an individual's overall sense of well-being and satisfaction with life, consisting of six dimensions: self-acceptance, positive relations with others, autonomy, environmental mastery, personal growth, and purpose in life. These dimensions provide a holistic understanding of an individual's psychological health and well-being. The findings of the study suggest that Syrian refugees in Turkey have moderately positive levels of PWB, with self-acceptance being the highest dimension and positive relations being the lowest. This highlights the need for interventions aimed at improving social connections and interpersonal relationships for refugees, as well as addressing individual factors related to autonomy, environmental mastery, personal growth, and self-acceptance. The study also found significant differences in the variance of certain latent variables across gender, indicating that gender-specific interventions may be necessary to effectively address the mental health needs of male and female refugees. Overall, this research highlights the importance of addressing the mental health needs of refugees and developing culturally sensitive interventions to promote their psychological well-being. This is particularly important given the significant challenges and stressors faced by refugees, including trauma, displacement, and social isolation, which can impact their mental health and well-being.

217 Commodified by displacement: the case of Syrian women in Lebanon's agricultural sector

Jessy Nassar

Drawing on ethnographic research conducted in Lebanon's Bekaa Valley, being the largest refugee host in the country and a prime agricultural zone, the paper discusses the implications of Syrian displacement on the agricultural workforce composition and the conditions of refugee-workers on large labour-intensive holdings. Given their dual positioning as female and as refugees in a context where labour relations are very much gendered and patriarchal, female refugees have become easier scapegoats of commodification. Findings reveal that as much as the post-displacement order has re-asserted pre-existing structures of power and labour relations, it also crafted new gender dynamics that are continuously shaped by the evolving reality of forced displacement. By exposing the intricacies of these dynamics, the research attempts to reconcile the complex relationship between labour, forced displacement, and gender.

1121 Challenges and Well-being of Pakistani Students: Evidence from Germany

Sadaf Mahmood, Beatrice Knerr, Izhar Ahmad Khan, Muhammad Shabbir, Muhammad Idrees, Uzma Niaz

There is an increasing trend of young people from economically marginalized or less developed countries studying in higher-income countries for the sake of quality education which is globally recognized afterward. This trend is observed in Pakistani students too who are scattered around the world while Germany is the top destination country rank for accommodating Pakistani students into their Higher Education Institutions (HEIs). Pakistani students preferred German universities because of the quality of education, advanced research, educational services, and the top nominal tuition fees. Although, there are very few pieces of literature in which the focus was the situation of Pakistani students in Germany. Our study is based on the human capital theory by Schultz and Becker as they stated that the schooling and capabilities of an individual are called human capital that maximizes their lifetime earnings (Schultz, 1971; Wossmann, 2001). Younger people are more interested to invest in migration and education as in our case,

Pakistani young students invested in both than other groups in the interest of better return on this decision (Becker, 1975; Sjaastad, 1962; Taylor, 2001). This paper explores the situation and well-being of Pakistani students and the challenges they face during their stay in Germany and discusses their coping strategies at the same time expanding their human capital. For this purpose, a questionnaire-based survey was conducted at different universities in Germany. A total sample of 264 respondents was screened for data analysis and 40% of the total sample was students. Among them, the ratio of female students remained significantly low. The data was collected through the face-to-face interview with Pakistani students enrolled in several universities in Germany, The data was analyzed with the help of the Statistical Package for Social Sciences (SPSS), and STATA. The outcome reveals that they are satisfied with their quality of educational life in Germany and their stay in Germany considerably enhances their educational attainments. Although, their social ties are much stronger within their Pakistani community rather than with the host community and other nationals. Whereas, their professional and social bindings to their home country influenced their decision of going back to Pakistan.

References

Becker, G. (1975). Human Capital: A theoretical and empirical analysis, with special reference to education, second edition, NBER. 0-226-04109-3, p. 13-44

Becker, G. (1994). "Human capital: a theoretical and empirical analysis with special reference to education", The University of Chicago Press, Chicago.

Becker, G. S. (1962). Investment in human capital: A theoretical analysis. The journal of political economy, 70(5), 9-49.

Becker, G. S. (1985). Human capital, effort, and the sexual division of labor. Journal of labor economics, 3(1), S33-S58.

Mahmood, S., & Knerr, B. (2015). Asian Students in Germany: Contexts of their Studies, Living Conditions and Future Plans 2. (Chapter 7: Students from Pakistan Social relations and human capital formation of Pakistani students in Germany), Volume: 11, pp. 156-175, *Kassel University Press GmbH.*

Mahmood, S. (2017). Human capital, occupational status, and social integration of Pakistani immigrants in Germany: Gender Perspectives, (Vol. 20). Pp. *Kassel University press GmbH.*

Mahmood, S., Knerr, B., Khan, I. A., Shabbir, M., & Mahmood, R. (2022). A Gender-Sensitive Analysis of Social Integration Challenges. Evidence from the Pakistani Diaspora in Germany. *Migration Letters, 19*(4), 437-448.

Schultz, T. (1971). Investment in human capital: the role of education and research, free press, New York, Mac Millan.

Sjaastad, L. A. (1962). The Costs and Returns of Human Migration, Journal of Political Economy, 70(1), 80-93

Wossmann L (2001). "Specifying human capital: A review and some extensions", KielInstitute of World Economics, [August 2001].

11:00-11:15 BREAK

Day Four 26 August 2023 - 11:15-13:00

13A   Migration and Urban Integration V1

Chair: Sahizer Samuk, University of Pisa, Italy

294   Internal Bordering in the Turkish Context: Inferences from Syrians' housing process in urban áreas

Ulaş Sunata and Feriha Nazda Güngördü

Borders are not just physical lines of separation between nation-states but also socially-constructed barriers used in filtering and controlling human mobility, which proliferates into and outside of the nation-state territory (Yuval-Davis et al., 2018). Currently, the bordering exercises have become urbanized with the decentralization of power to local authorities and the everyday barriers that refugees/migrants face in different aspects of city life (Balibar, 2002; Fauser, 2019). This study contributes to the border studies literature by unveiling Türkiye's unique role in internal bordering, apart from its heavily discussed role in the externalization of European borders (Stock et. al., 2019; Muftuler-Bac, 2022). Given the ongoing war in Syria since 2011, Türkiye has hosted 3.7 million Syrians. Most research to date has extensively focused on Türkiye concerning the macro-level policy-making and border externalization in the European context. However, the country also fits in the debates on internal bordering given the following circumstances: (i) The border control exercises in Türkiye have penetrated into the urban space as no strict procedures have been implemented at the gates (especially during the open-door policy of 2011-2016) and as Syrians have dispersed to urban areas in the lack of concrete settlement policies. (ii) Non-state actors (i.e., realtors, mukhtars) have remarkably taken over the role of central/local authorities in determining Syrians' settlement and integration (given the lack of comprehensive policies), which have resulted in different practices of recognition, control, ordering, and othering.

This study aims to present a snapshot of internal bordering practices that Syrians face in everyday life in Türkiye, particularly through a neighbourhood-level analysis focusing on Syrians' housing experiences and othering/filtering mechanisms in the housing market. The analysis is based on forty-two semi-structured interviews held with Syrian refugees, local authorities, and non-state actors (e.g., NGOs, mukhtars, and realtors) in Basmane, an inner-city settlement in Izmir attracting Syrians having different ethnic, socio-economic backgrounds and migration motivations. The findings suggest that there are two main forms of internal bordering concerning Syrians' housing in Basmane: othering and selective engagement/recognition. The othering mechanisms are based on Turkish-Syrian tension and Syrians' legal status in Türkiye, and the ethnic filtering applied by the actors in the local housing market (where being Syrian Turkmen, Arab or Kurdish affects which houses to be accessed and under what conditions). Besides being exposed to ethnic filtering/othering, Syrians are selectively engaged in the housing market by landlords, realtors, and often mukhtars based on their religion, cultural habits, political orientation, income, and household size/dynamics. Overall, in the absence of policies that manage/regulate the settlement and housing process of Syrians, many non-state actors come into play, and each actor plays a role in Syrians' access to housing according to their own interests, solidarity preferences, and ethnic and socio-political background. The type and degree of bordering practices that Syrians have been exposed to in the housing market depend primarily on their ethnic background and their negotiations with the actors involved in the housing process.

312   The Cretan Refugees in the Province of Adana

Aslı Emine Çomu

From the middle of the nineteenth century onwards, the Province of Adana had received a large number of Muslim refugees from different regions and ethnic backgrounds. Besides their impact on the consolidation of Muslim population in the province, they contributed to the agricultural development of their settlement points. One of these groups, Cretan Muslims, also sought refuge in the Ottoman Empire and some of them were sent to Adana at the end of the century for settlement. A short while after their arrival, they began to voice their complaints loudly and bitterly about their living conditions. They also demanded help from foreign consuls, which was not common among Muslim population. Their act finally caught the attention of the Porte following various reports from British, Russian and French consuls. Soon after, it was realized that these credulous refugees fell victim to a power struggle between the local government and Muslim notables. The paper will examine this power struggle in the light of the Ottoman and British primary sources and present the perception and assessment of the Cretan case in official and consular reports.

386   Reading the Production of Space in Syrian Neighborhoods in Ankara

Damla Isiklilar

In recent years, new urban codes and new public space practices have emerged with global changes and urban social movements. While the world is dealing with the increasing number of refugees crisis that has become one of the biggest challenges of the 21st century, almost all people are facing significant changes in the urban environment and especially in Turkey both citizens and "Urban Refugees" are facing socio-spatial changes. With this effect, numerous different disciplines have conducted on Syrian refugee crisis. Yet, it is examined that larger part of these research are oriented towards the outcasts of living within the refugee camps and there is a need of inquire about the refugees so called "Urban Refugees" settled in the cities in spite of the expanding significance of this concept. While urban environments are also affected by this social trend and the struggle for survival of this new concept, as urban designers, we need to look for answers to new urban questions and crises from a wider viewpoint in order for this newly developing agora to have a new social inclusiveness.

In this sense, with the aim of contributing in order to enrich the inadequacy in the literature, this research focuses on the recent and predicted future socio-spatial situation and effects of Syrian urban refugees within the cases of specific neighborhoods such as Önder and Ulubey Neighborhoods, which are called as Syrian Neighborhoods hereafter, in Ankara, Turkey. In this research, a reading of the new socio-spatial texture formed in the Syrian urban refugee neighborhoods in Ankara will be made from a Lefebvrian perspective. The phenomenon of socially produced space is being reshaped in the context of urban crises that occur in the neighborhoods, where refugees have settled as a result of forced migration. Afterall, derived information from the literature review on concept of social space and refugee movements, and case studies on daily life of refugees in the context of social spatial practice discussions will be analyzed.

126   Understanding Turkish return migration from Germany

Funda Yildirim

The first migration flow from Turkey to Germany started in the 1960s with the Bilateral Labor Agreements. Those that went were referred to as Guest Workers as they were employed only on short-term contracts, and they were expected to return to their home country after providing the workforce Germany needed. However, it did not go as planned, and, they started a life there and settled in Germany1.

According to the German Federal Statistical Office, the total population of Germany is currently 84,3 million. The total foreign population is almost 11,8 million. 26% of the population has a 'migration background' and 12% of the foreign population is from Turkey. Turkey has still one of the biggest diaspora communities in Germany[2]. The presence of the Turkish community in Germany has now moved away from the concept of guest workers.

Descendants of guest workers, who were born and raised in Germany, and mostly acquired German citizenship, are settling in Turkey, the motherland of their ancestors.

It is interesting to understand the second/third-generation migrants' main motivations for settling in Turkey. Thus, in this study, I aim to try to categorize the reasons for return by analyzing pre-return life in Germany, the return decision process, and life experiences in Turkey after the migration of the Turkish immigrants who lived in Germany.

Although the issue of return migration has become a hot topic among migration studies in recent years, it can be argued that there are different factors causing the second/third generation's return migration, especially as it occurs between relatively developed countries to less developed countries. Through this study, I intend to analyze individual reasons for the return decisions of people born and raised in Germany.

By comparing the quality of life in Germany and Turkey, I will go on using the indicators which are used by the European Commission to measure the quality of life such as income, consumption and housing, employment, health, education, leisure, and social interactions, economic security and physical safety, governance and basic rights, natural and living environment, life satisfaction[3].

The development in the literature on return migration dates to the 1980s, the return of the post-war labor migrants. If we look at the recent studies on the return migration of second-generation Turkish migrants; King & Kılıç, in their studies focusing on the return decisions of Euro - Turks, categorized the reasons for return as a family decision, a traumatic experience, an escape, and a new start; a project of self-realization and the attractions of the 'Turkish way of life[4]. Kunuroglu et al. analyzed the interview data and narrowed the common reasons into two groups: those generated from the host country and those generated from Turkey[5]. Considering that any decision of migration is a very comprehensive, and multi-layered issue, it does not seem possible to explain the decision of second/third generations to settle in their ancestral lands with a single theory. For this reason, I will similarly classify the main reasons for return as done in the above-mentioned studies.

13B   Wellbeing and Migration V3

Chair: Lan Lo, University of Nottingham, UK

345   The maternity experiences of women seeking asylum, in Australia

Glenys Frank, Deborah Fox, Nicky Leap

Introduction:

Australia's harsh immigration policy causes poor mental health for those who have been held in detention while seeking asylum (Macken 2019). Previous research indicates that asylum seekers are at high risk of PTSD and depression (Blackmore et al. 2020), but little research has been carried out looking at asylum-seeking women's experiences of engaging with maternity services. This research aimed to explore the maternity care experiences of women seeking asylum in Australia and the experiences of the midwives and doulas who cared for them.

Methods:

A feminist lens was appropriate as the research aimed to address the power imbalances faced by asylum-seeking women engaging with maternity services in Australia. This is in keeping with feminist research, which aims to give a voice to marginalised women while addressing inequalities and promoting social change (Kelly & Gurr 2020).

Phenomenology was used to understand the life worlds of participants. In-depth semi-structured interviews were conducted with women seeking asylum during their pregnancy and in the postnatal period in Australia. Midwives and doulas who care for women seeking asylum were also interviewed about their experiences.

I used the first person in writing the research in order to reflect on how I have situated myself within the research, including my values, attitudes and opinions.

Findings:

I interviewed 17 midwives and nine doulas based in Australia. In addition, I interviewed ten women seeking asylum and three undocumented migrants during their pregnancies and after their babies were born. The women were originally from Iran, Pakistan and Asia. Professional interpreters were used when required.

Many women spoke of their loneliness and lack of support, without family and friends in Australia. A key theme was 'living with uncertainty,' which included facing the barriers to accessing maternity care and the barriers to ensuring clear communication with interpreters. In contrast, support from midwives and doulas helped women to feel safe and informed, described in terms of 'sisterhood.' This was particularly evident where there was continuity of care.

Midwives were uncertain about asking identifying questions about visa status. They spoke of making an educated guess based on the woman's language preference, year of arrival and country of origin. The recommendation of the Australian Commission on Safety and Quality in Health Care to take a migration history was not in evidence.

Conclusion:

The thread of uncertainty for women seeking asylum was woven throughout this research. Women seeking asylum must be identified in order to understand the issues they experience during their maternity care and to provide appropriate support. Policy change is needed to prioritise the needs of asylum-seeking women in accessing midwifery continuity of care programs and models of care, such as group antenatal care, that promote social support. The experiences of pregnant women seeking asylum in Australia has been under-researched, and warrants increased focus on the development and evaluation of services that address their individual needs.

76   A comparative study on access to contraceptives and abortion services among Nepalese migrants in Japan and New York City, USA

Masako Tanaka

Nepalese is rapidly increasing both in Japan and the USA. This study aimed to identify the gaps in fulfilling their sexual and reproductive health and rights in destinations where available services differ from their home country. The research collected data through the online survey and Focus Group Discussions of Nepalese migrants and key informant interviews with healthcare professionals. The survey found that a few migrants brought oral contraceptive pills or emergency contraceptives from Nepal to their destinations. The paper concludes with the importance of including SRHR in pre-departure training in Nepal and organizing post-arrival training at their destinations.

Reference

Tanaka Masako 2020 Migrant women and SDGs: Access to sexual and reproductive health services in Japan, Impact, Volume 2020, Number 9, December 2020, pp. 38-39(2) https://doi.org/10.21820/23987073.2020.9.38

407   Implications of male migration on the decision-making and autonomy of the migrants' wives: Evidence from Middle Ganga Plain Survey, India

Reshmi R S, Ram Babu Bhagat, Gulshan Kumar, Sumit Narayan Dwivedi

This paper aims to understand the effects of male migration on the decision-making autonomy of the migrants' wives. The study setting is Middle Ganga Plain (MGP), a meso-level physiographic region of the Northern Indo-Gangetic Plains of India. This region has been the epicenter of distress-led male out-migration as an adaptive mechanism. The study hypothesizes that the absence of spouses increases the decision-making autonomy of the migrants' wives. A cross-sectional survey was conducted across 64 districts of MGP using a multi-stage systematic random sampling technique to develop a holistic understanding of the migration phenomenon while also assessing the consequences of migration on families' economic and social well-being. The effective sample size of our study is 2716 women, comprising 1106 migrants' wives and 1610 non-migrants' wives. The dependent variable of our study is decision-making autonomy, derived by utilizing confirmatory factor analysis. The primary independent variable was the husband's migration status, based on which women were categorized as migrants' wives and non-migrants' wives. In this study, descriptive and bivariate statistics have been performed to determine the summary statistics of decision-making autonomy by background characteristics across migrants' and non-migrants' wives. Pearson's Chi-square test was employed while cross-tabulating to examine the significance level between the decision-making and selected background factors. Further, to fulfill our prime objective, i.e., to study the association between selected background factors and decision-making among migrants' wives, multinomial logistic regression was conducted and expressed as Relative Risk Ratio (RRR) form. The male's migration strongly and positively impacts the migrants' wives decision-making autonomy independent of background characteristics. In addition, the findings suggests that the husband's migration outside India, Self-help groups(SHGs) membership are positively associated with migrants' wives decision-making autonomy, whereas joint family system shows a negative association.

The husbands' migration plays a crucial role in enhancing the decision-making and autonomy of the migrants' wives. Several factors play a role in affecting the ability of migrants' wives to take part in decision-making in the household. There is a need for more specifically designed and tailored empowerment programs for migrants' wives in the MGP to achieve SDG 5, which seeks to ensure gender equality and empower all women and girls by 2030.

This study has adopted a cross-sectional study design. Thus, the findings may generate biased estimates of the impact of male migration on women's decision-making autonomy because the propensity to migrate may be more in relatively better-off families than others. Cross-sectional data also incite a question about a causal relationship. For example, it might be possible that women with high autonomy may be more likely to encourage their spouses to migrate. A further longitudinal study and qualitative research are also required to thoroughly explain the causal influence of male migration on their wives' autonomy.

102   Immigrants' adaptation strategies in the (post)pandemic reality

Joanna Kulpińska, Katarzyna Górska, Anna Wyrwisz

The aim of our paper is to analyze the adaptation strategies of immigrants during and after the COVID-19 pandemic, in a comparative perspective of Poles in the UK and Germany. Particular attention will be paid to the impact of regulations and changes in the migration policies of these countries on the extent of immigrants' adaptation. Thus, an important variable taken into account in the data analysis will be the conditions existing in the place of migrant settlement and the changes introduced in their scope as a result of COVID-19, such as, among others, migration and social policy, labour market and employment conditions, access to health services, formal and informal institutions, scope of activities of non-governmental organisations, etc. Differences and similarities will be pointed out both in relation to the adaptation strategies of immigrant groups, and to the range of aid activities aimed at these populations: governmental and non-governmental, and their impact on the aforementioned processes of readaptation in the two selected countries.

The very notion of immigrant adaptation has already been explored quite extensively (Berry 1997; Spencer, Cooper 2006.; Castles, Korac, Vasta and Vertovec 2003.; Bosswick, Heckmann 2006.; Grzymała-Kazłowska 2016). However, new circumstances have emerged that have not previously been considered more widely in the context of the immigrant adaptation process - namely the crisis caused by the COVID-19 pandemic (Brzozowski et al. 2020, Arditis, Laczko 2020, Guadango 2020, Liem et al. 2020).

The pandemic completely changed the reality and functioning of societies almost all over the world. Subsequent regulations aimed at combating the virus also had many adverse effects. Among other things, they exacerbated the already existing inequalities between different social groups, including vulnerable groups such as immigrants. The inability to return home or, on the contrary, the necessity to leave the country of emigration, the loss of a job or reduced salary, the lack of or poor access to information, are just a few of the mentioned by the respondents consequences of the restrictions introduced as a result of the COVID-19 pandemic. These above-mentioned implications, as it were, made it necessary to reintegrate into the host society and the new (post)pandemic reality. As part of the presentation, we will try to answer the question of whether and how the adaptation processes of the group under study have changed as a result of the COVID-19 pandemic?

The paper will examine how migration policies and the COVID-19 epidemic restrictions introduced within them affected migrants' adaptation strategies from the comparative perspective of 2 case studies conducted among Poles in Germany and the UK. The project is based on both primary (official statistics, reports) and secondary data: both quantitative (CAWI survey) and qualitative (in-depth interviews) research. Within our presentation we will outline the changes and limitations that occurred during the COVID-19 pandemic in the adaptation strategies of immigrants.

537   Unpacking the magnitude and heterogeneity of the impacts of reverse migration in environmentally vulnerable locations in Bangladesh

Mohammad Kabir

This study focused on the international migrants who came home in the context of COVID-19 global crises. Due to workplace shutdown amongst few other reasons, about half a million Bangladeshi workers returned home during 2020-2022. Abrupt return and associated loss of income affected the migrant families' food security, social protection and coping mechanism. This study explored return migrants in Noakhali, one of the top five foreign remittance recipient districts in Bangladesh. This coastal district is comprised of both low lying mainland and islands, which are frequently affected by natural hazards such as cyclone, flood and riverbank erosion. Primary data was collected at two consecutive stages. Firstly, a spatial distributions of return migrants was identified by local key informants. Secondly, in depth interviews with identified return migrants and their household members were conducted. These qualitative interviews investigated the impact of return migration on the migrant's life trajectory and the required measures (e.g., how informal economies can be a source of resilience in periods of complex crises) most beneficial for such return migrants at home country. Moreover, how to extend such components to the migrants voluntarily returning at the end of their natural migration cycle – was unpacked throughout the empirical fieldwork. The outcome of this study provides greater nuance on involuntary return migration and will have implication in other similar contexts.

13C   Migration and Integration V2

Chair: Ruchi Singh, Tata Institute of Social Sciences, India

65   Assessing the integration of Ukrainian refugees in the Romanian labour market: Case study: the city of Oradea

Edina Lilla Meszaros

Anyone familiar with the history of Romania regards it mainly as a country of emigrants and not of immigrants, thus, the problem of integrating refugees hasn't been on the top of its national agenda. However, the 2015 refugee crisis, the war in Ukraine and the still increasing trend in asylum applications have demanded the reconsideration and reforming of its migration and integration policies. Accordingly, the current paper is aimed at assessing the level of integration of

Ukrainian refugees on the Romanian labour market, more specifically in our hometown, the city of Oradea, since the eruption of the war in February 2022. After the qualitative analysis of the polls, legislation in vigour and of the programmes elaborated at national (macro) level facilitating the integration of Ukrainian refugees, our attention focuses exclusively on evaluating the efficiency of the policies elaborated at local (micro) level. Local institutions (County Agency for Employment, Payments and Social Inspection, County Health Insurance House, Town Hall, Territorial Labour Inspectorate etc.) were requested to provide specific information that they register about foreigners, in our case Ukrainian refugees living in the city, about their participation in Romanian language courses, medical insurance, help for job search, social benefits, child allowances, unemployment benefits, social housing etc. Corroborated with the data provided by the local authorities, an online questionnaire distributed among the Ukrainian refugees living in Oradea by using the method of snowball sampling, offer a genuine picture about their level of integration in the labour market of Oradea, a medium sized city in the North-Western part of Romania. The analysed polls and the acquired data reveal a positive and inclusive approach at both national and local level concerning refugees from Ukraine, in contrast with the predominantly negative and exclusive stance registered at country/local level following the debut of the 2015 refugee crisis upon the arrival of asylum seekers from Africa and the Middle East. As regards the theoretical framing, while emphasis shall be put on the structural integration of refugees, namely on their incorporation into the core institutions of the host society, such as the labour market or the educational system, Hartmut Esser's sociological integration theory provides the theoretical backbone for the study.

222   Experiences of migrant nurses in Japan: Building diversity in workplace interpersonal relationships

Yoshiyuki Nagaya, Nicola Gillin, David Smith

Objectives

This study aimed (1) to explore the experiences of foreign nurses who had arrived in Japan under the Economic Partnership Agreement (EPA); and (2) to suggest measures to improve current policies or training schemes at hospitals.

Relevant literature

Although 3.6 per cent of the global population are international migrants (IOM, 2021), approximately 15 per cent of all health-care workers are working outside their country of birth (WHO, 2022). In OECD countries, the number and percentage of foreign-trained nurses in the workforce continued to rise throughout the second decade of the twenty-first century (OECD, 2021). International health-care professional relocation, and difficulties in attracting and retaining health-care professionals, are among several factors impacting upon the quality of health-care and those who deliver it (WHO, 2016). In Japan, according to the regulations currently in force, nurses who have been trained overseas and wish to register for employment must pass the National Nursing Examination (NNE). First of all, though, these applicants must be assessed for eligibility to take the examination. This requires them to pass a Japanese language proficiency test and have nursing qualifications at the same level as their Japanese counterparts (MHLW, 2022). Less than proficient communication impairs collaboration with colleagues, which leads to negative outcomes in the provision of safe, efficient, and high-quality care.

Methods

The research is part of a doctoral study titled 'Exploring decisions as to whether to remain or to leave made by Indonesian, Filipino and Vietnamese registered nurses relocating to Japan under the Economic Partnership Agreement (EPA)'. The research took an inductive qualitative approach, adopting the methodology of Charmaz's Constructivist Grounded Theory (2014) as its philosophical underpinning. The target participants were EPA nurses who had passed the Japanese National Nursing Examination and were currently or formerly working in Japan. Because of the COVID-19 pandemic, all twenty participants chose to be interviewed online. Ethical approval for the study was given by Anglia Ruskin University's Ethics Committee.

Results

Although this article focuses on workplace interpersonal relationships, the interviews had explored not only work-related but also non-work-related topics. In the analysis, problems with workplace interpersonal relationships were established as one of the main themes. Initial coding derived two sub-categories from the transcripts: 1) a general tendency for relationships in the workplace to become unpleasant; and 2) workplace difficulties that affected EPA nurses only.

Conclusions

The findings point to a need for further improvements in the workplace, such as more generous provision of in-service training, and better opportunities for staff to socialise with one another, so that migrant nurses encounter fewer difficulties in their relationships with colleagues.

COI disclosure

There are no entities or relationships, etc. presenting a potential conflict of interest requiring disclosure in relation to this study.

440   Chinese Migration to Africa: The Case of Cameroon

Jocelyne Kenne Kenne

Chinese Migration to Africa: The Case of Cameroon

Globalization leads to important mobility and an unprecedented multiplication of diasporic communities in various centers of the world, making them sites of "super-diversity" (Vertovec 2007). A bulk of the literature reports the increasing presence of the Chinese transnational community in Africa in recent decades. Some scholars even refer to the influx of Chinese on the African continent as a "Chinese invasion" (see e.g. Abdulai, 2016; Gagliardone, 2019; Insaidoo, 2016; Ngome, 2007). According to Bodomo (2012), there are about two million Chinese in Africa. At present, this number would have increased from what it was in 2012 due to China's foreign policy and development strategy which encourages the migration of Chinese people out of their country. Similarly, China has been Africa's largest trading partner since 2009. China's position as an important trade and development partner further consolidates Africa-China relations, which is reflected in the strong presence of Chinese immigrants who settled in Africa for economic reasons. The present paper focuses on the Chinese community living in Cameroon. It aims to examine their sociodemographic profile, mainly, who are the Chinese living in Cameroon. What is their age group? level of education? family status? how long have they been in Cameroon, and what is their migratory project? Further, which language are they exposed to speaking once they arrive in Cameroon? Cameroon in this situation is a particular case due to its complex linguistic situation. It is the African country with the highest number of languages, after Nigeria. It has almost 300 languages among which are two official languages: French and English, two "hybrid" languages: Pidgin English and Camfranglais, and more than 250 local languages (Ngefac, 2010).

The present study uses a mixed research method. First, a questionnaire survey, written in Chinese and English, has been administered to 432 Chinese migrants living in Yaounde, Douala, and Bamenda. The goal was to elicit detailed information about the sociodemographic data of the Chinese and their language use and proficiency. Secondly, semi-structured interviews have been conducted. The main goal of this research method was to collect the Chinese migrants' narratives about their stay in Cameroon and to allow them to express their attitudes and opinions about language matters. Lastly, observations have been used besides questionnaires and interviews. The use of these three research instruments augmented the validity and reliability of the data and their interpretation. The analysis of the sociodemographic profile of the Chinese respondents shows that Chinese immigrants in Cameroon are diverse in their level of education, marital status, socio-economic class, profession, and age, among others. However, the point they share in common is their motivation for migrating: almost all of them migrated to carry out various economic activities in Cameroon. The majority are engaged in family retail and wholesale business. Additionally, the findings reveal that the presence of Chinese in Cameroon is relatively recent. Indeed, 99% of them have arrived since 2000.

1107   Boatmen and Decent Work: Insights from Varanasi District

Akhilesh Vishwakarma and Ruchi Singh

Migration is not a new phenomenon in developing countries and is described as a long-term change in a person's place of residence. This change can occur inside the limits of a single nation or across borders, from rural to urban or from urban to rural areas. Water tourism is one of the major source of employment in Varanarsi (Doron, 2005) which leads to complicated and varied phenomenon of migrantion of boatmen to the city with important social, economic, and cultural implications. Migrant boatmen have developed a unique type of social identity and engage in a specific type of circulatory or "transversal" labour migration.Current study focusses on boatmen in Varanasi, which is located on the banks of the holy river Ganga, where boatmen have different lifestyles, patterns of interaction, and socioeconomic conditions. Boatmen, play a vital role in the economy of Varanasi district, despite this the decent work frameowork and ILO Conventions are still distant dream for these migrants. They are often denied of basic civic ammenities, have poor working conditions, and have limited access to healthcare. A variety of elements, including economic possibilities, political unpredictability, and social and cultural conventions, influence the migration of boatmen.With the given context , the major objective study is is to understand the issues, challenges and livelihood issues of migrant boatmen in Varnasi district. The study is based on primary survey of 100 boatmen at shores of river Ganges in Varanasi district of Uttar Pradesh. Surprisingly, in spite of over 3.2 million domestic and foreign tourists visiting the city annually, these boatmen lead a life of deprivation, destitution and poverty. Data have been collected employing simple random sampling and simple statistical techniques have been used for analysis of the data. The major finindg of the study is majority of these communities belong to vulnerable and marginalised section of the society in Varanasi and are less educated and have barely any awareness regarding their rights both at national and internationla level inclusding ILO frameworks on decent work. Even though they are a low-status and underprivileged minority, it demonstrates how boatmen manage to fight and contest state dominance and upper-caste dominance. Boatmen work long hours in difficult conditions. They are often excluded from social and cultural events and face stigma and prejudice are often prone to discrimination. Many boatmen in Varanasi are denied of civic amenities and lack access to basic facilities such as sanitation, clean drinking water, and healthcare. Despite these challenges, the boatmen of Varanasi continue to play an important role in the city's economy and culture.To guarantee that boatmen may work in safe and equitable conditions and that their human rights are safeguarded, policymakers, employers, and other stakeholders must collaborate.

13D   Migration, Religion, and Religious Groups V1 - VIRTUAL ACCESS

Chair: Eric M. Trinka, Emory and Henry College, USA

455   Religious Studies and Migration Research: Exploring Methodological Mysteries and Interdisciplinary Insights

Ingrid Løland

While expanding literature addresses the intriguing nexus of religion and migration through different theoretical lenses and empirical case studies, there is still a need to delve more deeply into the methodological subtleties that encourage new insights on these topics. When setting out to explore the many competing and contradictory manifestations of religion in diverse migratory settings, our research endeavours reflect highly complex phenomena that cannot always be understood within the scientific vocabulary of one single tradition. This paper offers a dynamic gaze on the interdisciplinary link between religious studies and migration research and argues for an inquisitive openness towards the theory-data relationship in qualitative research. Although vastly dissimilar and bound by their respective and longstanding scientific traditions, both religious studies and migration research cover broad areas of study and represent chiefly interdisciplinary types of scholarship. Despite belonging to divergent and sometimes contending paradigms, the paper questions how these disciplines may critically enhance and work as combined sources of knowledge in contemporary and increasingly complex research problems. Drawing on Alvesson and Kärreman's (2011) compelling 'mystery as method' approach, the study proposes to encounter religion and migration-related issues through combined "repertoires of lenses" (Deetz, 1992, cited in Alvesson & Kärreman, 2011, p. 34). Acknowledging the interdependence of theory and data allows for a critical and reflexive view of their constructed interrelationship. Multiple perspectives may thus envision interpretative portals into empirical realities in broader and more creatively inspired ways. When applying this dynamic methodology to the cross-disciplinary conversations of religious studies and migration research, alternative ways of understanding can help challenge hegemonic discourses and blur hitherto strict boundaries between scientific genres. Moreover, such a methodology acknowledges the messiness and hybridity of empirical data, in which mysteries, anomalies and tensions may come to the fore, contest established theories, as well as inspire ever-new and evolving perspectives. The imaginative component of conducting/constructing qualitative research, therefore, rests upon a mutually enhancing and complementary interplay between theory and data which, the paper argues, is beneficial for cross-fertilizing disciplines such as religious studies and migration research. This study seeks to illustrate these interdisciplinary linkages by showcasing a few research examples in which the richness, depth and intricacies of the religion/migration nexus are inquisitively imagined and creatively accounted for.

118   Identity Matters: Culture and Religion as Key Factors in the Migration of Muslims

Joseph Abraham Levi

Using as a springboard the Islamic concept of الْهِجْرَة Hijrah (migration)—whereby migration is conceived as a way of saving the faithful from religious persecution[1]—I analyze how culturally, economically, and socio-politically disfranchised and marginalized Muslims decide or, better yet, have no other choice but to leave their homeland in search for a better life in non-Muslim lands. Adaptation, assimilation, and compromise vs. maintaining their cultural, linguistic, and religious identity while living in دَار الْحَرْب dār al-Ḥarb (land of the enemy, i.e., non-Muslim territory) are oftentimes a barrier to fully enjoying the benefits of living free from danger in their adopted homeland. Finally, cultural, ethnic, racial, religious, and (trans)gender issues will be analyzed as these modern-day مُهَاجِرُون muhājirūna (migrant Muslims) negotiate their identities away from home (دَار الإِسْلام dār al-Islām, lands under Muslim sovereignty).

[1] See Qur'ān 2:218; 4:100; 8:72; 8:74-75; 9:20; 16:110.

111   A Tale of Two Regions: Perceptions of Syrian Forced Immigrants in Lebanon through a Religious Lens

Ziad Alahmad

Previous research has shown that religion, culture, and identity play a role in forced immigrants' acceptance. This study aimed to explore how religion influences the relationship between the host community and forced immigrants in Lebanon. The study focused on the perceptions of Lebanese citizens in the North Governorate, a predominantly Sunni area, and the Greater Beirut Area, a multi-faith region, towards Syrian forced immigrants. A total of 1000 randomly selected respondents, equally distributed between the two regions, were surveyed through door-to-door visits. Using statistical tests, the study confirms significant differences in perceptions between the two regions. Respondents in the North Governorate perceived Syrians as guests rather than members of the community, expected them to go back home sooner or later, and were more willing to offer them housing and employment. Conversely, respondents in the Greater Beirut Area perceived Syrian refugees as a part of the Lebanese community, competing with them for resources, and were less likely to offer them housing and employment. The findings suggest that personal and collective identity and perceived threat to shared resources are significant factors in attitudes towards Syrian forced immigrants in Lebanon, particularly through a religious lens. This research provides valuable insights into the complexities of forced immigrant acceptance and integration in a country where religion plays a significant role in society. The study's findings have significant implications for policymakers, practitioners, and academics working in the fields of forced migration and refugee resettlement. To foster greater acceptance and integration of forced immigrants, there is a need for targeted interventions that take into account the unique cultural and religious contexts of host communities. By providing insights into these complexities, this research contributes to a better understanding of the challenges and opportunities for forced immigrant acceptance and integration in Lebanon and beyond.

www.ingramcontent.com/pod-product-compliance
Lightning Source LLC
Chambersburg PA
CBHW052122270326
41930CB00012B/2725